Homeric Stitchings

Greek Studies: Interdisciplinary Approaches
General Editor: Gregory Nagy, Harvard University
Assistant Editor: Timothy Power, Harvard University

On the front cover: A calendar frieze representing the Athenian months, reused in the Byzantine Church of the Little Metropolis in Athens. The cross is superimposed, obliterating Taurus of the Zodiac. The choice of this frieze for books in *Greek Studies: Interdisciplinary Approaches* reflects this series' emphasis on the blending of the diverse heritages—Near Eastern, Classical, and Christian—in the Greek tradition. Drawing by Laurie Kain Hart, based on a photograph. Recent titles in the series are:

Homeric Stitchings

The Homeric Centos of the
Empress Eudocia

M. D. Usher

ROWMAN & LITTLEFIELD PUBLISHERS, INC.
Lanham • Boulder • New York • Oxford

ROWMAN & LITTLEFIELD PUBLISHERS, INC.

Published in the United States of America
by Rowman & Littlefield Publishers, Inc.
4720 Boston Way, Lanham, Maryland 20706

12 Hid's Copse Road
Cumnor Hill, Oxford OX2 9JJ, England

British Library Cataloguing in Publication Information Available

Library of Congress Cataloging-in-Publication Data

Usher, Mark David, 1966 –
    Homeric stitchings : the Homeric Centos of the Empress Eudocia /
M.D. Usher.
        p. cm. — (Greek studies : interdisciplinary approaches)
    Includes bibliographical references and index.
    ISBN 0–8476–8999–9 (alk. paper). — ISBN 0–8476–9050–4 (pbk. :
alk. paper
        1. Eudocia, consort of Theodosius II, Emperor of the East, d. 460 —
Criticism and interpretation. 2. Christian poetry, Greek — History
and criticism. 3. Homer — Appreciation — Turkey — Istanbul.
4. Byzantine Empire — Intellectual life. 5. Oral tradition — Turkey —
Istanbul. 6. Centos — History and criticism. 7. Oral–formulaic
analysis. 8. Transmission of texts. 9. Literary form. I. Title.
II. Series: Greek studies.
PA3972.E86Z88 1998
881'.01 — dc21   98–6369
                                                          CIP

Printed in the United States of America

⊖™ The paper used in this publication meets the minimum requirements of American National
Standard for Information Sciences—Permanence of Paper for Printed Library Materials, ANSI
Z39.48–1984.

As a good house-wife out of divers fleeces weaves one peece of cloth
. . . I have laboriously collected this *Cento* out of divers Writers.

—Robert Burton, *The Anatomy of Melancholy*

Contents

Greek Studies: Interdisciplinary Approaches

Foreword
by Gregory Nagy, General Editor

Building on the foundations of scholarship within the disciplines of philology, philosophy, history, and archaeology, this series spans the continuum of Greek traditions extending from the second millennium B.C.E. to the present, not just the Archaic and Classical periods. The aim is to enhance perspectives by applying various disciplines to problems that have in the past been treated as the exclusive concern of a single given discipline. Besides the crossing over of the older disciplines, as in the case of historical and literary studies, the series encourages the application of such newer ones as linguistics, sociology, anthropology, and comparative literature. It also encourages encounters with current trends in methodology, especially in the realm of literary theory.

Homeric Stitchings: The Homeric Centos of the Empress Eudocia, by M. D. Usher, is a definitive study of the Homeric Centos, an epic-style biblical poem composed in the early fifth century C.E. by the Empress Eudocia, wife of Theodosius II. The building blocks of the Centos are verses taken directly from the *Iliad* and *Odyssey*. Such versification, known by the technical designation of *cento* or "stitching," has not until now received the attention it deserves. Previous scholarship has tended to underestimate the Homeric Centos and the form of the cento in general. Usher's book forces a radical reassessment.

Concentrating on the historical context of audience reception, Usher demonstrates the artistry and communicative power of the Homeric Centos. This poem, as Usher shows convincingly, was intended for performance before audiences who were intimately familiar with both Homer and the Bible. To say "familiar" may well be an understatement: the Homeric Centos presuppose a veritable internalization of both Homer and the Bible for both the composer and the audience. In the case of Homer, the composer has internalized not only the themes of the *Iliad* and *Odyssey* but also—and this is essential—the formulaic system of Homeric poetry.

Eudocia's consummate understanding of both the mechanics and the esthetics of Homeric diction cannot be understood purely in terms of composition. Applying the techniques of formulaic analysis pioneered by Milman Parry and Albert Lord, Usher argues that the art of the Homeric Centos grew out of mnemonic traditions that perpetuated the actual performance of the Homeric poems. The reading of the Homeric Centos, in the culture of later antiquity, was merely the means toward the end of *hearing* them—the same way that audiences would hear the *Iliad* and *Odyssey* at public performances. The Homeric Centos, like Homer, were meant to be heard. In the historical context of later antiquity, as *Homeric Stitchings* proves, it is essential to keep in mind the performative aspects of reading in general. The Homeric Centos of the Empress Eudocia bring to the fore the cultural synergism of reading and performing the Classics.

Acknowledgments

Some debts are a pleasure to pay. My heaviest and most pleasant one is to Laura Slatkin—Μέντορι εἰδομένη ἠμὲν δέμας ἠδὲ καὶ αὐδήν—for her inspiration, insight, and constant support. My thanks go out also to other readers: Bob Kaster, Chris Faraone, and Michael Roberts, for their generous contributions of time, counsel, and energy; to Elizabeth Asmis, for the research opportunity that led to my discovery of this fascinating poem; to Bob Allison, for his role in obtaining access to the manuscript on which this study is based; to Robert Lamberton, Mark Edwards, and Gregory Nagy, for carefully reading and commenting on various parts of this project.

Above all, I would like to thank my wife, Caroline, and my children, Isaiah, Estlin, and Gawain, for making it a life of the heart as well.

Note on Citation Style

The style of citation and reference used here is adapted from that used in the journal *Oral Tradition*. Full bibliographic information (including volume numbers for multivolume works) for all sources cited in the text will be found in the references. For older books and essays that have been reprinted, or translated from another language into English at a later date, I have given the author's name and (when known) original year of publication in the body of the text and the year of the standard or most accessible modern edition or English translation in the references. For example:

Wood 1775   R. Wood. *An Essay on the Original Genius and Writings of Homer*. New York: Garland (1971).

An ancient author is sometimes cited according to the modern editor's date and pagination, when that edition is standard.

In order to give the reader maximum exposure to this unfamiliar poem, I have been generous in citing Cento text. All extended citations have been translated, though many short passages and phrases that illustrate aspects of Homeric prosody and composition have not. The line of argument in such instances, however, should be intelligible even to the nonspecialist. All translations are my own, though for biblical passages I have occasionally fallen into the cadences of King James.

Introduction

> Eudocia—in the twenty-first year of the fifth century—wife of
> Theodosius, and empress of the world, thought good to
> extend her sceptre . . . over Homer's poems, and cento-ize
> them into an epic on the Saviour's life. She was the third fair
> woman accused of sacrificing the world for an apple, having
> moved her husband to wrath, by giving away his imperial gift
> of a large one to her philosophic friend Paulinus; and being
> unhappily more learned than her two predecessors in the sin,
> in the course of her exile to Jerusalem, she took ghostly
> comfort, by separating Homer's εἴδωλον from his φρένες.
> There she sat among the ruins of the holy city, addressing
> herself most unholily, with whatever good intentions and
> delicate fingers, to pulling Homer's gold to pieces bit by bit.
> . . . The reader, who has heard enough of centos, will not care
> to hear how she did it. That she did it was too much; and the
> deed recoiled.

This is how Elizabeth Barrett Browning characterizes the Homeric
Centos of Eudocia Augusta in her essay *The Greek Christian Poets*,
published in 1842. This passage is cited in the *Oxford English Dictionary* for the verb form "cento-ize," which one might gather from
Mrs. Browning's fulsome description is a metaphor drawn from the
fabrication of textiles. A *cento* is a patchwork quilt. This Latin loan-
word, derived from the Greek κέντρον, meaning "goad," "prick,"
"needle," and thus metonymically "a piece of needlework," is first
used as a metaphor for speech by Plautus in the proverbial phrase
centones sarcire (*Epidicus* 455), which Erasmus glosses in his *Adagia*
as *sermo mendaciis explere*, roughly our English "to spin a yarn"

(Delepierre 1875:7; Crusius 1899:1930; Salanitro 1997:2319-21).[1]

To this day the word retains this decidedly negative connotation. To compose a cento is thought to be proof positive of an author's mendacious lack of poetic ability; what is worse, centonism destroys the integrity of the source text: in Mrs. Browning's words, Eudocia separated Homer's εἴδωλον from his φρένες, and pulled his gold to pieces bit by bit. Like Mrs. Browning, no one has been interested in how she did it; *that* she did it has continued to be too much for most—too much for the eminent Homerist, Arthur Ludwich, who couldn't bring himself to complete the task of editing her poem; too much for Joseph Golega, an esteemed scholar of later Greek literature, who declared that the Centos aren't worth the paper they're printed on—"weder des Druckes noch des Lesens wert" (Golega 1960:1).

My purpose in writing this book on the Centos is to show to what extent such assessments lack understanding and imagination. Indeed, when we look closely at *how* Eudocia composed her poem, we find that her Centos reflect many of the concerns of modern philology, especially of Homeric studies.

As the quilting metaphor suggests, a centonist collects disparate scraps and strands from a source text and stitches them into a new artistic whole. "Cento is not a generic term but an *écriture*—such as parody, travesty . . . and pastiche—which can be realized in a lyric and an epic form as well as in the prose of political treatises and the literary essay, even in dramatic form" (Verweyen and Witting 1991:172). In fact, dozens of ancient and modern centos exist, some pious, some political, some obscene, patched together from the works of Euripides, Vergil, Ovid, Cicero, Petrarch, Shakespeare, Goethe, and Emily Dickinson.[2]

Homeric centos are poems made up entirely of verses lifted verbatim, or with only slight modification, from the *Iliad* and *Odyssey*. Of the several Homeric centos to have survived antiquity, Eudocia's is

---

1. The word is first used to designate a literary pastiche by Ausonius, who says he inherited the term from predecessors (Green 1991:132, 519).

2. Many specimens are collected in Delepierre 1875.

by far the longest at nearly twenty-four hundred lines.[3] The poem originated with a Christian cleric named Patricius in the fourth century C.E. and was expanded by the Empress in the early fifth. Eudocia's Centos comprise a single, continuous poem on a biblical theme that recounts the creation of the world, the temptation and fall of man, and the birth, life, death, resurrection, and ascension of Christ.[4]

In 1979, a voice crying in the wilderness called for a new edition of Eudocia's poem, emphasizing its great heuristic potential for classicists, medievalists, literary critics, and theologians (Smolak 1979:49; cf. Schembra 1995:17). Unfortunately, the recognition of this potential has been impeded, in the words of the prophet, by "the censorship of a *klassizistischen Ästhetik*." The reference here is to Ludwich, whose Teubner edition of 1897 (until recently the only modern edition of the Centos available) was based on a single, partially edited manuscript, which, as Ludwich himself was well aware, is a non-Eudocian eclogue of Homeric centos compiled in the Middle Ages by several hands (Ludwich 1897:87; *pace* Schembra 1995).

Ludwich left his editorial work incomplete because of his aesthetic disenchantment with the poem—not Eudocia's—that he had in front of him. As he confessed, "Books of this kind, only a few of which still lie hidden in libraries, are not worth the careful attention of anyone today." "I leave this sterile field," he adds elsewhere, "to others more patient than myself to plow" (Ludwich 1897:87-8). Within the past twenty years the ground has begun to be broken up again and the field is attracting workers. I too have given my neck to the yoke and have produced a new edition of the Centos, using an important but previously neglected manuscript. It is on the basis of the text of this

---

3. There exist three short Homeric centos in the *Palatine Anthology* (9.361, 381, 382; cf. Hunger 1978:98-101), a ten-line cento about Herakles quoted by Irenaeus (Wilken 1967), a six-line cento about Echo and Pan in the scholia to Dionysius Thrax (Hilgard 1901:480-1), and a seven-line cento grafitto inscribed on the leg of a statue of Memnon in Egypt, which dates from the reign of Hadrian (Bernand 1960:111-3; Bowie 1990:65). There are also several cento-like incantations from the *Greek Magical Papyri* that use lines from Homer (Maltomini 1995).

4. In using the capitalized plural "Centos" to designate Eudocia's work and to distinguish it from cento poetry in general, I am translating the title of her poem in Greek—Ὁμηρόκεντρα.

new edition, which I have argued elsewhere represents Eudocia's expanded and improved version of the poem, that I offer here an explanation and radical reevaluation of the Homeric Centos.[5]

❖

Oscar Wilde once said that "Art is at once Surface and Symbol" (Wilde 1891:236). Following Wilde, I have endeavored in this study to scan the one and sound the depths of the other—the symbol perhaps (as Wilde cautions) at my own peril, but nonetheless with eyes and ears open to appreciate the art of the Homeric Centos. The Centos' poetic surface is the topic of part 2, a detailed discussion of the linguistic techniques and devices used in the composition of this poem and their basis in Homer. The symbol is a central concern in part 3, where I attempt to place the Centos in their larger semiotic environment, namely the textual domains of Homer and the Bible, and their place in the world of late antiquity. The reasons (and the advantages) for taking a semiotic approach to this text are well stated by Mukarovsky, for without such an approach

> The theorist of art will always be inclined to regard the work of art as a purely formal structure or, on the other hand, as a direct reflection of the psychological . . . states of its creator or a direct reflection of the ideological, economic, social or cultural situation of the milieu in question. This train of thought will lead the theorist either to treat the evolution of art as a series of formal transformations or to deny evolution completely . . . or, finally, to conceive of it as passive commentary on an evolution exterior to art. Only the semiotic point of view allows theorists to recognize the autonomous existence and essential dynamism of artistic structure and to understand evolution of art as an immanent process but one in constant

---

5. Usher 1998. The manuscript in question is *Iviron* 4464 (Mt. Athos), catalogued and described by Lambros (1900:92) and collated by me against Stephanus's 1578 edition of the poem. For details, including arguments for identifying this recension with Eudocia's revision of Patricius, see Usher 1997. At the time of writing that article I was unaware of Schembra 1995, who wants to identify the Homeric cento eclogue edited by Ludwich with Eudocia's revision of Patricius. His arguments, however, are contradicted in Usher 1997:308-12.

dialectical relationship with the evolution of other domains of
culture. (Mukarovsky 1936:8)

This classic statement on the semiotics of art reflects my
objectives exactly. I am interested here in both the "autonomous
existence and essential dynamism" of the Centos' artistic structure
and the "constant dialectical relationship" they have "with the
evolution of other domains of culture." Before discussing either
surface or symbol, however, some preliminary information about the
text and its author is necessary. This is the purpose of part 1, which
places the Centos in their particular cultural and literary contexts.

As there is no preexisting body of criticism on this poem, I find
myself in the privileged, yet awkward position of having to start the
conversation. According to my privilege, I have drawn freely from
research in various disciplines—Homeric scholarship, biblical studies,
folktale analysis, linguistics, and semiotics. There are many ways I
might have approached this poem, and many other questions I might
have asked of it. The poem itself and the purpose of this study
seemed to call for eclecticism—even *centonization*. I sincerely hope
the patchwork offered here is useful and that it will be but the first of
many interpretations of this multifarious text.

Part One

Cento Contexts

1

Understanding the Homeric Centos

"Understanding art by means of its reception," writes Constance Perin,

> implies understanding culture itself. For what people find meaningful determines what will make them curious and pleased, anxious and fearful, distant and hostile. The reception of new, unusual, and difficult art—in all the arts—depends on interpreters who will speak as much to the culture as to the work of art. (Perin 1994:193)

The Homeric Centos are new, unusual, and sometimes difficult. They have not been well received, in either ancient or more modern times. One speaks then as much to the culture as to the work of art in saying that, despite their reception hitherto, the Homeric Centos are an intrinsically fascinating text, and a neglected document in the history of Homer reception.[1]

Eudocia's poem has especially much to contribute to the ongoing debate about the effects of orality and textuality in verbal art forms, and much to teach us about the aural and performative aspects of ancient reading, the processes of human memory, and the reception of Homeric poetry as oral poetry in later antiquity. The aural and mnemonic aspects of Eudocia's work were once admired: Petrus Candidus, the Centos' very first editor, described them in the Aldine edition of 1502 as a "model of mnemonic capacity" (τὰ τῆς μνήμης δείγματα), "a poem which proceeds eurhythmically, almost seamlessly, from the poetry of Homer" (ποίημα ἐκ τῆς Ὁμήρου προελθόν, εὐρυθμὸν

---

1. There is evidence, for example, that the Centos were known to, and perhaps used by, Milton and Joyce. For Milton see Harris 1898; for Joyce see Fàj 1968.

καὶ γλαφυρόν). To recast this assessment in the language of modern linguistics: the Homeric Centos may be said to stand to the *Iliad* and *Odyssey* as *parole* does to *langue.*

According to this familiar model, *parole* ("speech" or "*langue*-realization") corresponds to the activity of verbal combination, visualized as taking place on a horizontal axis. *Langue*, meaning "language as a complete system" or "*parole*-potential," corresponds to the process of verbal selection from a vertical axis. An individual's *langue*-awareness is, following Noam Chomsky, referred to as his "competence," and his *langue*-realization as verbal "performance" or "generation."[2] To apply the model to the Homeric Centos: Eudocia's competence in the text of the *Iliad* and *Odyssey*, her *langue*, is the basis for the generation of her cento poem.

Because she is a cento poet, Eudocia's *langue*-competence is much more specific than the kind of familiarity with the Homeric *Kunstsprache* and the habits or techniques associated with it (e.g., localization and colometric structure) that we see in Hesiod, the Homeric Hymns, the Alexandrian hexameter poets, or even Nonnus. Unlike them, Eudocia has no choice whether or not she will "imitate" Homer stylistically in a given line. As she scans the *langue*-axis of selection, the question is not "whether," but "which" line she will use. That is, the field open for selection is limited, because she is working from within a closed system (the actual Homeric texts), and linguistically that system, transmitted over centuries, reached her more or less intact. Leonard Muellner puts this beautifully: the Homeric *Kunst-*

---

2. For a succinct expression of Chomsky's notion of linguistic competence and performance, terms first used in *Aspects of a Theory of Syntax* (1965), see Chomsky 1985:7. On Chomsky's relationship to de Saussure, see Dresselhaus 1979. There is an excellent discussion of literary competence in a *parole-langue* system in Culler 1975:6-10; 113-30. The notion of linguistic competence in a traditional, formulaic language is well expressed by Cassidy and Ringler, who in discussing *langue* acquisition by the Anglo-Saxon *scop,* note that "language itself supplies a useful parallel. The child learns his language by abstracting recurrent patterns out of the apparent chaos he hears in the speech of adults. He learns how to substitute within grammatical 'frames'—substitute one noun for another, etc. The frames themselves remain constant. The oral poet learns, in a similar way, the grammar of formulaic substitution—and will ultimately be as flexible and spontaneous at oral poetical composition as we are at speaking our native language" (Cassidy and Ringler 1971:270-1).

sprache, he writes, "has an extension in time and place beyond that of natural languages, [and] comes with expressiveness and consistency built in and refined over generations of audience-performer inter-action" (Muellner 1990:98). Eudocia's own competence in the *Kunst-sprache*, as one expects of *parole* in general, generates idiosyncrasies, that is, solecisms within this closed system. In Eudocia's case, these are often ingenious, and we will be paying close attention to them in our analysis.

Eudocia's use of Homeric lines to express biblical themes also generates fascinating semiotic problems. Verweyen and Witting em-phasize that the cento, more so than other literary forms, "can serve two opposite purposes: on the one hand the constitution/ formation and confirmation/endorsement of norms" (by its use of canonical texts and authors), and "on the other hand their violation" (by the deconstruction and selective reassembly of those texts) (Verweyen and Witting 1991:173). In the Homeric Centos, the form serves both purposes at once: on the one hand Eudocia's use of the *Iliad* and *Odyssey* to express biblical and biblically derived themes affirms the cultural prestige of both Homer and the Bible in the world of late antiquity; and yet, because of the clash of these two very different sign systems in the Centos, her poem inevitably disturbs the integrity, and hence the authority, of both. This perhaps explains why the poem has received such bad reviews; yet it is precisely what makes the poem so attractive.

The cento aesthetic infuriated the Christian fathers Irenaeus and Jerome, two early critics of the cento form. In a well-known letter to Paulinus of Nola, Jerome says that cento poets "fit to their own private meaning passages that have nothing to do with that meaning, as if it were some great feat (and not a depraved method of exposition) to have an author's intention violated, and to make scripture conform to their own will, though in fact that same scripture flies in their face."[3] Irenaeus, in a discussion of the teachings of Valentinus, insists that cento-writing is a gnostic art. In taking over material from authoritative source texts, he argues, cento poets disregard the immediate context of the originals. As he puts it, "They

---

3. *Ad sensum suum incongrua aptant testimonia, quasi grande sit et non vitiosissimum docendi genus, depravare sententias, et ad voluntatem suam Scripturam habere re pugnantem* (Jerome *Ep.* 53.7 in Labourt 1953:15-6).

collect words and phrases lying about here and there in a text and transpose them from their natural context to an unnatural one."[4]

Natural or unnatural, there is nonetheless a logic to Eudocia's use of Homeric verses to communicate biblical themes. Frazer's definition of magic expresses it well, for the logic of the Cento aesthetic "is nothing but . . . [an] application of the very simplest and most elementary processes of the mind, namely the association of ideas by virtue of resemblance or contiguity" (Frazer 1906:52).[5] Indeed, the semiotic magic at work in this poem is pervasive, for beneath the apparent mismatch of material on the Cento surface, the two source texts are strongly bound by theme and structure. As stories of quest, cunning, suffering, recognition, and return, the tales of Christ and Odysseus are compatible, as we shall see, and their literary *Nachleben* attests to the adaptability of these two polytropic heroes.

It has been said that "the generations of men, throughout recorded time, have always told and retold two stories—that of a lost ship which searches the Mediterranean seas for a dearly loved island, and that of a god who is crucified on Golgotha" (Borges 1972:19). In the Homeric Centos, these two stories, the fabric of the Western imagination, are read one in terms of the other. Eudocia's poetic syncrasis of Homer and the Bible presents us with a unique comparative reading of those two texts. This "reading"—the *parole re-generation* of Homer's oral poetry—commands our attention as a feat of human memory, interpretation, and imagination; it also makes the Centos a case study in intertextuality, and in what the playwright Bertolt Brecht called *Verfremdung*, the aesthetic of "defamiliar-

---

4. Λέξεις καὶ ὀνόματα σποράδην κείμενα συλλέγοντες μεταφέρουσι . . . ἐκ τοῦ κατὰ φύσιν εἰς τὸ παρὰ φύσιν (Iren. *apud* Epiph. *Pan.* [Migne *PG* 41:532]).

5. Compare C. A. Faraone's observations on the appropriation of Homeric verses in late antique magical spells: "a single line cited in a magical recipe may be shorthand for citing a short passage . . . [where] the original context of the verse or verses in the Homeric poem usually dictates its power or usefulness in a magical ritual. Thus, for example, verses excerpted from an Homeric speech—used in epic to calm someone's anger or to assure the temporarily blinded Diomedes that the mist has been lifted from his eyes—could similarly be used to calm the anger or heal the eyesight of someone in day-to-day life" (Faraone 1996:85).

ization" (cf. Hunger 1978:99). As explained by Brecht himself, *Verfremdung* is a heuristic device: it aims "to deprive an event or character of any self-evident, familiar, or obvious quality, and to produce instead astonishment or curiosity about it" in order to "bring about heightened understanding."[6]

Cento lines 84-7, which describe "Man's first disobedience," neatly illustrate all these facets of Homeric Cento poetry. Eudocia here says of Eve:[7]

ἥ μεγὰ ἔργον ἔρεξεν ἀϊδρείῃσι νόοιο	ο 11.272
οὐλομένη, ἥ πολλὰ κάκ᾽ ἀνθρώποισιν ἔθηκε᾽	ο 17.287 †
πολλὰς δ᾽ ἰφθίμους ψυχὰς Ἄϊδι προΐαψεν	i 1.3
πᾶσι δ᾽ ἔθηκε πόνον, πολλοῖσι δὲ κήδε᾽ ἐφῆκεν.	i 21.524

She unwittingly did a monstrous deed,
and, destructive, she wrought many evils for men;
she cast many strong souls to Hades' abode,
wrought hardship for all, caused trouble for many.

Under close inspection, the text reveals the poet's manner of composition. First, in terms of the generation of the verse, we see how the appropriated Homeric lines are linked together by keywords (ἔθηκε, πολλά), a mnemonic aid frequently used in the composition of this poem, and with Homeric precedent (see chapter 6). In line 85, taken from *Odyssey* 17.287 (= 17.484), Eudocia substitutes the verb ἔθηκε for the Homeric reading δίδωσι at the end of the line. This and many other Cento substitutions, some accidental, others intentional, are often suggested to the poet by Homeric habits of word-collocation and word-localization (see chapter 3). Here the substitution is due to the influence, by association, of the first word of *Od.* 17.287, the enjambed participle οὐλομένη (see chapter 2), whose *locus classicus* is of course the second line of the *Iliad*: οὐλομένην, ἥ μυρί᾽ Ἀχαιοῖς ἄλγε᾽

---

6. "Einen Vorgang oder einen Charackter verfremden heisst zunächst einfach, dem Vorgang oder dem Charakter das Selbstverständliche, Bekannte, Einleuchtende zu nehmen und über ihn Staunen und Neugierde zu erzeugen" (Brecht 1933-41:301). Cf. Brecht 1935-41:364: "Die classische Verfremdung erzeugt erhöhtes Verständnis." On Brecht's theory and practice, see further Knopf 1986:102-6 and Brooker 1994:191-5.

7. An explanation of the sigla used here is given in chapter 2.

ἔθηκεν. *Iliad* 1.2, although unexpressed, suggests, on the principle of contiguity, *Iliad* 1.3 (used in Cento line 86), which in turn suggests a thematically related line (*Il.* 21.524), containing the verb ἔθηκε and the adjective πολλά, for line 87.

Eudocia's text also contains its own interpretation. The word οὐλο-μένη ("destructive") in line 85 (= *Od.* 17.287), for example, refers in Homer to the stomach (γαστέρα). Eudocia predicates the word here of Eve, implicitly equating her with a stomach, which is to say, a womb. For an audience steeped in Christian discourse, the Homeric referent (the unexpressed γαστέρα) suggests the curse of pain in childbearing mentioned in the Book of Genesis (3:16), and the adverse effects of "original sin" on the womb, which produced Cain, the world's first murderer (Gen 4:1). An audience steeped in the Homeric poems—and in late antiquity, this could be the same audience, as Irenaeus shows by his ready identification of the Homeric context and speaker for each verse in the ten-line cento he cites (Wilken 1967:32)—might appreciate the additional nuance that Homer himself uses οὐλομένη elsewhere in the *Odyssey* (though in a different metrical position) to describe Clytemnestra, the "destructive" wife of Agamemnon, party to the "fall" of the House of Atreus (*Od.* 4.92; 11.410; 24.97). In fact, earlier in this passage (77-9) Eudocia explicitly links Eve to Clytemnestra with these dire lines from *Odyssey* Book 24:

κουρίδιον κτείνασα πόσιν, στυγερὴ δέ τ᾽ ἀοιδὴ   ο 24.200
ἔσσετ᾽ ἐπ᾽ ἀνθρώπους, χαλεπὴν δέ τε φῆμιν ὄπασσεν   ο 24.201
θηλυτέρῃσι γυναιξί, καὶ ἥ κ᾽ εὐεργὸς ἔῃσιν.   ο 24.202

She destroyed her lawfully-wedded husband, and the song of it
will make men shudder; she has also given women
a bad reputation, even the woman who does what is right.

The word οὐλομένη in line 85, especially with the verb ἔθηκε substituted for δίδωσι and followed by *Iliad* 1.3 in line 86, also evokes the wrath of Achilles, the catalyst that sets the whole story of the *Iliad* in motion, just as Eve's unwitting role in the fall of man from Paradise is the initial crisis in the biblical story. Here too Eudocia had precedent in the Homeric *langue*. At a crucial point in his narrative, the *Iliad* poet himself evokes this initial crisis when in Agamemnon's apology to Achilles he qualifies Ἄτη ("Folly") with an enjambed οὐλο-μένη in initial position: πρέσβα Διὸς θυγάτηρ Ἄτη, ἣ πάντας ἀᾶται /

οὐλομένη (*Il.* 19.91-2).[8]

Cento line 84 (= *Od.* 11.272), like οὐλομένη used of the womb and of Clytemnestra, also evokes images of fateful marriage and curse. This Homeric line is taken from the parade of nefarious women Odysseus meets in Hades and refers to Epikaste (Jocasta), the mother and unwitting spouse of her son, Oedipus. The appropriation of this line here implies for the reader who knows Homer and Greek tragedy that Eve's sin was not just destructive, but incestuous as well. Here we feel the full effects of defamiliarization: to assimilate Eve, "Mother of All the Living," with the mother of Oedipus is (momentarily) disconcerting.

Whether or not Eudocia intended to defamiliarize her audience in this or in any given Cento passage is difficult to gauge.[9] We do not have statements from Eudocia as clear or explicit as the one from the German poet Erich Weinert, for example, who in his cento poem "Einheitsvolkslied" (published in 1924) stitches together popular verses from Germanic folklore and *Lieder* in order to deconstruct those texts which he felt articulated the identity of certain social classes.[10]

All the evidence we possess about her life and interests suggests the Empress was a pious Christian; it is therefore unlikely that she intended to undermine Christian belief and doctrine.[11] The defamiliar-

---

8. On the "deictic" potential of localized words and runovers in Homer, see the study of Kahane (1994).

9. This problem was acknowledged by Bakhtin in reference to centonic, parodic, and macaronic treatments of Christian themes in the Middle Ages (Bakhtin 1981:68-9).

10. "When I saw the bourgeoisie and petite-bourgeousie with whom I had contact in my day-to-day affairs rise up in all their cowardly arrogance and lies," Weinert tells us in his autobiography, "I reacted with spite. I felt the urge to yank down the shorts of these patriots in top coat and tails—stained with the blood of the workers—and expose their warts to the world. My intent in this poem was to make them look ridiculous" (Quoted in Verweyen and Witting 1991:173, my translation).

11. "Für Eudokia war der christliche Glaube keineswegs ein blosses Lippenbekenntnis. Er formte vielmehr ihr Leben und Denken und war die wichtigste Inspiration ihrer Dichtung" is an accurate assessment (West

ization aesthetic in the Homeric Centos is unmistakable, but it is primarily an *attendant* effect, the result of Cento intertextuality, dependent upon, or activated by, a third-party reader's knowledge of Homer. This is not to say that Eudocia was incapable of irony, humor, or even intentional *Verfremdung*. Indeed, ambiguity is Eudocia's strong suit, showing, as we shall see in due course, all seven of William Empson's types.[12] What is clear from her treatment of the Fall, however, is that Eudocia drew deeply from the repository of Homeric poetry to tease meanings out of Homer and the Bible that she as a reader found there; and this exhilarating mixture of narrative ambiguity and logic exhibited in this Cento vignette is characteristic of the poem as a whole.

Decades before Brecht, the Russian Formalists had argued that defamiliarization, which they termed *ostranenie*, constitutes the very "literariness" of literature,[13] a proposition revived recently by Harold Bloom, who finds "strangeness" the common thread that runs through the Western literary canon (Bloom 1994:3). The Centos are strange. They are not, however, a high work of fine art, but are more akin to folk art. That too is part of their appeal. Eudocia's mismatch of Homeric and biblical text-worlds brings to mind the magnificently naive painting of American folk artists Morris Hirshfield, Howard Finster, and Oscar de Mejo, whose flat surfaces teem with visual contradictions: stunted limbs, disproportionately elaborate costumes, biblical mixed with secular iconography. Finster's work in particular

1978:110; cf. Haffner 1996:223 and the studies of Cameron 1982 and Holum 1982).

12. Listed in *Seven Types of Ambiguity* as follows: (1) "a detail is effective in several ways at once, e.g. by comparison with several points of likeness, antitheses with several points of difference"; (2) "two or more meanings are fully resolved into one"; (3) "two apparently unconnected meanings are given simultaneously" (as in puns); (4) "alternative meanings combine to make clear a complicated state of mind in the author"; (5) "fortunate confusion[s], as when the author is discovering his idea in the act of writing"; (6) "what is said is contradictory or irrelevant and the reader is forced to invent interpretations"; (7) "full contradiction, marking a division in the author's mind" (Empson 1966:v-vi).

13. On the Formalist conception of "literariness" (*literaturnost*), see Erlich 1965:172; Todorov 1973:70; and P. Steiner 1984:212-3. On *ostranenie* see Birnbaum 1985:148-50 and Fowler 1987:101.

smacks of the Cento aesthetic: "Finster's episodic and multi-panel paintings . . . read like medieval narratives in their parataxis which, rather than unfold in a sequential ordering of events, abruptly joins them side by side in a manner that is filmic or televisionistic as images shift from panel to panel" (J. Murray 1980:161).

Like Finster and his ilk, Eudocia created a work of what art historians call "Outsider Art" (Cardinal 1994:21-43). Artist Outsiders have certain traits in common: they are largely self-taught; they often reuse discarded materials; their work stands outside established canons of taste; the artists themselves are often marginalized socially. In terms of their reception, the Centos qualify as Outsider Art on all counts. Even their author can be constructed as somewhat of an Artist Outsider: Eudocia, history's "first writing empress" (van Deun 1993:273), composed this work while in exile in Jerusalem on charges of adultery (Holum 1982:193-4). The story of Eudocia's affair with Paulinus, Theodosius's most trusted advisor, and the Emperor's discovery of it through an erotic "apple of discord" is legendary—at once biblical and Homeric. Behind that legend, however, lies an important truth, that in Eudocia the fantasies of critics like Harold Bloom, and before him Samuel Butler, find perfect historical expression. Butler and Bloom sought, and found, a woman in the author of two of western literature's greatest works: Butler for Homer in his *Authoress of the Odyssey* (1897), and Bloom for the biblical Genesis in his *Book of J* (1990). The fantasy entertained here is that the Empress sits enthroned between both critics like a πότνια θηρῶν as she mediates between Homeric text and biblical theme. That mediation, and not Eudocia herself, is the focus of this study—Eudocia, that is, not as an historical figure in the traditional sense, but as a Homeric reader of the Bible.

2

Eudocia Augusta: Reader-Rhapsode

The Homeric Centos are the product of a manuscript culture and thus share with the *Iliad*, the *Odyssey*, and the books of the Bible problems relating to date, authorship, and the transmission of the text. The particular situation we face is also similar to the problems encountered in establishing the texts of early print culture, including some of the finest Renaissance poetry, for example, the works of Donne, Wotton, and Sir Philip Sidney. As a recent editor describes it (Norbrook 1993:xxxv),

> The concept of an accurate, correct text representing what an author had finally decided on was . . . an unfamiliar one in the Renaissance. Once in circulation, a poem could easily change its form, being adapted for different purposes at different times by different people. The whole notion of authors' control over, or ownership of, their texts was a relative one.

This is precisely what has happened to the Homeric Centos. As we learn from Eudocia's prologue to the poem, an otherwise unknown bishop named Patricius composed the work in the latter third of the fourth century C.E. but left it, in Eudocia's judgment, "half-finished" (ἡμιτέλεστον). The Empress later edited and greatly expanded Patricius's poem during her exile in Jerusalem, sometime after 443 C.E. (Holum 1982:220).

As suggested in the previous chapter, Eudocia's Centos effectively prove that Homer continued to be appreciated aurally as an oral poet in late antiquity, and, more importantly, could be reproduced as such. This does not mean that actual texts played no role in the process of composition. Indeed, Eudocia speaks of Patricius's poem as his "columns" (σελίδες), his "writing tablet" (δέλτον) and "book" (βίβλος), and of course she knew her Homer from manuscript copies of the

Iliad and *Odyssey*. However, the information we possess about the origin and context of the cento form and the nature of Eudocia's editorial work on Patricius's poem as revealed in her prologue indicate that oral/aural factors loom large in the composition and transmission of the Centos. These two areas of evidence suggest that Eudocia, a late antique *reader* of Homer, is heir to the ancient tradition of rhapsodic *performance* as well.

In her verse prologue (5-8), Eudocia says that the reason for undertaking her revision of Patricius's poem was that her predecessor "did not declare (ἀγόρευσεν) everything accurately . . . nor in singing (ἀείδων) did he remember (ἐμνήσατο) the actual verses that Homer uttered (εἶπεν)." Eudocia's description here emphasizes the vocal, aural, and mnemonic aspects of Patricius's cento, and by extension, those of the poetry of Homer himself. The same qualities are stressed in her assessment of another predecessor in the art of composing Homeric centos, the praetorian prefect of the East under Theodosius I, Flavius Eutolmius Tatianus[1] (Prologue 19-27):

> And if anyone listens to (εἰσαΐων) the formal beauty (μορφήν[2]) of wise Tatian the poet (ὑμνοπόλοιο), and if he likes what he hears (τέρψειεν ἀκουήν), it was on account of the 'double' that Tatian composed his epic poem (ἀοιδήν) out of Homeric song, using verses of his own composition as well.[3] It is a terrible song that sings (ἐνέπουσαν αὐτήν) of warlike Trojans, about how the sons of Achaians destroyed the city of Priam, Troy itself holding out against them; it sings of gods and men raging in the terrible din of battle, the same ones Homer once sang with his voice of bronze (χαλκεόφωνος . . . αὔτησεν Ὅμηρος).

---

1. *PLRE* I 876-8 ('Tatianus 5'); see Usher 1997:314.

2. Cf. the Homeric μορφὴ ἐπέων (*Od.* 11.367).

3. "Doubles" (δοιάδες) are passages taken over from Homer in sequences of two or more lines. According to the so-called rules of cento composition laid down by Ausonius in the preface to his *Cento nuptialis* such doubles were to be avoided. Tatian avoided them by interspersing lines of his own composition. Eudocia does not avoid them and thus "apologizes" for them in her prologue. See further Usher 1997:313-5 and chapter 3 below.

Eudocia's synaesthetic metaphors of sight and sound, text and voice, remind us that the frequent practice of reading (or being read to) aloud in antiquity necessarily blurs any sharp distinction between spoken word and written text (Gamble 1995:204, 321).[4] In the fourth and fifth centuries C.E., this aspect of Greco-Roman culture is perhaps appreciated most by scholars of Christian prose literature, where it is often difficult to determine which texts were originally sermons actually delivered to a congregation and which are treatises intended primarily for a reading public (Dihle 1994:521).

Picking up on Paul Zumthor's notion of *vocalité* in medieval poetry, Doane and Pasternack (1991) describe the interplay between orality and textuality in later antiquity and the Middle Ages with the apt phrase *vox intexta*, "sound sewn into text" (cf. Gamble 1995:203-4). In part 2 we will see in detail how many features of the orally derived poetry of the *Iliad* and *Odyssey*—the sound sewn into text—actually facilitated the composition of the Homeric Centos. The question here is: In the *parole-langue* model proposed earlier, what would be the nature and significance of Eudocia's revisions of Patricius? The answer is to be found in line 6 of the prologue, which states that Patricius "did not preserve the harmony of the verses" (οὐδὲ μὲν ἁρμονίην ἐπέων ἐφύλαξε), and in line 14 where Eudocia says she therefore conferred it upon them (ἁρμονίην ἱερὴν ἐπέεσσιν ἔδωκα).

It is clear from the prologue that Eudocia performed her harmonizing on the actual Homeric verses (ἔπη), and that this somehow involved correcting them. The need for such corrections arose, we recall, because Patricius "did not declare all his verses accurately" (οὐ πάμπαν ἐτήτυμα πάντ᾽ ἀγόρευσεν), "nor in singing did he remember only those verses sung by the brazen heart of blameless Homer" (οὐδὲ μόνων ἐπέων ἐμνήσατο κεῖνος ἀείδων / ὁππόσα χάλκεον ἦτορ ἀμεμφέος εἶπεν ῾Ομήρου). Her response was "to *draw out* what was *not in order*" (ὅσσα μὲν ἐν βίβλοισιν ἔπη πέλεν οὐ κατὰ κόσμον / πάντ᾽ ἄμυδις κείνοιο σοφῆς ἐξείρυσα βίβλου), "and to add what he left out" (ὅσσα δ᾽ ἐκεῖνος ἔλειπεν, ἐγὼ πάλιν ἐν σελίδεσσι / γράψα).

---

4. While it is fair to say that the ancients could and did read silently (or with some small degree of subvocalization) to themselves (cf. Knox 1968), I find the conclusion of A. K. Gavrilov that "the phenomenon of reading itself is fundamentally the same in modern and ancient culture" (Gavrilov 1997; cf. Burnyeat 1997) rather overstated.

As described here, Eudocia's editorial work was clearly a form of *emendatio*, which according to Quintilian (*Instit.* 10.4.1) entails "addition, excision, and alteration" (*adiicere, detrahere, mutare*). Eudocia, we have just seen, claims to have performed all three tasks. I have argued elsewhere that she is responsible for nearly three-quarters of the poem's twenty-four hundred lines (Usher 1997). These are her additions. The character of her excisions and alterations is bound up in the notion of ἁρμονία, the very quality of Homer's poetry that Patricius did not preserve. It is here that we can detect an aural dimension in her revisions, for ἁρμονία is an ancient critical term for proper accentuation in the vocalization of texts (Arist. *Rhet.* 1403b with Allen 1987:116).

Dionysius Thrax, for example, speaks of ἁρμονία as an important element in act and art of reading (ἀνάγνωσις), and hence recitation, which he defines as the "unfaltering pronunciation" (ἀδιάπτωτος προ–φορά) of poetry or prose (Uhlig 1883:6). By reading "with an ear for accentuation" (κατὰ προσῳδίαν), he suggests, we apprehend a poet's art or skill (τέχνη), which according to Dionysius of Halicarnassus is what produces ἁρμονία (*De comp. verb.* 3). For Dionysius of Halicarnassus, the aural quality ἁρμονία is the desired object of "composition" (σύνθεσις), the effective combination and arrangement of syllables, words, and clauses; this includes the harmonius arrangement of μέλος, ῥυθμοί, μέτρα, and of various speech-sound phenomena involving "slurring" (συναλοιφή) (*De comp. verb.* 6; with Rutherford 1905:158 n. 2, 164 n. 14). Reading or reciting κατὰ προσῳδίαν, then, preserves the ἁρμονία of a poetic composition.

Two of Dionysius's principal examples of ἁρμονία come from Homer, and his analysis sheds some light on Eudocia's use of the word in the prologue. To prove that σύνθεσις is more important than word-selection (ἐκλογή), Dionysius cites the homely description of Odysseus's breakfast in his swineherd's hut (*Od.* 16.1-16), the beauty of which, he says, consists not in the use of figurative language, but in the composition (σύνθεσις), specifically in the meter (*De comp. verb.* 3). "If the meter were broken up," he writes, "the very same lines would appear cheap (φαῦλα) and unworthy of our emulation (ἄζηλα)."

Iliad 12.433-5 is offered as another example of ἁρμονία. To demonstrate the same point he made with *Odyssey* 16.1-16, Dionysius performs some experiments upon these lines, changing the word order several times to create several different "heroic" rhythms (*De comp.*

verb. 4). He concludes that such rearrangements spoil the original: "While the choice of words remains the same and only the σύνθεσις is altered, the rhythm and meter changes along with it, as well as the structure, complexion, character, and emotion—indeed, the whole meaning—of the verses."[5]

As an aesthetic principle, ἁρμονία, the sound-quality of a verbal composition, is paramount: it affects the poetic meaning of an entire passage. Dionysius does not transpose whole Homeric lines in his verbal experiments, only the words within them, so what he would have made of the cento poet's stichic rearrangements one can only guess. His identification of Homeric ἁρμονία with Homeric μέτρα, however, is surely a clue to understanding the nature of Patricius's cento-poetic flaws.

Good composition, according to Dionysius, has a "beauty" or "order" consisting of ἁρμονία (κόσμον ἁρμονίας). Patricius, according to Eudocia, lacked both qualities because he did not declare Homer accurately. In fact, she says much of his poem was οὐ κατὰ κόσμον. Patricius's σύνθεσις was somehow faulty. Perhaps his original cento— at least as it had been transmitted to her—contained non-Homeric forms, displaced words, and/or poorly joined half-lines and metrical flaws caused by phonological changes in the Greek language and by the incipient shift from accentuation based on pitch to accentuation based on stress in the fourth and fifth centuries (Allen 1987:130-1; Browning 1983:24-6). Traces of his work, or the Empress's own limitations in this regard, may perhaps remain in the few non-Homeric lines left in Eudocia's recension, and in the occasional metrical fault. By and large, however, Eudocia successfully took it upon herself to restore the proper (i.e. Homeric) ἁρμονία of such lines and expanded Patricius's poem on the same principle, keeping as close as possible to Homeric wording (cf. Alan Cameron 1982:284).

Eudocia's editorial work, then, was not entirely unlike the work involved in the production of the διορθώσεις of the Homeric text undertaken by Aristotle and the Hellenistic critics, Zenodotus, Aristophanes, and Aristarchus. In fact, the verb διορθόω is the word used in

5. Τῆς μὲν ἐκλογῆς τῶν ὀνομάτων τῆς αὐτῆς μενούσης, τῆς δὲ συνθέσεως μόνης μεταπεσούσης τά τε μέτρα μεταρρυθμίζεσθαι καὶ συμμεταπίπτειν αὐτοῖς τὰ σχήματα, τὰ χρώματα, τὰ ἤθη, τὰ πάθη, τὴν ὅλην τῶν ποιημάτων ἀξί-ωσιν.

the testimonia and manuscript epigraphs to describe her activity, just as συντίθημι is used of Patricius's original composition (Usher 1997: 310). As Gregory Nagy has recently emphasized, the production of the Hellenistic corrected editions or copies of Homer essentially involved two things: the correct accentuation and thus pronunciation of Homeric verse (Nagy 1996a:118-27),[6] and the athetesis of lines and passages judged to be interpolations. In each type of correction Nagy argues persuasively that both the variants (including the so-called concordance interpolations) and the Hellenistic critics' notions of correctness and authenticity (e.g., proper pronunciation marked by diacritics; the *numerus versuum* of each poem) were established by the performance traditions of rhapsodes. Consequently, many textual variants in the papyri and medieval manuscripts, Nagy argues, should be regarded as "authentic" variants stemming from those living performance traditions (Nagy 1996a:146-7).

Of course, in comparing Eudocia's concern for ἁρμονία with the Hellenistic critics' methods of textual criticism, I do not mean to suggest that she is a critic of that caliber or stripe, much less that we should value her Centos primarily as a *textual* witness for Homer. Although this has been the direction of recent work on the poem (e.g., Alfieri 1987; 1989), it is not the most rewarding path to follow, for in the Centos, we are dealing not with a "reperformed composer," to borrow Nagy's phrase, but rather with a "recomposed performer" (Nagy 1996a:60), whose text is in effect a "recomposition-in-performance" (Nagy 1996a:78). Indeed, I suggest that Eudocia's Centos have their own peculiar place in the rhapsodic tradition of authentic variation and creative manipulation of the Homeric repertoire, a proposition supported by our sources.

Eustathius, for example, citing Pindar *Nemean* 2.2 on the Homeridae (Ὁμηρίδαι / ῥαπτῶν ἐπέων τὰ πόλλ' ἀοιδοί), explicitly compares the Homeric cento poet to the ancient rhapsode. In his discussion of the use of the term ῥαψῳδία to designate the books of the *Iliad*, Eustathius notes that the Homeric Centos are "a clear example of this kind of stitching" (τῆς δὲ τοιαύτης ῥάψεως παράδειγμα σαφὲς καὶ οἱ κέντρωνες, τουτέστι τὰ λεγόμενα Ὁμηρόκεντρα), and that centonism, like ῥαψῳδία, is

---

6. Aristotle is reported to have made notes on diacritics in the margin of the text, while Aristarchus confined such remarks to his commentaries (cf. Nagy 1996a:135).

"song stitched together from either of the two poems of Homer in a manner appropriate to the business at hand, be it a wedding or a festival" (καὶ ῥαψῳδία δὲ ἡ ἐξ ἑκατέρων τῶν Ὁμηρικῶν ποίησεων συρραφεῖα ᾠδὴ ἀναλόγως τῷ ὑποκειμένῳ πράγματι, γάμῳ τυχὸν ἢ ἑορτῇ, van der Valk 1971:I.10.18-29).

Heliodorus, a seventh-century commentator on Dionysius Thrax, questions this derivation of ῥαψῳδία from the verb ῥάπτειν (preferring instead the popular—and morphologically untenable—derivation from ῥαβδός, "staff") by citing a short seven-line Homeric cento about Echo and Pan, arguing as follows (Hilgard 1901:480-1):

> Some say that rhapsody is song stitched together out of different Homeric passages (τόποι). However, if this were true, then this little passage [the short cento about Echo and Pan] would be called rhapsody, even though these verses are no longer in their proper Homeric order. Actually, such compositions are called centos; just as a cento is said to be a coverlet made out of various swatches of fabric, so too the themes (νοήματα) which have been composed out of various epic poems are called centos.[7]

In surveying the many textile metaphors for poetic composition in classical antiquity (for example, Latin *texo*, Greek ῥάπτω, ὑφαίνω), Nagy concludes that in ῥαψῳδία "many and various fabrics of song, each one already made (that is, each one already woven), become remade into a unity, a single new continuous fabric, by being sewn together" (Nagy 1996b:86). This is a fitting description of the centonism of Eudocia, who too took a fabric of song, already made, and remade it into a "single new continuous fabric" by sewing it together. When we review the ancient evidence, however, we see that the centonist and rhapsode share more than a metaphor drawn from the making of textiles, regardless of whether the verses in Homeric centos remain in their proper order or not.

---

7. Ῥαψῳδίαν δὲ εἶναι λέγουσι τὴν ἐκ διαφόρων τόπων Ὁμηρικῶν ἐρραμμένην ᾠδήν . . . ἀλλ᾽ εἰ τοῦτο ἦν ἀληθές, αὐτὰ ἂν μόνα ἐκαλεῖτο ῥαψῳδία, καὶ οὐκέτι τὰ κατὰ τάξιν Ὁμήρου· εἴρηται δὲ ὅτι τὰ τοιαῦτα κέντρωνες καλοῦνται· καὶ ὥσπερ κέντρων λέγεται περιβόλαιον τὸ ἐκ διαφόρων ῥακῶν συγκείμενον, οὕτω καὶ τὰ ἐκ διαφόρων ἐπῶν συγκείμενα νοήματα κέτρωνες καλοῦνται.

We know that the first stitchers of Homeric verse, the archaic rhapsodes, recited Homer and other texts from memory—both at public festivals and in private settings—and were believed to have borrowed lines or passages from other poems, or other places in the same poem, and to have patched them onto the texts they (or their competitors) recited.[8] The disciples of the rhapsode Kynaithos of Chios, for example, the reputed author of the *Homeric Hymn to Apollo* (with its notable suture of Delphic and Delian material), were even believed to have "inserted many verses of their own composition" into the Homeric poems.[9]

The elasticity of the Homeric repertoire during the archaic period is underscored by Aelian's remark that for ancient rhapsodes what we now possess as the *Iliad* and *Odyssey* were not thought of as continuous poems but as discrete episodes: "The Doloneia, The Aristeia of Agamemnon, The Catalogue of Ships . . . The Ransom . . . What Happened in Pylos . . . The Cyclopeia, The Nekuia."[10] Similarly, Dionysius Thrax, in the same portion of his treatise in which he discusses reading, defines ῥαψῳδία as "the part of a poem that contains the major 'theme' or 'main subject' (ὑπόθεσις) in a given book of the *Iliad* or *Odyssey*" (Uhlig 1883:8). Another ancient commentator on Dionysius, Melampos, explains (Hilgard 1901:28):

> The poem is the whole book—for example, the whole *Iliad* or *Odyssey*—whereas the sections of these poems are called ῥαψῳδίαι. Dionysius is correct to say each part contains its

---

8. For the ancient testimonia see Herington (1985:167-76). Andrew Ford (1988:300-7) points out that the word ῥαψῳδία as used in antiquity extends beyond the genre of epic to any type of recited or chanted poetry that was unaccompanied by music.

9. Οἱ ῥαψῳδοὶ οὐκέτι τὸ γένος εἰς Ὅμηρον ἀνάγοντες, ἐπιφανεῖς δὲ ἐγένοντο οἱ περὶ Κύναιθον, οὕς φασι πολλὰ τῶν ἐπῶν ποιήσαντες ἐμβαλεῖν εἰς τὴν Ὁμήρου ποίησιν (schol. Pind. *Nem.* 2); cf. Eustathius: οἱ περὶ τὸν Κύναιθον καὶ πολλὰ τῶν ἐπῶν αὐτοὶ ποιήσαντες παρενέβαλον (van der Valk 1971:I.11.40).

10. Τὰ Ὁμήρου ἔπη πρότερον διῃρημένα ᾖδον οἱ παλαιοί. οἷον ἔλεγον Τὴν . . . Δολώνειάν τινα καὶ Ἀριστείαν Ἀγαμέμνονος καὶ Νεῶν κατάλογον καὶ . . . Λύτρα καὶ . . . Τὰ ἐν Πύλῳ καὶ . . . Κυκλώπειαν καὶ Νέκυιαν (*Var. Hist.* 13.14; cf. Nagy 1996b:78 following Sealey 1957).

own ὑπόθεσις, and this ὑπόθεσις is not contained in the other parts. For example, *Iliad* Book 1 contains the "The Battle between Achilles and Agamemnon," Book 2 "The Dream Sent to Agamemnon from Zeus," Book 3 "The Single Combat between Alexander and Menelaus," and so forth. Each of these "comprises" (in Dionysius' words), or rather, "contains," its own ὑπόθεσις, which is a part of the poem as a whole.[11]

Eudocia's poem also unfolds as a chain of episodes: "Adam, Eve and the Serpent's Trick" (Περὶ τοῦ Ἀδὰμ καὶ τῆς Εὔας καὶ περὶ τῆς ἀπάτης τοῦ ὄφεως) . . . "The Annunciation" (Περὶ τοῦ εὐαγγελισμοῦ) . . . "The Betrayal" (Περὶ τῆς προδοσίας), and so forth. That the Centos were actually composed by "theme" (ὑπόθεσις—on which more below) is the topic of chapters 4-7. The important point here, *à propos* Eudocia, is the connection Dionysius makes between reading and ῥαψῳδία.

In a revealing comment, Melampos traces Dionysius's flow of thought from reading to rhapsody, reasoning that "when children begin to read, they latch onto the Homeric poems before all other books" (οἱ ἀρχόμενοι ἀναγίνωσκειν παῖδες πρὸ πάντων τῶν βιβλίων ἅπτονται τῶν Ὁμηρικῶν); thus "[Dionysius] wants to teach them what the word ῥαψῳδία means" (Hilgard 1901:28; cf. Pecorella 1962:94). We have evidence from Asia Minor and Chios dating to the first century B.C.E. that rhapsodic exercises were actually practiced in the schools. In Teos, for example, competitions took place in which secondary level students read Homer aloud, "each competitior taking up the text at the point where his predecessor had left off" (Marrou 1956:166).[12]

---

11. Ποίημα μὲν γάρ ἐστι τὸ ὅλον βιβλίον, ὡς ἡ Ἰλιὰς καὶ ἡ Ὀδύσσεια, τὰ δὲ τμήματα αὐτῶν ῥαψῳδίαι καλοῦνται· καλῶς οὖν εἶπε μέρος περιέχει τινὰ ἰδικὴν ὑπόθεσιν μὴ ἐμφερομένην ἐν τοῖς ἄλλοις μέρεσιν, ὡς τὸ μὲν Α περιέχει τὴν μάχην τοῦ Ἀχιλλέως καὶ Ἀγαμέμνονος, τὸ δὲ Β τὸν ὄνειρον τὸν πεμθέντα ὑπὸ τοῦ Διὸς πρὸς Ἀγαμέμνονα, τὸ δὲ Γ τὴν μονομαχίαν τοῦ Ἀλεξάνδρου καὶ Μενελάου, καὶ τὰ ἑξῆς. ἕκαστον οὖν τούτων ἐμπεριείληφε, τουτέστι περιέχει, ἰδικήν τινα ὑπόθεσιν, ὃ μέρος ἐστὶ τοῦ ὅλου ποιήματος.

12. I mention in this context an Attic red-figure kyathos of the fifth-century B.C.E. that portrays a seated youth peering into a book, flanked by two other youths holding what appear to be ῥαβδοί (Berlin 2322 in Beazley 1963:239.134; 1645).

In the sixth century B.C.E., Hipparchus, son of the Athenian tyrant Pisistratus, enacted the so-called Panathenaic rule, whereby "the episodes of Homeric story-telling were arranged in a constant order for rhapsodes to follow" (Sealey 1957:349). The rule of Hipparchus was also an attempt to limit the performances of epic poetry (which earlier had probably included episodes from the Epic Cycle as well) to the material in our *Iliad* and *Odyssey*, an action which constituted "a narrowing of the repertoire . . . with no freedom to 'stitch together' episodes in different ways" (Shapiro 1993:104).[13] In a sense, centonism represents an innovative return to that lost freedom.[14] The Homeric cento, which perhaps originated as a spoof on rhapsodic exercises in the schools, becomes, in Eudocia's hands, a serious poetic medium. In their rhapsodic treatment of non-Homeric themes, Eudocia's Centos mark a significant chapter in the cultural and literary history of the Roman empire.

Inscriptional evidence indicates that rhapsodic performances of Homer continued at games and festivals until at least as late as the third-century C.E. (West 1981:114)—the period to which our first centos date—and it is possible that professional rhapsodes or *Homeristai* in the Roman empire were also cento poets. A short Homeric cento graffito found inscribed on the leg of a statue of Memnon in Egypt, for example, was composed by a man who appears to have been a professional poet working in the age of Hadrian, one "Areios, an Homeric poet from the Museum" in Alexandria (Ἀρείου Ὁμηρικοῦ ποιητοῦ ἐκ Μουσείου Bernand 1960:111-3; cf. Bowie 1990: 65).

Whether this Areios was a rhapsode or not, our two earliest sources of information about Homeric centos give us a clear picture of the cento poet as a performance artist. "They set themselves subjects at random and then try to declaim them extemporaneously in lines from Homer," writes the church father Irenaeus (τοῖς ὑποθέσεις τὰς

---

13. Nagy, adducing evidence and terminology from the study of contemporary Indian performance traditions, sees the Panathenaic rule as the culmination of a process of "even" or "equalized" weighting of individual episodes, "a communalization of repertoire" (Nagy 1996b:76-82).

14. This was intimated by Fabricius (1790:552): *verisimile sane videtur, centones eiusmodi Homericos decantatos fuisse a Rhapsodis, antequam de vero ordine carminum Homericorum constaret.*

τυχούσας αὐτοῖς προβαλλομένοις, ἔπειτα πειρωμένοις ἐκ τῶν Ὁμήρου ποιημάτων μελετᾶν αὐτὰς [Iren. *apud* Epiph. *Pan.* II, 29.9]). Or, as the author of the *Life and Writings of Homer* describes the activity, cento poets "propose non-Homeric themes (ὑποθέσεις) and fit Homeric verses to them, transposing them and stringing them together" (ἑτέρας ὑποθέσεις προθέμενοι ἁρμόζουσιν ἐπ᾽ αὐτὰς τὰ ἔπη μετατιθέντες καὶ συνείροντες Keaney and Lamberton 1996:310-11).

Both references place this art form squarely in the ancient rhetorical tradition of declamation, where μελετάω, the verb used by Irenaeus, is a technical term meaning "to declaim," or, to reduce that Latin word to its etymological base, "to raise one's voice aloud" (in Greek, ἀναφώνησις), while ὑπόθεσις, used by both authors, is a technical term for the specific "theme" declaimed (Russell 1983:141; Heath 1995:17-18).[15] A memorable description of an accomplished practitioner of this art, Isaeus, is given by the Younger Pliny (*Ep.* 2.3). "He always speaks extempore," Pliny writes to a friend:

> He lets his audience choose the topic, and often the side he is to argue. He gets up, wraps himself in a cloak and begins. Almost instantly every sort of word comes readily to this learned man's mind—just the right words. In these spontaneous performances his wide reading and experience in composing shines forth. His memory is unbelievable. He can repeat what he has just spoken extempore without missing a word.[16]

If the Homeric cento poet is a successor to the ancient rhapsode,

---

15. Wilken (1967:30), who is concerned primarily with Irenaeus's theological attack on the Valentinian Gnostics, translates the word ὑπόθεσις in this passage as "system." This is true enough to the meaning of the word in Christian theological discourse (Lampe 1961 *s.v.* ὑπόθεσις 3.a. and b.), but it fails to recognize the analogy Irenaeus is drawing between the Valentinians' haphazard concatenation of unrelated proof texts from Scripture and the *impromptu* performances of cento-declaimers of Homer.

16. *Dicit semper ex tempore . . . electionem auditoribus permittit, saepe etiam partes; surgit amicitur incipit; statim omnia ac paene pariter ad manum, sensus reconditi occcursant, verba—sed qualia!—quaesita et exculta. Multa lectio in subitis, multa scriptio elucet. . . . Incredibilis memoria: repetit altius quae dixit ex tempore, ne verbo quidem labitur.*

then declamation, I suggest, is their historical intermediary, and Homeric centos are best viewed as a rhapsodic expression of it, requiring of their practitioners the same great mnemonic capacity and technical expertise (cf. P. Murray 1996:98). Long after Homer and his primary oral culture had passed away, declaimers, both schoolboys and professionals, practiced a form of oral composition in their improvised speech-performances. In fact, Greek declamation, like Eudocia's centonism, is a generative system dependent upon a speaker's *langue*-competence for verbalization: "Typically, a speaker will aim to generate a superabundance from which to select an effective combination of mutually supporting material," according to a recent study of Hermogenes' treatise on declamation, *On Issues*. "To make a selection the speaker must already have an eye on the way the material will be organized" (Heath 1995:7).

This, as we shall see in subsequent chapters, is an apt characterization of Eudocia's method. A crucial difference between Eudocia's cento poetry and declamation, however, lies in the fact that Eudocia does not handle her themes according to the rules of rhetoric, with its five-step process of *inventio, dispositio, elocutio, memoria,* and *pronuntiatio* (Quint. *Inst.* 3.3.1-10), but rather "according to Homer," that is, according to the Parryan principles of economy and extension, and guided by the semiotic principles of resemblance and contiguity.

The centonists of Eustathius's day were encomiasts (van der Valk 1971:IV.758.1-4). Eudocia too was adept in this art. In the year 438, on her way to Jerusalem where she would eventually compose the Centos, the Empress visited Antioch, delivered an encomium on the city before the Senate, and brought the house down (ἔκραξαν αὐτῇ οἱ τῆς πόλεως) with a pastiche from Homer (Ludwich 1897:12-13; cf. Holum 1982:117, 186). Eudocia's use of the cento form as encomium suggests that her Centos may actually have been composed with performance in mind, perhaps even during performance. Sadly, like the performances of Homer and the recitations of rhapsodes, these are forever lost to us with the living culture that produced them.

This much, however, is certain: like Xenophon's friend Niceratus before her, Michael Psellus after her, and in our time, the late Steven Powelson, "a retired C.P.A. and amateur Homeric rhapsode," Eudocia knew Homer by heart.[17] Mnemosyne presides over every aspect of Cento poetics and aesthetics, suggesting appropriate Homeric verses to express her biblical themes from the *langue*-axis of selection, and harmonious adjustments to a given line to make it fit its new environment on the *parole*-axis of verbal combination: as Pliny says of Isaeus, Eudocia's "wide reading and experience in composing shines forth." On that note, ἄρχομ᾽ ἀείδειν.

---

17. For Niceratus see Xen. *Symp.* 3.5-6 (Herington 1985:169); for Psellus's claim to have memorized the whole *Iliad* (*Ep.* 1.14), see Marrou (1956:341); for Powelson see his advertisement in the *American Philological Association Newsletter* (October 1993:7 [obituary: October 1995:14]). Ausonius knew first-hand that cento composition is "a task for the memory only" (*solae memoriae negotium*, Green 1991:132).

Part Two

Cento Poetics

3

Accommodations

> I cannot greatly honor minuteness in details, so long as there
> is no hint to explain the relation between things and thoughts.
>
> —Ralph Waldo Emerson

"Every poetics," it is true, "must . . . be based, either explicitly or implicitly, on a theory of language and, behind that, on a theory of mind, mind being the maker of language" (Preminger and Brogan 1993:932). This in not the place for purveying theories of mind or of language *per se*. However, the following discussion of Eudocia's compositional habits will necessarily entail such theories seeing that "nearly all the topics of psychology are raised at one point or another by criticism" (Richards 1928:2). In offering in the next two chapters a detailed description of Cento poetic techniques, I am aiming at a generative model, or as Todorov defines poetics, at "the establishment of general laws of which this particular text is the product" (Todorov 1973:6). To establish a generative model of Homeric Cento versification, we must look in detail at two features of the poetic surface: first, the relationship of the elements in the individual Cento line to the elements in the Homeric line, and second, the various relationships Cento verses have to one another compared to the relationships verses have to one another in Homer. The first set of relationships is discussed in this chapter. The second set of relationships receives full treatment in the next chapter under the heading "Enjambement."[1] In both her accommodations and her use of

---

1. Homeric lines appropriated in couplets and blocks (e.g., similes) will not be discussed as such here, either under "Accommodations" or "Enjambement." Although couplets and blocks of lines show accommodation and (naturally)

enjambement Eudocia proves to be fully conversant with important conventions of Homer's oral style, yet she brings to that style the peculiar verve of a cento poet.

Adaptation of the source text is a necessary part of the process of cento composition. I follow Stephanus in calling such adaptations *accommodations* (Stephanus 1578:Praefatio). Accommodation takes several forms in the Homeric Centos, but most often it is a response to the syntax set up by a verse the poet has already chosen to appropriate as she moves from one verse to another. In many cases, the reader "will be unsure," as Stephanus himself observed, "whether the variation is done on purpose or is due to a mistake."[2] Such instances usually involve a semantic change and must be judged on a case-by-case basis. However, categories can be drawn up and some generalizations made from Eudocia's practice.[3]

There are two basic types of accommodation used by Eudocia to make Homeric verses fit together in their new context: the grammatical and the semantic (cf. Alfieri 1988:140-1). The two are distinguished by various sigla in the Cento text cited throughout this book. As these sigla appear frequently in the following discussion where knowledge of them is presumed, I give here a brief overview and explanation of my system of annotation.

Most Cento verses have undergone no change. These are identified simply by an i (*Iliad*) or an o (*Odyssey*) with the book and line numbers printed in Arabic numerals. A reference given in *italics* indicates that the line or a close variant of the line occurs elsewhere

---

contain enjambements, they do not in and of themselves reflect the stitching techniques involved in Cento composition as the poet moves from one individual line to the next. What couplets and blocks *do* suggest is that Eudocia was thinking of their particular context when she took the lines over. In this capacity, they will receive due attention in chapters 5-7.

2. *Alicubi vero ea est diversitas quae an ex errore sit, an consulto mutatio illa facta fuerit, dubites.*

3. Alfieri, revising the early work of Sattler (1904), has discussed Eudocia's accommodations in some detail (Alfieri 1987; 1988; 1989). However, because her work is based on Ludwich's edition, her observations about Eudocia's technique have limited application here. Schembra (1993; 1994; 1995) has added further observations based on his own inspection of several unpublished Homeric cento manuscripts that may represent Patricius's shorter poem.

in the Homeric poems. Italicized lines are usually formular verses, which are often repeated verbatim by Homer in similar contexts, for example speech introductions and type-scenes (cf. Alfieri 1988:140); they may also be lines repeated only once elsewhere in the same Homeric book, a common phenomenon distinct from type-scene or formular repetition known as "clustering" (Hainsworth 1993:27-8).[4]

An asterisk (⁕) placed after the reference indicates that there has been a change in grammatical form. This is the most common type of accommodation in the Centos and affects one or more of the following elements in a verse: the number, case or gender of nouns and pronouns; the person, tense and mood of verbs; and participles when they are substituted for finite verbs and vice versa.[5]

The sigla ⸂ ⸃ indicate a semantic change. These sigla enclose semantic or lexical variants of one or more than one word.[6] A dagger (†) placed after the reference in the margin conveniently alerts the reader of the change. Semantic deviation from the Homeric text usually involves either the substitution of one noun, verb or adjective for another, or variation in the use of a conjunction, particle or particle chain. I have also used raised brackets (⸢ ⸣) when a non-

---

4. When I give a book- and line-reference in italics, it usually means that the verse occurs verbatim *only* in that place in Homer (or, if it occurs verbatim more than once, that the reference given is to the first occurrence in the respective poem). Wherever necessary, I have made an editorial decision for the source of a repeated line based on context. This was easy in the majority of instances since a given formular line in the Centos is often surrounded by other lines unquestionably from the same Homeric book. It is, of course, reasonable to suppose that Eudocia had any one of several similar Homeric verses in mind and that she chose the precise wording of the one that fit her syntax. Due to the generic nature of formular verses, however, for example those introducing speeches, the uncited references for italicized lines do not add much nuance to the intertextual associations between Homeric context and biblical theme. Moreover, *exact* repetition of whole lines within the Homeric corpus does not occur as much as one might think.

5. In the interest of keeping the text uncluttered, the Homeric readings for verses marked with an asterisk are not given; the reader may look up the reference or not at his or her discretion.

6. In each instance, the Homeric reading may be found in the apparatus of Usher 1998, or the reader may consult the Oxford text of Monro-Allen.

semantic change (✻) requires the addition or deletion of other words in a verse (usually particles) for the sake of the meter. Where the Cento reading is itself attested somewhere in the textual tradition of Homer but not printed in the standard text of Monro-Allen (e.g., ἔρδεσκεν for ἔρρεξεν at line 36 = *Il.* 22.380), I enclose the word or words in raised brackets (ʽ ʼ), and put the sign @ next to the reference.[7]

A line with two references, such as i 23.536 + 107, indicates that the verse is made up of two half-lines. References given as cf. i 1.149 mean that there is no or only an approximate match in Homer. These two varieties are rare, yet such conflations of Homeric phraseology are to be expected of a recomposition-in-performance, and, since they too reveal the processes involved in Cento verse generation, they will be discussed in some detail below.

Grammatical accommodation (✻) involves the least change to the Homeric line. It is in principle always intentional, motivated by the need to maintain syntactical coherence. Although central to the centonist's technique, it is not peculiar to the Centos. Grammatical accommodation often occurs within Homer when the words of one protagonist are reported to another. *Iliad* 2.11-15, a well-known example, is repeated verbatim at 2.28-32 and 2.65-9, except for the minor adjustment of the third-person pronoun ἑ to second-person σε (or σ'), and the corresponding adjustments to the verb.

Fortunately, the identical metrical shape of short words and inflected endings in Homeric Greek allows the cento poet great flexibility in this regard. It is important to emphasize this flexibility and Eudocia's free use of grammatical accommodation, for although it involves minimal change to the Homeric line, it is in some respects the most important type. As will be argued in more detail in chapter 4, the easy change of number, person, even gender of nouns and pronouns makes the Homeric Centos what they essentially are: a comparative reading of Homer and the Bible, a reading in which the *function* of a character serves as the stable, constant element in the respective narrative, "independent of how and by whom it is fulfilled" (Propp 1928:21).

Semantic substitution (†) is a more complicated affair. When semantic accommodation occurs it is by no means certain whether it

---

7. Here too the Homeric reading may be found in Usher 1998, or the reader may consult Monro-Allen directly.

is intentional or not. Sometimes the motive for semantic accommodation seems obvious, as at the baptism scene (446 = *Od.* 5.230) where the word νυμφή ("bride"—the subject of the Homeric sentence), is replaced by the adjective θεῖον ("divine") agreeing with the object, φᾶρος ("cloak"), in the same line. Simply in terms of the story, the Homeric νυμφή is inappropriate to a scene requiring the presence of John the Baptist (however, at line 450 a παρθένος ἀδμής, "an unwed maid," hands Christ a cloak). Other semantic accommodations seem to have been influenced by dogmatic concerns (cf. Alfieri 1988:141n.11; 154; Schembra 1994:320-7), as was often the case in the Christian appropriation of the Classics.[8] Eusebius, for example, in a manner characteristic of the Cento technique, alters a passage from Plato's *Phaedo* (114c3) to make it suit his purposes (*Praep. Evang.* 13.16.10): where Plato had said that the souls of those who have purified themselves sufficiently through philosophy will live forever "without bodies," that is, without being reincarnated (ἄνευ σωμάτων), Eusebius says they will do so ἄνευ καμάτων, "without trouble," altering the reading so as not to violate the Christian doctrine of bodily resurrection (cf. Wilson 1983:17). In the Centos, accommodation on dogmatic grounds may be present, for example, in the Crucifixion scene (1889 = *Od.* 11.584) where the Homeric verb εἶχεν in the phrase πιέειν δ᾽ οὐκ εἶχεν ἑλέσθαι is changed to ἤθελ(εν). Εἶχεν, "could not," may have been thought inappropriate for a god revered by Christians as Pantokrator, and was therefore intentionally softened to ἤθελεν, "did not will it."

Moral and religious considerations play an important role in Cento composition, and the Centos invite further study with such considerations in mind. I will for the most part bracket such considerations here, however, for as Todorov notes, the fact that "the relation of poetics and interpretation is one of complementarity

---

8. And it was, of course, not only Christians. The archaic poet Tyrtaios (Frag. 12.3 West) changes one word in a half-line from *Il.* 16.262 to make a common "woe" into a public "good." Aristarchus and Zenodotus, on the Hellenistic critical principle of "propriety" (τὸ πρέπον), athetized and sometimes omitted passages in Homer, famously the reference to Phoenix's intent to kill his father at *Il.* 9.458-61 (on these lines see Janko 1992:27-9; on athetesis see Apthorp 1980:xv). Philosophers especially, like Plutarch, positively recommended adjusting or "glossing" Homer where necessary (*Mor.* 22 B, F).

par excellence," both being "'secondary'. . . must not keep us from distinguishing, in the abstract, the goals of the one attitude from those of the other" (Todorov 1973:7-8). Moreover, as will be argued in chapter 4, the appropriation of *Od.* 5.230 to the baptism scene already suggests *ipso facto* a comparison of the Baptist with the nymph, Calypso, a comparison which invites its own set of speculations in light of a passage like John 3:29 where Jesus describes himself as a bridegroom (νυμφίος) and the Baptist as his "best man" (ὁ φίλος τοῦ νυμφίου).

Even in the one case where the Cento text itself seems to explain an accommodation, we cannot be certain of the motivation: this involves the substitution of the verb μυθέομαι ("speak") for μαντεύομαι ("prophesy") at lines 396 (= *Od.* 15.172), 469 (= *Od.* 2.170) and 1678 (= *Il.* 1.107), which follows logically from Christ's statement at 472 (= *Od.* 1.202) that he is "not a prophet (μάντις) or an augur (οἰωνῶν σάφα εἰδώς) / but the son of the great God." However, some manuscripts of Homer actually read μυθήσομαι for μαντεύσομαι at *Od.* 15.172, and it is entirely possible that the other instances of this particular reading in the Centos arose by analogy, since μυθήσομαι regularly occurs in this *sedes* in Homer.

Before we look closely at semantic accommodation of Homer in the Centos, it is important to emphasize that the phenomenon appears also in Plato, where the motive for the variation from the received text of Homer poses similar problems. In the *Ion*, for example (538d1-3), Plato cites Homer's description of Iris's descent from Olympus at *Iliad* 24.80-2,

ἡ δὲ μολυβδαίνῃ ἰκέλη ἐς βυσσὸν ἵκανεν,
ἥ τε κατ᾽ ἀγραύλοιο βοὸς κέρας ἐμμεμαυῖα
ἔρχεται ὠμηστῇσι μετ᾽ ἰχθύσι πῆμα φέρουσα

She plunged down to the depths like a sinker made of lead,
which, attached to a piece of ox-horn, persistently
makes its way down, bringing woe in its wake to flesh-eating fishes

which shows the same kinds of accommodation found in the Centos: the verb ἵκανεν substituted for the Homeric ὄρουσεν , the participle ἐμ–μεμαυῖα for ἐμβεβαυῖα at line-end; the preposition μετά substituted for the Homeric ἐπί, and the noun πῆμα for the Homeric reading, κῆρα . As Jules Labarbe concluded in his study of Plato's use of Homer, such variation is due to many factors, ranging from legitimate variation, grammatical necessity, mnemonic imprecision and "rhapsodic" habits of word- and phrase-association, to deliberate revisionism and even parody (Labarbe 1949:108-20). We must allow for the same range of explanations of accommodation in the Centos.

Frequently, semantic substitution in the Centos seems to occur simply in order to avoid repetition with a previous line,[9] or to fit the new syntax a line may acquire in the Centos. This is analogous to the use of synonymns in Homeric formulas for stylistic *variatio* in order to "avoid the repetition of a noun in the same or adjacent sentences" (Hainsworth 1993:15, 25). At line 6, for example, the conjunction ὡς is substituted for ὄφρ᾽ in a purpose clause so as not to repeat the (temporal) ὄφρ᾽ in the previous line. Other times, the close proximity of a word or phrase in an adjacent line seems to have brought to mind a similar line involving that word or phrase and then that line, once used, required accommodation.[10] An example of this is lines 229-31 (the angel's speech at the Annunciation):

χαῖρέ μοι, ὦ βασίλεια, διαμπερές, εἰς ὅ κεν 'ἔλθοι᾽	o 13.59 †
ἀνδράσιν ἠδὲ γυναιξὶν 'ἐπὶ᾽ χθόνα πουλυβότειραν	o 19.408 †
'γῆρας᾽ καὶ θάνατος, τά τ᾽ ἐπ᾽ ἀνθρώποισι πέλονται.	o 13.60 †

Hail, my queen, forever and ever, until there come
upon the men and women inhabiting the fertile earth
old age and death, which do indeed come upon men.

Here Eudocia accommodates a line well suited to the Gospel setting (cf. Lk 1:28 χαῖρε κεχαριτωμένη), changing the γῆρας of *Od.* 13.59 to ἔλθοι. The resulting end-line phrase is analogous to several *Iliad* end-

---

9. Just as often, however, such repetition is not avoided (e.g., at 890-1) and lines are strung together catena-style, bound by keywords. This Cento poetic technique, a mnemonic device, is discussed in chapter 5.

10. Compare Parry's observations on the enjambement at *Il.* 8.74-5 (πολλῶν δ᾽ ἀγρομένων τῷ πείσεαι ὅς κεν ἀρίστην / βουλὴν βουλεύσῃ): "Homer, putting together his traditional phrases, remembered first such common expressions falling at the end of the verse as ὅς μέγ᾽ ἄριστος, ὅς τις ἄριστος, and then such expressions used at the beginning of the verse as βουλὰς βουλεύει . . . βουλας βουλεύειν . . . βουλὰς βουλεύουσι . . . and their joining made the enjambement" (Parry 1929:264-5).

line formulas, such as εἰς ὅ κεν ἔλθῃ / νὺξ (*Il.* 14.77), and εἰς ὅ κεν ἔλθῃ / δείελος ὀψὲ δύων (*Il.* 21.231). In fact, as we shall see in a moment, the words εἰς ὅ κεν of *Od.* 13.59 probably brought ἔλθοι to the poet's mind. As for the optative form at line-end, though not used in the particular verse she accommodates, it is worth noting that this is perfectly consistent with Homeric practice elsewhere: 24 of 34 total occurrences of the optative form ἔλθοι appear at line-end.

Having committed herself to the *Odyssey* line and the accommodation, Eudocia could have supplied any nominative expression to finish the thought, that is, "there shall come to that place (point in time) / X, Y or Z." However, she expands the thought, inserting a line containing datives, then perhaps remembers γῆρας, or associates it with θάνατος owing to the frequent Homeric collocation ἀθανατ– καὶ ἀγήρ–, which always occurs in the first half of the line (11x *Il.* and *Od.*). In any event, once γῆρας becomes the first word of the line (a normal *sedes*, 4x in Homer), Eudocia completes the line with the rest of *Od.* 13.60, καὶ θάνατος . . . κ.τ.λ.

A related phenomenon may be observed at line 299 (= *Od.* 4.526), where Mary "receives with wonder two talents of gold" from the Magi and "keeps them in her home" (φύλασσε δὲ ταῦτ᾽ ἐνὶ οἴκῳ). The substitution of the phrase δὲ ταῦτ᾽ ἐνὶ οἴκῳ for the Homeric δ᾽ ὅ γ᾽ εἰς ἐνιαυτόν ("for/towards the year") does not seem to be motivated by a need to make the text agree with some biblical or apocryphal detail, but rather by a desire to avoid the masculine pronoun (ὅ) by substituting a neuter plural (τά) to agree with τάλαντα. But it is interesting to note that the word ἐνιαυτόν, omitted in Eudocia's accommodation, occurs in the first line of the next scene (301 = *Od.* 10.469): ἀλλ᾽ ὅτε δή ῥ᾽ ἐνιαυτὸς ἔην, περὶ δ᾽ ἔτραπον ὧραι. Once again, it is likely that the unexpressed (in the Centos) ἐνιαυτόν of *Od.* 4.526 actually brought *Od.* 10.469 to mind. This is certainly the case with line 794 (= *Il.* 24.181) where Eudocia substitutes the word θυμῷ for τάρβος at line-end, and then continues in 795 with a line from the *Odyssey* (7.51) that begins with the form τάρβει.

Compare also Cento lines 42-3 where Eudocia takes a verse closest to *Il.* 7.28 (ἀλλ᾽ εἰ μοί τι πίθοιο, τό κεν πολὺ κέρδιον εἴη) apparently accommodating the particle chain in the first half of the line to ἦ ῥά νύ μοί τι πίθοιο . . . κ.τ.λ. She continues with *Il.* 14.191, ἦέ κεν ἀρνήσαιο, κοτεσσαμένη τό γε θυμῷ, which in Homer is directly preceeded by a verse, the first half of which—ἦ ῥά νύ μοί τι πίθοιο—is identical to the first half of the "accommodated" Cento line 42. *Il.* 14.191 here provides the second limb of the disjunctive sentence set up by the poet's accommodation and that particular line came to mind because of her association of it with ἦ ῥά νύ μοί . . . κ.τ.λ. We will have more to say about this phenomenon momentarily.

While each instance of semantic accommodation must be evaluated with various criteria in mind, we can be sure that semantic accommodation involving proper names is always intentional (cf. Schembra 1994:323-4). This was a potentially difficult problem for Eudocia to overcome since names and naming are such a large and integral part of the Homeric style (von Kamptz 1982; Higbie 1995). While some names are allowed to stand as personifications, for example, Ἀμφιτρίτη (17), Ὠρίων (11, 13), Χάριτες (753), Δημήτηρ (323, 666) and Ἡφαῖστος (559), as a rule Eudocia tends to avoid lines that contain personal names. Thus, semantic accommodation of Homeric names does not occur very often.

Still, though she needs to avoid names, the poet must nonetheless specify who's who in her story. This she does either by periphrasis, the use of a Homeric "significant name," or by the misuse of some other Homeric word. Some of the substitutions used in semantic name-accommodation are non-Homeric in that either the word substituted in is not a Homeric word (e.g., ὑποκυσσαμένη for ῥ' Ἡρακλῆα at 275; Συκείμων for Φαιήκων at 1122[11]), and/or a Homeric word is placed in a position where it never occurs in Homer (e.g., βίη for Διί at 1524; ἥρωι for Ἄρει at 1792).

At line 273, we find μώνυχες for Διομήδεος in the phrase μώνυχες ἵπποι Μώνυχες ἵπποι is a common Homeric formula (25x in this *sedes* in the accusative case; 7x in the nominative), whereas Διομήδεος ἵπποι, the particular version of that formula in the line she adapts from *Iliad* Book 10 (568), occurs in Homer only there, and—unless some word or words have been lost—we must scan the word as μῶνῠχες to fit the meter. However, even in the Homeric corpus adaptations of metrically sound formulas sometimes result in faulty derivations, for

---

11. Συκείμων is a Septuagint word for the inhabitants of the biblical town Συχάρ or Συχέμ (= Shechem). The same form of the name is found in the biblical paraphrase of Theodotus, a Hellenistic Jew who paraphrased the story of Shechem in the Book of Genesis (Harris 1898:10-1; on Sychar see Brown 1966:169).

example μερόπων ἀνθρώπων becomes μέροπες ἄνθρωποι. As the poet Martial complained, Homer himself is not hidebound with regard to word localization and metrical quantity. In the well-known line Ἄρες Ἄρες βροτολοιγέ, μιαιφόνε, τειχεσιπλῆτα (*Il.* 5.31, 455) and elsewhere, the poet "wilfully adapts" the position and hence the metrical quantity of a word, here a proper name (a relatively inflexible metrical unit), in composition (so Kahane 1994:9).

However, most of Eudocia's substitutions are consistent with Homeric practice, and this consistency applies to all types of accommodation, semantic and/or grammatical, whether intentional or not. For example, the phrase δ' ἄρα πάντες, substituted for δὲ καὶ ἄλλοι at 921 and 981 (= *Il.* 24.484), is in perfect keeping with Homeric practice: δ' ἄρα πάντες is localized to this position 45 out of the 47 times the phrase occurs in Homer, once in a line rather close in sense to ours (μνηστῆρες δ' ἄρα πάντες ἐς ἀλλήλους ὁρόωντες *Od.* 20.373), and lines containing the phrase occur four other times in the Centos. Eudocia was clearly familiar with this formula and could easily slip into it here. Her substitution νεκύεσσι for Δαναοῖσι in line 1991 (*Il.* 8. 227), in spite of the fact that the word occurs in this position only at *Od.* 12.383, is truly in the Homeric manner. Line 1991 is an *Iliad* formula used by Homer six times, always reproduced verbatim except for *Il.* 12.439 and 13.149 where Homer, like Eudocia, substitutes a dative plural, Τρώεσσι, for Δαναοῖσι to suit *his* context. The name substitution of ἔξοχα πάντων for Πάλλας ' Αθήνη at end-line in 1763 is also perfectly Homeric (5x in this *sedes*). It is interesting to observe that at *Il.* 5.61, the words ἔξοχα and Πάλλας ' Αθήνη occur in the same line. As will emerge again and again the closer we look at Eudocia's method of composition, the association of ἔξοχα and Πάλλας ' Αθήνη at *Il.* 5.61, reinforced by the effects of localization, may in fact have suggested this substitution. Such word association is clearly at work in 1285 ('πάντας' δὲ τρόμος αἰνὸς ὑπήλυθε γυῖα ἑκάστου = *Il.* 7.215): while the change from the *Iliad*'s Τρῶας to πάντας has no exact Homeric precedent, πάντας (in a different *sedes*) is often associated with τρόμος, occurring in the same line four times in Homer (*Il.* 14.506, 18.247, 19.14; *Od.* 24.49), and in the Centos themselves (1978), where Eudocia makes the same substitution, once in a distinctly different line from the *Odyssey* (2015 = *Od.* 20.44).

Another type of Cento name-accommodation involves imperatives and vocatives. Here too Eudocia works in the Homeric manner.

While the phrase ὦ φίλε substituted for Τηλέμαχ᾽ at 691 (*Od.* 2.303) occurs exactly so only at *Od.* 14.115, the plural ὦ φίλοι occurs 42 times in initial position. So too with the *Odyssey* phrase ὦ ξεῖν᾽ substituted for Δημόδοκ᾽ at 1112 (= *Od.* 8.469; also at 891 and 1408). This phrase is always localized to the same pre-caesural position in Homer (10x). However, we find the plural ὦ ξεῖνοι in initial position at *Od.* 3.71 and 9.252. Like Homer himself we see Eudocia here displacing formulas (Hainsworth 1968:45-57) and composing by analogy.

Periphrasis serves to identify characters beyond the mere use of a demonstrative (e.g., ὅ, ὅδε, or ἐκεῖνος). In the Centos, periphrases are employed like formulas; in some instances they *are* formulas lifted from Homer, and employed in exactly the same way. Examples: Jesus is designated by *Il.* 12.242 as ὃς πᾶσι θνητοῖσι καὶ ἀθανάτοισιν ἀνάσσει, "He who rules over all the gods and men" (73, 91, 270, 428, 1537, 1998, 2240); Judas by *Il.* 22.380, ὃς κακὰ πόλλ᾽ ἔρδεσκεν ὅσ᾽ οὐ σύμπαντες οἱ ἄλλοι, "He who did more harm than everyone else put together" (1423, 1613, etc.), and *Il.* 9.313, ὅς χ᾽ ἕτερον μὲν κεύθῃ ἐνὶ φρεσίν, ἄλλο δὲ εἴπῃ, "A man who hides one thing in his heart and says another" (1411). The Virgin Mary is referred to by *Od.* 23.325 as μήτηρ θ᾽ ἥ μιν ἔτικτε καὶ ἔτρεφε τυτθὸν ἐόντα, "The mother who bore him and nursed him when he was young" (290, 298, 354, 2040, 2169, 2328); Peter is ὅς οἱ κήδιστος ἑτάρων ἦν κεδνότατός τε, "His dearest and most thoughtful companion" (= *Od.* 10.225; at lines 529, 772, 1758); the other disciples are, in the words of *Il.* 9.586, ἄλλους θ᾽, οἵ οἱ κεδνότατοι καὶ φίλτατοι ἦσαν, "The others, his most thoughtful and beloved" (1303, 1436). As in Homer, the comments of anonymous spectators are regularly introduced by *Od.* 2.324 (etc.), ὧδε δέ τις εἴπεσκε νέων ὑπερηνορεόντων, "Thus one of the arrogant young men would say" (1742, 1891, 1939, 2087), or the related formula ὧδε δέ τις εἴπεσκεν ἰδὼν ἐς πλησίον ἄλλον, "Thus someone would look at his neighbor and say" (722, 983, 1287, 1912, 1995, 2233). Once, at a particularly poignant moment during the Crucifixion (1956), Eudocia uses Homer's apt modification of his own formula describing the violation of Hector's body: ὥς ἄρα τις εἴπεσκε, καὶ οὐτήσασκε παραστάς, "Thus a man would say and stand there wounding him again and again" (*Il.* 22.375).

Another way to refer to individuals in the Gospel story is by using an Homeric significant name as an adjective. Some significant names in Homer do in fact occur as ordinary adjectives. For example the Trojan counselor Ἀγήνωρ gets his name from the adjective ἀγήνωρ, "manly," which at *Il.* 12.300 modifies the noun θυμός. In the Centos, this feature of Homeric poetry has a broader application: Christ is the God-fearing itinerant prophet, Θεοκλύμενος (13x), "he who hears from God" (so Eust. 1780.20 [Stallbaum 1825:II.97]);[12] elsewhere he is the healing divinity Ἰητρός (1127) or Παιήων (1128); the Baptist is the herald Πεισήνωρ, "a persuasive man" (or "persuader of men" 224, 258, 362).

Conversely, Ἔχετος, the personal name of a wicked king in the *Odyssey* (18.116), becomes a common adjective meaning "powerful" (1827). Ἀλιθέρσης, Odysseus's close friend from Ithaka and counsel to Telemachus, is used as an adjective to describe the "old man" Peter, and means either "sweaty," if we follow Eustathius's suggestion (1439.40-1 [Stallbaum 1825:I.90]: παρὰ τὸ ἐν ἁλὶ θέρεσθαι ὑπὸ τοῦ ἡλίου), or "daring in wit" if we connect -θέρσης with θάρσος—either meaning well-suited to the context of Peter's denial of Jesus under pressure (1757 = cf. *Od.* 2.57). Place-names too receive such treatment: the spring Ἀρτακίη at 1054 (= *Od.* 10.108), if from ἄρτι + κίεν, is "close-moving"; the plain Ἀλήϊον at 929 (= *Il.* 6.201), if from ἀλᾶσθαι, means "for wandering" or, if an α-privative of λήϊον, means "without wheat or booty," that is, "desert" (cf. Eust. 636.49 [van der Valk:II.290.10-4]). A mirror image of this onomastic technique is seen at 771 (= *Il.* 16.734) where the common noun πέτρον is used for "Peter."

Akin to this use, or rather misuse, of Homeric words is the frequent exchange of δρήστηρ and μνήστηρ. The word μνήστηρ ("suitor") was not in itself objectionable since it is regularly used in a positive way (13x) to describe the disciple-suitors of Christ, as, for example, at 467 (= *Od.* 18.351). However, δρήστηρ ("manservant"), is sometimes substituted (or confused) for μνήστηρ where the context requires a villain or villain's accomplice, and seems to verge on the meaning "perpetrator" (note especially 1862 = *Od.* 22.211, and 2029 = *Od.* 22.270).

To various degrees, all these examples of semantic name-accommodation involve the use of the rhetorical figure known as

---

12. However, von Kamptz derives -κλύμενος from κλυτός and takes the name to mean "God-renowned" (1982:203).

catachresis (κατάχρησις = Latin *abusio*), which is defined by Tryphon the grammarian in *De tropis* as "the transference of a word or phrase from what is its original, proper, and true meaning to some other thing for which no name exists, against common usuage."[13] Tryphon gives the expressions γόνυ καλάμου ("the knee of a plant stalk," i.e., "joint"), ὀφθαλμὸς ἀμπέλου ("the eye of the vine," i.e., "bud") and χεῖλος κεραμίου ("the lip of a jar," i.e., "rim") as characteristic examples. The author of the *Essay on the Life and Writings of Homer* gives an example specifically from Homer, αἰγείην κυνέην, noting that a helmet (περικεφαλαία) is called κυνέη ("of or pertaining to a dog") by the poet because helmets were traditionally made out of dogskin, though this particular helmet, modified by the adjective αἰγεία, was made out of goatskin (Keaney and Lamberton 1996:84-5; so too Apion in Neitzel 1977:246). As we see by pseudo-Plutarch's example, catachresis does not involve word substitution, but "abuses" or stretches a given word's ordinary or apparent meaning.

A fine example of catachresis is Cento line 1378 (= *Il.* 22.255) where the Homeric words ἐπίσκοποι("observers") and μάρτυροι ("witnesses") clearly have their Christian connotation, "bishops and martyrs." Similarly, *Od.* 5.194—ἷξέν γ᾽ ἐς σπεῖος γλαφυρὸν θεὸς ἠδὲ καὶ ἀνήρ—which describes two persons in Homer (Calypso and Odysseus), is used in the Raising of Lazarus scene (line 1270) as a hendiadys to describe the god-man, Jesus (cf. also Cento line 6 = *Il.* 5.128). In the Feeding of the Five Thousand scene (line 1222 = *Il.* 23.58), the Homeric word κλισίη ("shanty" or "cabin") seems to be used catachrestically to represent the biblical word κλισία, found in the plural in the Gospel of Luke (9:14), where it describes the "companies" or "dining groups" into which the disciples have divided the crowd. In this instance, Eudocia may have been influenced by the Homeric phrase κατὰ κλισίας, which often occurs in meal type-scenes, for example, at *Il.* 8.53-4. As Quintilian puts it in his discussion of catachresis, the trope "non ad nomen, sed ad vim significandi refertur, nec auditu, sed intellectu perpendenda est" (*Inst.* 8.2.6). "Non verbum pro verbo ponitur," he notes elsewhere, "sed res pro re" (*Inst.*

---

13. Λέξις μετενηνεγμένη ἀπὸ τοῦ πρώτου κατονομασθέντος κυρίως τε καὶ ἐτύμως ἐφ᾽ ἕτερον ἀκατονόμαστον, κατὰ τὸ οἰκεῖον (Walz 1835:182).

8.6.36).[14]

Catachresis, then, extends a word's ordinary meaning without resorting to substitution. Sometimes, however, even when semantic accommodation does involve word substitution, it does not greatly affect the sense: for example, αὐτὰρ ἐπεὶ ῥ᾽ for αἶψα δ᾽ ἔπειθ᾽ in 774 (= *Il.* 6.370 etc.), or ἔθηκε for δίδωσι at 85 (= *Od.* 17.287). Sometimes the substitution is simply an antonymn, as is especially the case with prepositions (ἀνά for κατά in 320; ἀπό for εἰς in 346; cf. also 136, 1365 and 2081). Often the accommodation involves particles and particle chains. Variants like τι for τοι, δὲ and τε for γε, and so forth, are probably mnemonic errors on the part of Eudocia, or, alternatively, scribal errors in the transmission of the text of a kind commonly found in the textual tradition of Homer (cf. Salanitro 1987:233; Alfieri 1988:142n.12, 154). In her non-Cento poetry, Eudocia was rather indiscriminate in her use of such particles, for example in her hexameter paraphrase of the life of St. Cyprian, "where she does not seem to be aware of the essential meaning of these particles. . . . They have become stop gaps . . . to give her poems a Homeric touch" (Van Duen 1993:280; cf. Cameron 1982: 279). C. J. Ruijgh, however, suggests that some of the confusion goes much farther back, and that archaic rhapsodes introduced τε in many instances of what was originally γε, for example, at *Od.* 13.238 and 15.484, for the sake of euphony (Ruijgh 1971:839). In fact, many variants in the Homeric corpus involving γε, τε and δέ are attributable to the rhapsodic performance and transmission of the epics (Ruijgh 1971:118-22). Eudocia herself—in her own way—stands in this tradition.

While it is sometimes difficult to decide which is responsible, the poet or the textual tradition, we may proceed on the premise that if a substitution does not appear as a variant somewhere in the manuscript tradition or papyri of Homer, it may fairly be counted as a mnemonic variation. But this, even if it is a sound assumption, is not enough. It is important for Cento poetics to try to account for how and why such mnemonic variation—and, in some cases, innovation—arises. I

---

14. For the phrases κυρίως and καταχρηστικῶς λεγόμενα in Greek scholia, see further Rutherford 1905:209-11. Porphyry frequently uses these terms in his "Aristarchan" work, *Homeric Questions* (Sodano 1970:index). On Stoic views of catachresis, see Barwick 1957:88-97.

offer a few observations in this regard, which have a wider application and significance for the Cento technique.

In the example of Homer's use of grammatical accommodation from *Iliad* Book 2, we saw that the difference between verse 11 and verses 28 and 65 was minimal: θωρῆξαι ἑ κέλευε versus θωρῆξαί σε κέλευσε. While technically a grammatical change has taken place involving the pronoun and the verb, the phrases are metrically identical and nearly homophonous. Homophony is by definition a function of speech and sound, not limited to single words, and sometimes dependent on the pace of speech for its effect, as in the pronunciation of the French *à votre tour* and *à votre retour* (Jakobson and Waugh 1979:7-8).

That homophony plays an important role in the oral poet's technique has been argued for Homer by Michael Nagler. Nagler has expanded Milman Parry's notion of *calembour* ("punning"), or the sound corresponsion between elements in variations of the same Homeric formula, to include words that are not semantically related (Nagler 1967:274, 296).[15] For example, in Homer the words ἀϋτμή ("breath") and ἀϋτή ("battle cry") both occur with the verb ἀμφήλυθε ("went 'round'"); πίονι δημῷ ("rich fat") and the homonym, πίονι δήμῳ ("a rich country"), always occur in the final colon of the line, though they are semantically distinct and appear in a wide variety of grammatical and syntactical combinations.

Nagler argues, contra Parry's definition of a formula, that while the "overwhelming similarity of rhythm and phonetic sound among these phrases is formulaic . . . they do not express one 'given essential idea'" (Nagler 1967:275). Such phrases he calls "allomorphs of a single [mental] template."[16] Hainsworth (1993:15) cites other similar substitutions in Homer, such as δηλήμονες ("harmful") for ζηλήμονες ("jealous") in the phrase σχέτλιοί ἐστε, θεοί, ζηλήμονες, and γερόντων ("old men") for θανόντων ("dead men") in τὸ γὰρ γέρας ἐστὶ θανόντων, noting

---

15. Stanford (1939:7-8; 26-34) is careful to note that homophones (same sound, different form, different meaning) and homonyms (same sound, same form, different meaning) are distinct phenomena, yet that in oral speech homophones are effectively homonyms, and both are covered by the ancient (Aristotelian) term ὁμωνυμία. Cf. also Rutherford 1905:223 n. 51.

16. Hoekstra (1965), observing the same phenomenon from a slightly different angle, had previously referred to them as "conjugations" of a formula.

that *calembour* is "striking evidence for the basic orality of the Homeric style." However, while *calembour* may be "atypical" of the Homeric style, we cannot deny it, as Hainsworth is too ready to do, "a place among the resources of ἀοιδή."[17] In fact, an example of a Homeric formula cited by Hainsworth himself, ἄγχι παραστάς (4x *Il.*; 3x *Od.*), shows homophonic reflexes, or "conjugations" of a type identical to Cento accommodations: ἄγχι παρέστη, ἄγχι παρίστατο, ἄγχι παρισταμένη, and even ἄγχι δ᾽ ἄρα στάς, accommodated to take the connective (Hainsworth 1993:16).

Clearly, if not a primary resource to the ancient ἀοιδός, *calembour* was an appreciable feature of Homeric verse, and was exploited as such by the poet of the Homeric Centos (cf. Alfieri 1988:143), where homophony and allomorphism play a large role in the generation of the verse. Both phenomena account for many grammatical accommodations since this type often involves conjugated verb forms or the declension of nouns that are themselves allomorphs of a word stem. The slight phonetic difference at 1064 (= *Od.* 23.101) between πόλλ᾽ ἐμόγησε and the Homeric πολλὰ μογήσας is a good example, as are ἰών κε for the Homeric dual ἰόντε (1515 = *Il.* 10.468), τάρβησάν τε for ταρβήσαντε (1437 = *Il.* 1.331), οὐκ ἄν for οὔ κεν (1964 = *Od.* 4.223), δάκρυ χέουσα for δακρύσασα (2055 = *Od.* 17.38), ἠδὲ τιθῆσι for ἠδ᾽ ἐπιθήσει (1016 = *Il.* 4.190), μάκαρ ἐκτελέῃσι for μάκαρες τελέσωσι (1187 = *Od.* 18.134), or even θεῷ ἰδὲ for θεοῖσι δὲ (1214 = *Il.* 7.177).

The poet's choice of a particular word for semantic accommodation is also often facilitated by homophony: the frequent substitution or confusion of γάρ for ἄρ and vice versa (777, 788, 1010, 1341, 1689), the intentional name accommodation βίη for Διί at 1524, μιν for μέν (824), με for τε (883), and perhaps even θεοῦ for θ᾽ ἐὸν (1151), to cite but a few. Some semantic substitutions show considerable ingenuity. Out of Homer's ὤριστος (crasis for ὁ ἄριστος) in the chariot-race scene at *Il.* 23.536 (= Cento line 33), Eudocia makes the verb-form ὤριστο ("was traced out"), which she uses to describe the creation of the "last" (λοῖσθος —meaning, of course, the "first") man, Adam.

17. Nor does Hainsworth's implicit criticism of Nagler's mental template— "A pleasing sound is perhaps a reason for keeping an expression rather than a template for its creation" (1993:10)—do justice to Nagler's position, which is based on homophony, not euphony.

Σώματα ("bodies") substituted for δώματα ("palace") in the phrase κατὰ σώματα is used to describe the physical strength of the villain Judas at 1696 (= *Od.* 21.372); ἠρνήσατο for ἠρήσατο at 1796 (= *Il.* 17.568) makes Peter "deny" in the Garden of Gethsemane with a Homeric line that describes Menelaus "praying" to Athena on the battlefield. In order to avoid the name ᾿Αντίνοον at 2283 (= *Od.* 17.414), the phrase αὐτὸν ἰών is used; at 294 (= *Od.* 8.419; cf. *Il.* 8.280), in order to avoid ᾿Αλκινοοῖο, the poet coins the word ἀγνοτόκοιο. The homophone εἰ for ἦ at 1951 (= *Il.* 11.433) makes what is in Homer a disjunctive sentence into an indirect question. Λῖς ("lion") for the indefinite pronoun τις at 1529 (= *Od.* 4.535) lends additional force to a rather weak Homeric simile.

The conformity with Homeric practice in homophonous semantic accommodation varies. The epithet ἀγνοτόκοιο at 294, for example, is a Homeric formation, but not a Homeric, or even epic, word. However, most substitutions involve common Homeric words, and are consistent with Homeric practice. For example, γάρ for δ᾿ ἄρ at line 777 (= *Od.* 15.134) is a variant reading found in the textual tradition of Homer at *Od.* 15.495. The Centos' semantic accommodation mentioned above of δρηστῆρ- as μνηστῆρ- is a variant also found in the Homeric textual tradition. Cento line 425 (= *Il.* 1.79) contains the semihomophonous substitution ἀνθρώπων for ᾿Αργείων in semantic name-accommodation at the beginning of the line, a non-Homeric substitution in that ἀνθρώπων is regularly localized at the end of a line. However the end-line substitution ἅπαντες for ᾿Αχαιοί in the same verse —ἀνθρώπων κρατέει καὶ οἱ πείθονται ἅπαντες—is clearly patterned after the phrase πειθώμεθα πάντες, a formula occurring ten times in Homer, always at line-end. The phonetic difference between πειθώμεθα πάντες and πείθονται ἅπαντες is slim indeed. In one instance in Homer (*Od.* 22. 269), we find this homophonous "allomorph of a single template" relocalized to the beginning half of the line: οἱ μὲν ἔπειθ᾿ ἅμα πάντες ὁδὰξ ἕλον ἄσπετον οὖδας.

Another aspect of homophony and allomorphism in the Centos is metathesis (cf. Jakobson and Waugh 1979:3-4), seen in the sub-stitution at 1829 (= *Il.* 6.167), μυθῷ ("word") for θυμῷ ("heart"), which involves a metathesis of consonants, as does 616 (= *Od.* 12.440), κίρνων ("mixing") for κρίνων ("selecting"), the ingenious (or unintentional?) σώζοντες ("saving") for ζώοντες ("living") at 945 (= *Od.* 18.76; cf. σῶσον for ζῶσαι at 1950 = *Od.* 18.30), and λαομέδοντα ("ruler of his people[?]" an epithet for Christ) for the name Λαοδάμαντα at 92 (= *Od.* 7.170). The regular confusion of the words ἐναίσιμος ("just") and (the non-Homeric, unmetrical) αἰνέσιμος ("praiseworthy") in the Iviron manuscript involves a metathesis of vowels of a type frequent in Homer, for example, ἀτραπιτός for ἀταρπιτός or κράτιστος for κάρτιστος, which itself occurs at Cento line 172 (= *Od.* 8.17), and in the manuscript tradition of Homer.

A related phenomenon is the transposition of words that go together: πάτηρ τε μήτηρ τε for μήτηρ τε πάτηρ τε at 1098 (= *Od.* 8.550); πέλεν αἴγλη for αἴγλη πέλεν 2191 (= *Od.* 7.84); δόμου ἔσαν for ἔσαν δόμου 2269 (= *Od.* 1.126); τοῖς εὖ for εὖ τοῖς 1592 (= *Il.* 12.369); φίλα τέκνα for τέκνα φίλα at 605 (= *Od.* 3.418); and ὡς βοῦς for βόες ὡς 2019 (= *Od.* 22.299). One example of word transposition in the Centos, Ζέφυρος νέφεα for νέφεα Ζέφυρος at 1155 (= *Il.* 11.305), is found so written in papyri, three manuscript families of Homer, and Strabo. As with this example, it is possible that the other word metatheses were part of some vulgate with which Eudocia worked. However, τέκνα φίλα occurs thus only at *Od.* 3.413 (and once in the singular at *Od.* 23.26), whereas Eudocia's φίλα τέκνα is the order used at *Il.* 2.313 (but at line-end) and *Il.* 10.192. As for ὡς βοῦς, while this phrase does not occur in Homer, βοῦς is often localized in this *sedes*, and twice is juxtaposed with ἀγελαίας (*Il.* 23.846 and *Od.* 10.410) as it is in the Cento line. As we see again here, association and analogy play an important role in Cento composition.

A few Cento lines are made up of two half-lines. Such lines are far fewer in the Homeric Centos than in the Vergilian Cento of Proba. This is largely because Homeric and Vergilian lines are not organized internally in the same way. The Homeric poet, composing during performance, does not strive to attain literary effects like chiasmus or the adjective-noun displacements (often organized around an articulating caesura) that characterize any given line in Vergil.[18] In spite of these differences between the Latin and the Homeric hexameter, it has been suggested (Alfieri 1988) that Eudocia's use of

---

18. Alfieri notes this difference between the Vergilian and Homeric Centos but attributes it not to orality or performance, but to the "depersonalized" (*spersonalizzato*) nature of the Homeric style (1988:140), apparently meaning by that term Homer's so-called objective (as opposed to Vergil's "subjective") narrative style.

half-lines is in keeping with the so-called rules of Cento composition as outlined by Ausonius in the preface to his *Cento nuptialis*. Yet when we look at Ausonius's rules and Eudocia's practice, we find only the most superficial relationship and many striking differences.

Most obvious among the discrepancies between the two methods is Eudocia's complete disregard for Ausonius' aesthetic ideal that the cento poet should avoid reproducing whole lines from his source in blocks. To use two lines in a row, according to Ausonius, is *ineptum*; three or more in a row are *merae nugae* (Green 1991:133). Yet over 35 percent of Cento lines come in blocks, ranging from two to six successive lines to consecutive runs of blocks from different places in Homer as long as twelve lines (see Usher 1997:314-5).[19]

Further evidence of Eudocia's disregard for Ausonian rules is the presence of what I call conflated lines, which are distinguished from half-lines proper. Conflation occurs when two successive Homeric

---

19. Though Ausonius himself occasionally falls into ineptitude by using two successive lines from Vergil, his practice is for the most part as he describes it (Green 1991:133): *Diffinduntur autem per caesuras omnes, quas recepit versus heroicus, convenire ut possit aut penthemimeres cum reliquo anapestico chorico aut <lacuna> post dactylum atque semipedem* ("There are divisions at all caesurae which the heroic hexameter allows so that one may find a penthemimeral caesura followed by an anapestic/choral rhythm . . . or [one may find a division] after a dactyl [i.e., a dieresis] or after the half-foot [i.e., a "weak" caesura])." It is worth emphasizing that there is nothing overly technical about this. Eudocia too joins Homeric half-lines at the caesuras (Where else would she join hemistichs?). Eleven of her thirty half-lines are joined at the weak penthemimeral caesura: Lines 33 (= *Il.* 23.536 + 107), 121 (= *Il.* 11.761 + 1.397), 384 (= *Il.* 19.101 + 84), 1274 (= *Il.* 18.178 + *Od.* 3.123), 1392 (= *Il.* 11.632 + 3.338), 1548 (= *Od.* 23.117 + 17.274), 1739 (= *Il.* 4.85 + *Od.* 17.488), 1796 (= *Il.* 15.144 + *Od.* 19.362), 1840 (= *Il* 7.264 + 5.34), 1597 (= *Il.* 2.786 + 19.130), and 206 (= *Il.* 11.118 + 619). Seven more lines are joined at the strong penthemimeral caesura, one of which (214) requires lengthening a short vowel in thesis before the break: Lines 207 (= *Il.* 11.184 + 17.425), 214 (= *Il.* 14.504 + 9.480), 648 (= *Il.* 10.10 + 19.77), 805 (= *Il.* 23.235 + 6.66), 1203 (= *Il.* 8.380 + *Od.* 3.44), 1388 (= *Il.* 5.216 + 1.450), and 1412 (= *Il.* 21.445 + 11.405). Unlike Ausonius, however, we find in Eudocia one three-colon line (801 = *Od.* 8.554 + 4.36 + 1.120), and divisions at other metrical breaks: at the second-foot diaeresis (1389 = *Il.* 21.32 + 23.235), and at the bucolic (1410 = *Od.* 1.33 + *Il.* 10.378; 1869 = *Od.* 22.189 + 477; 685 = *Il.* 15.262 + 572).

54   Chapter 3

lines, or lines in close physical or contextual proximity to each other,
are compressed into one Cento line.[20] As we have already seen,
elements from two or more very similar Homeric lines are often
mixed and matched in the Centos, as in line 1: κέκλυτε, μυρία φῦλα
περικτιόνων ἀνθρώπων. The phrase in the second half of this line, if
from *Il.* 17.220, substitutes ἀνθρώπων for ἐπικούρων; if from *Il.* 2.804,
where the collocation is πολυσπερέων ἀνθρώπων, we have an adjectival
substitution. Either way, two different but related genitive phrases,
which comprise the latter half of the line, have been conflated, and,
as Alfieri remarks, this probably happens spontaneously because of
the similarity of the two lines (Alfieri 1988:144).

   Conflation involving half-lines occurs several times in the Centos.
Lines 657 (from the healing of a paralytic) and 1008 (the woman
with a flow of blood) are perfect examples, both of which conflate
two successive lines from the *Iliad* (657: σοὶ γὰρ ἐγὼ καὶ ἔπειτα
διαμπερὲς ἤματα πάντα [= *Il.* 16.498 + 499]; 1008: ἕλκος μὲν γὰρ ἔχω τόδε
καρτερόν. οὐδέ μοι αἷμα [= *Il.* 16.517 + 518]). Line 103 involves conflation and line-transposition: οὐχ ὁράᾳς ὅτι δ᾽ αὖτε βροτοὶ ἐπ᾽ ἀπείρονα
γαῖαν (= *Il.* 7.448 + 446). Analogous to the examples of grammatical
and semantic accommodation discussed above, conflation is caused by
the close proximity of familiar material, as if today one were to
misrecite e. e. cummings's familiar dactylic poem as "what if a much
of a which of a wind / bloodied with dizzying leaves the sun," skipping
the part about giving truth to summer's lie. Conflation, then, is often
the result of a mind thoroughly acquainted with Homeric verse and
Homeric technique thinking ahead of itself.

   As in semantic accommodation, the association of words and
phrases contribute to the generation of Cento half-lines too, though
they be comprised of Homeric hemistichs which lay hundreds of lines,
books, even poems apart. Take for example line 1863 (ἴθυσαν δὲ

---

20. The scholia to Venetus A, which preserve several examples of this kind
of line conflation (e.g., at *Il.* 1.219-20, 1.446-7; 4.88-9), attribute them to the
ancient Homeric critic, Zenodotus of Ephesus (see Bird 1994:43-4). For a
similar conflation of lines from *Iliad* Book 11—with accommodation—at Plato
Ion 538c2-3, see Labarbe 1949:101-8, who comments: "La resemblance des
éléments . . . a déterminé l'association psychologique." Some such association
is also discernible in the conflated Homeric lines and passages in "Longinus,"
On the Sublime (e.g., 9.6 and 9.8), which are virtually centos.

'λύκοισιν᾽ ἐοικότες ὠμοφάγοισιν), which is comprised of *Il.* 17.725 and *Il.* 5.782. This Cento line is in effect a "mixed simile" in which two Homeric similes of similar phrasing have been assimilated by Eudocia and Homer's datives (κύνεσσιν, "dogs" at 17.725, λέουσιν, "lions" at 5.782) accommodated with λύκοισιν ("wolves"), apparently to suit a Gospel saying (Mt 7:15, Lk 10:3, Jn 10:12, etc.).[21] Note also line 717: βῆ δ᾽ ἴμεν ὥς 'περ λῖς᾽ ὀρεσίτροφος ἀλκὶ πεποιθώς (= *Il.* 12.299 + 17.61). Although the Homeric reading in the first half-line is τε λεῶν, the synonym λίς used by Eudocia occurs in a closely related simile at *Il.* 17.109. So too line 2141: ἠδὲ γυναῖκας ἐϋζώνους καὶ νήπια τέκνα (= *Il.* 23.261 + 22.63). No exact equivalent is to be found in Homer, though women and children co-occur in a variety of formulas (cf. *Od.* 14.264).

Such overlap between elements is common to all types of Cento half-lines. The conflated line 1869—σὺν δὲ πόδας χεῖράς τε δέον κεκοτηότι θυμῷ—is composed of two similar lines from the *Odyssey*, 22.189 (σὺν δὲ πόδας χεῖράς τε δέον θυμαλγέι δεσμῷ) and 22.477 (χεῖράς τ᾽ ἠδὲ πόδας κόπτον κεκοτηότι θυμῷ), both of which mention "hands and feet." Compare the conflated line at 1969—αὐτίκα δ᾽ ἐβρόντησεν ἀπ᾽ οὐρανοῦ ἀστεροέντος—which is made up of *Od.* 20.103 (αὐτίκα δ᾽ ἐβρόντησεν ἀπ᾽ αἰγλήεντος Ὀλύμπου) and *Od.* 20.113 (ἣ μεγάλ᾽ ἐβρόντησας ἀπ᾽ οὐρανοῦ ἀστερόεντος).[22] In each instance the poet has collapsed two related lines based on their shared lexical and structural elements.

There are a handful of lines and half-lines in the Centos for which an exact Homeric equivalent is lacking,[23] and one (1918: ἴσχεο, μηδὲ περισθενόων δηλήσεο τούσδε) that is a conflation of line-fragments with no exact half-line matches, but closely resembling *Od.* 22.367 +

---

21. For wolves in Homeric similes, cf. *Il.* 16.156. For the substitution of one animal for another in otherwise identical Homeric similes (e.g., "boar" for "lion"), see Scott 1974:58-60 and Muellner 1990:63.

22. Other examples include lines 1548 (= *Od.* 23.117 + *Od.* 17.274) and 1840 (= *Il.* 7.264 + *Il.* 5.34).

23. For whole lines and hemistichs with no exact equivalent, consult Usher 1998.

368.[24] The source for most of these lines, however, is readily apparent, either because of their context in the Centos (i.e., they are followed by or preceded by lines from the same Homeric book), or by other verbal features that limit the possibilities for their source in Homer (e.g., the name Πεισήνωρ occurs only at *Od.* 2.38). Moreover, roughly half of these lines are made up Homeric material used to introduce speeces, adapted to fit the particular Cento speaker or context, and one of them (667) is repeated elswhere in the Centos; another (599) involves little more that the displacement of one word. Both features suggest that these lines result from a combination of mnemonic variation and/or *impromptu* composition using Homeric diction. The presence of such lines, coupled with the presence of conflated lines, underscores a basic and fundamental difference between the rather mechanical Ausonian model of cento versification (which was followed by Proba) and the more organic poetics of Eudocia in the Homeric Centos. This difference will be brought into higher relief when we look at Cento enjambement.

---

24. Using Ludwich's text, Alfieri analyzed sixteen such lines whose sources in Homer eluded Sattler (Alfieri 1988:147-53). However, of those sixteen lines, eight are not in the Stephanus-Iviron text. Five others are in Stephanus-Iviron, but match (or nearly do) the Homeric wording, and their Homeric source is easily found, without appeal to hemistichs. Of the other three (lines 144, 295, 371 of my text), only 144 and 295 involve a multiple or unknown source. Both lines receive excellent treatment in Alfieri's study (to which the interested reader is referred).

4

Enjambement

> . . . as that of Homer in Greek . . . the sense variously drawn
> out from one verse into another.
>
> —John Milton

It is a mark of Eudocia's skill as a poet and seamstress that lines taken
from different places in the Homeric poems occur as successive,
enjambed lines in the Centos, often without alterations. Enjambement
is an important aspect of the Homeric style and has received due
attention in recent years. Carolyn Higbie, for example, has thoroughly surveyed and slightly revised earlier categories of Homeric enjambement proposed by Milman Parry (1929) and G. S. Kirk (1966;
1985:17-34), and has, for the first time in Homeric studies, tabulated
statistics based on the entire *Iliad* (Higbie 1990). Though I myself
disagree somewhat with the rationale behind some of her distinctions,
which I think result in the overclassification of Homeric enjambement types, I offer Higbie's basic categories here as a control so as to
demonstrate Eudocia's command of Homeric oral technique, and her
divergences from it, in terms familiar to the modern student of
Homer.

Homeric enjambement is described by Higbie as either "adding,"
"clausal," "necessary" or "violent." The Centos show the full range
of these types, and they occur with about the same relative frequency
as they do in Homer.[1] They will be treated here, with exception of

---

1. In the *Iliad*, end-stopped lines are just slightly more common than
"adding" enjambement (39 percent compared to 36 percent), "necessary" enjambement accounts for 19 percent, "clausal" for 5 percent, and the rare
"violent" type of enjambement for 0.5 percent (Higbie 1990:29, 82).

the clausal type, roughly in reverse order, according to their frequency.

So-called violent enjambement is caused by the separation of a clause's introductory material from the clause itself (Higbie 1990:51). Higbie restricts this category of enjambement to particle chains and "adverbs that are sentence adverbs, that color the meaning of an entire clause rather than modify only the verb, an adjective, or another adverb" (Higbie 1990:53). According to this definition, violent enjambement occurs twice in the Centos:

1. At 361-2 (John the Baptist's recognition of Jesus):

ἷξέν γ᾽ ἐς πεδίον πυρηφόρον, ἔνθα δ᾽ ἔπειτα   o 3.495 ※
κῆρυξ πεισήνωρ, πεπνυμένα μήδεα εἰδώς,   o 2.38

[Jesus] then came to a grassy plain, whereupon
the persuasive herald, an inspired advisor

2. At 1457-8 (at the Last Supper):

αὐτὰρ ῾ἐπεὶ᾽ δῶκέν τε καὶ ἔκπιον, αὐτίκ᾽ ἔπειτα   o 10.237 †
μύθοισιν τέρποντο πρὸς ἀλλήλους ἐνέποντες.   i 11.643

When he had given them [the cup] and they had drunk from it,
    thereupon
they began to enjoy conversation together.

There are, however, three other examples that come close to qualifying as violent.

1. Lines 674-5 (Christ speaking to a healed paralytic):

ὄρσεο, κυλλοπόδιον, ἐμὸν τέκος· ἄντα σέθεν γὰρ   i 21.331
οὔ τις ἀνὴρ προπάροιθε μακάρτατος οὔτ᾽ ἄρ᾽ ὀπίσσω   o 11.483

Rise up, little cripple, my son. For compared to you
no one in times past nor in future was ever so fortunate.

2. Lines 1681-2 (Jesus to Judas, in the garden of Gethsemane):

ταῦτα μὲν οὕτω πάντα πεπείρανται· σὺ ῾δὲ αἶψα᾽   o 12.37 †
῾ρέξον᾽ ὅ τι φρονέεις· τελέσαι δέ σε θυμὸς ἀνώγει.   o 5.89 † ※

All things have now been fulfilled. <u>Quickly, you,</u>
do what you have in mind to do. For your heart bids you to bring it to pass.

3. Lines 2081-2 (the burial of Christ by the disciples):

ὣς οἵ γ᾽ ἐμμεμαῶτε νέκυν φέρον. <u>αὐτὰρ᾽ὕπερθεν᾽</u>   i 17.746 †
χερσὶ μέγαν λίθον ἀείραντές τε προσέθηκαν,   cf. o 9.240

And so the two of them carried out the corpse with some effort. <u>And high</u>
with their hands they lifted a huge stone and put it in place.

The second major type, "necessary" enjambement, is more common. In this type, any one or two of three essential elements of a clause—subject, verb, or object—is separated by verse end. In 129-31 (God in heaven speaking to the preexistent Christ about the human condition), the verb is enjambed:

ἠέρι καὶ νεφέλῃ κεκαλυμμένοι· οὐδέ ποτ᾽ αὐτοὺς   o 11.15
<u>εἴα</u> ἵστασθαι, χαλεπὸς δέ τις ὦρορε δαίμων   o 19.201
δαίμοσιν ἀρήσασθαι, ὑποσχέσθαι δ᾽ ἑκατόμβας.   i 6.115

[Humankind] shrouded in mist and cloud. For did never them
[Death] <u>allow</u> to arise, but some demon spurred them on
to pray to demons, and to promise the sacrifice of hecatombs

In 202-3 (the Annunciation), it is the object:

καὶ τότ᾽ ἄρ᾽ ἄγγελον ἧκεν, ὅς ἀγγείλειε γυναικὶ   o 15.458 ✵
<u>βουλήν,</u> ἥ ῥά ᾽τότε σφιν᾽ ἐφήνδανε μητιόωσι.   i 7.45 †

At that time he sent a herald to inform the woman
<u>of the plan,</u> since it pleased them who devised it.

These two passages may serve to show that Eudocia often enjambs lines that Homer does not, as with *Od.* 19.201 in the first example and *Od.* 15.458 in the second.

Examples of "adding" (Parry's "unperiodic") enjambement, the most common type in Homer, abound in the Centos as well. Adding enjambement often involves a runover adjective or participle in agreement with, or a noun in apposition to, some element in the previous line, or a runover adverb or adverbial phrase. The verse is then extended to line-end usually by either a relative clause, or a new sentence connected to the preceding one by δέ or, if negative, οὐδέ. An example of the first type is Cento lines 474-6 (Christ's teaching about God the Father):

πατρὸς δ᾽ εἴμ᾽ ἀγαθοῖο, θεὸς δέ με γείνατο 'πατὴρ'   i 21.109 ⁂ †
ἤπιος ὅς δή τοι παρέχει βρῶσίν τε πόσιν τε,   o 15.490 ⁂
ξείνιος, ὅς τε μάλιστα νεμεσσᾶται κακὰ ἔργα.   o 14.284 ⁂

I stem from a good father, and a god, my father, begat me;
<u>gentle is he</u>, who provides you with food and with drink,
<u>a protector of strangers</u>, who is sure to avenge evil deeds.

Examples of the second include lines 1733-4 (Christ on the way to the cross)

ἐν δ᾽ αὐτὸς κίεν ᾗσι προθυμίῃσι πεποιθὼς   i 2.588
<u>καρπαλίμως κατὰ ἄστυ</u>· φίλοι δ᾽ ἅμα πάντες ἕποντο   i 24.327

And he set off, trusting his own earnest resolve,
<u>swiftly through the city</u>; and his friends followed in train.

the description of the wine at the Last Supper (1450-1)

νίψατο δ᾽ αὐτὸς χεῖρας, ἀφύσσατο δ᾽ αἴθοπα οἶνον,   i 16.230
<u>ἡδὺν ἀκηράσιον, θεῖον ποτόν</u>. οὐδέ τις αὐτὸν   o 9.205

He washed his hands and drew a draught of gleaming wine,
<u>sweet and pure, a drink fit for a god</u>. No one

and 1805-7 (Peter's denial):

ἦ ῥ᾽ ὁ γέρων, πολιὰς δ᾽ ἄρ᾽ ἀνὰ τρίχας ἕλκετο χερσί,   i 22.77
αὐλῆς ἐκτὸς ἐών· οἱ δ᾽ ἔνδοθι μῆτιν ὕφαινον   o 4.678
<u>νωλεμέως</u>· ἀτὰρ αὐτὸς ἐλίσσετο ἔνθα καὶ ἔνθα   o 20.24

The old man spoke, then ran his fingers through his grey hair,
outside the courtyard; those inside were weaving a device,
<u>empty of pity</u>, while he himself tossed about this way and that.

Another type of adding enjambement occurs when a sentence fragment that takes up a whole verse is placed in apposition to a word in the previous line. This characteristically Homeric technique is very useful to the centonist for it "allows the poet simply to add items without affecting the grammatical construction" (Higbie 1990:33). Take for example the Centos' hymnic proem, which recounts the creation of the world: after the verb ἔτευξ᾽ in line 8 (= *Il.* 18.483), there follow twenty lines of things created in the accusative case, bound here and there by relative clauses. As in Homer, the pattern is usually noun (and/or adjective) + τε καί, or + τε . . . τε καί, or + τε . . . ἰδέ . . . ἠδέ, as in lines 21-4 (= *Il.* 14.347 + *Il.* 14.448 + *Od.* 5.72 + *Od.* 4.604), where flowers are catalogued in the accusative case after the phrase νεοθηλέα ποίην, or lines 26-8 (= *Od.* 7.115-6 + *Od.* 5.64), where varieties of trees are enumerated in the nominative case after δένδρεα ὑψιπέτηλα. In the Wedding at Cana scene, this type of adding enjambement is used to tally the guests, their activities, and their pleasures (e.g., lines 623-5 = *Od.* 1.150 + *Od.* 23.145 + *Od.* 8.99). It is not surpising that both the creation and Cana scenes are populated with lines taken from Homer's description of Achilles' shield where the same cataloging style is used.

Often in Homer, adding enjambement follows pronominal adjectives (e.g., ἕτερος, ἕκαστος, οὐδείς, μηδείς, and πᾶς), and the deictic pronouns ὁ, ἡ, τό, both of which the poet uses in a quasi-substantival way. This Homeric peculiarity also proves convenient for the cento poet who can simply end-stop such lines, or enjamb them *ad libitum*. For example πᾶσι in *Od.* 10.38—ὦ πόποι, ὡς ὅδε πᾶσι φίλος καὶ τίμιος ἐστίν—at line 984 is end-stopped, whereas in Homer it is enjambed, being glossed with ἀνθρώποις . . . κ.τ.λ. in 10.39.[2] So too with the deictic pronoun οἱ we find *Od.* 9.334 end-stopped in the Centos (1349-50), followed by an explanatory γάρ verse-clause from the *Iliad*:

οἱ δ᾽ ἔλαχον τοὺς ἄν κε καὶ ἤθελεν αὐτὸς ἑλέσθαι.　　o 9.334 ※
οἱ γάρ οἱ εἴσαντο διακριδὸν εἶναι ἄριστοι.　　　　　　 i 12.103

These were his lot, whomsoever he wanted to choose.
For it was clear to him that they were the best.

In Homer, *Od.* 9.334 is enjambed with the runover τέσσαρες in the following line.

Higbie's otherwise comprehensive study does not attempt to explain how the rest of a line that begins with enjambement from the previous verse is related to the runover word. This is the subject of a

---

2. *Od.* 10.38-9 occur as a couplet at 1337-8.

study by Matthew Clark (1994, 1997), who insists that "in order to understand the condition and function of runovers . . . we must examine not only what precedes the enjambement, but also what follows." When dealing, as in the Centos, with essentially stichic units, this becomes even more important.

Clark uses the term "binding" to refer to the probability that two words will occur together and borrows terminology from the analysis of musical fugues to describe the two limbs involved in enjambement: the *dux* is the preceding whole-verse or, if punctuated, verse-fragment before the runover; the *comes* is what follows, either to line end or to some point of punctuation in the line that contains the enjambement. Runovers themselves can be *free, pendant, embedded* or *orphan*.

An example of a free runover is an adjective like νήπιος, which, while often followed by οὐδέ or a relative clause, shows great variety in the *dux* and *comes*. A pendant runover is associated with a particular *dux*, but not with a particular *comes* (Clark 1994:96). The term "orphan" refers to runovers that are *not* associated with a particular *dux* but are associated with a specific *comes*. An example is γυμνόν in the line γυμνόν· αὐτὰρ τά γε τεύχε᾽ ἔχει κορυθαίολος Ἕκτωρ (*Il.* 17.122 and 693; 18.21) where "the runover and the *comes* are in different clauses, and have no grammatical relationship; nonetheless they co-occur. Lines of this sort," Clark observes, "are in effect whole line formulas, [even though] the boundaries of the line do not coincide with the boundaries of the grammar" (Clark 1994:101). Homer's free, pendant, and especially orphan runovers are of tremendous importance to our understanding of Cento composition. On the one hand, Eudocia adheres to the principles involved in each type; but she also diverges from Homeric practice and creates thereby some ingenious, disconcerting effects.

An example of an orphan runover occurs in lines 904-6 (Christ speaking to the man born blind):

ἦ μέν σ᾽ ἐνδυκέως ἀποπέμπομαι, ὄφρ᾽ ἂν ἵκηαι   o 10.65 ⁂
χαίρων καρπαλίμως, εἰ καὶ μάλα τηλόθεν ἐσσί,   o 7.194 ⁂
πατρίδα σὴν καὶ δῶμα, καὶ εἴ πού τοι φίλον εἴη.   o 10.66 ⁂

Now I am sending you off in good stead so that you may <u>come,</u>
<u>speedily, with rejoicing</u>, even though you are far off,
to your own country and household, assuming that is to your liking.

The enjambement of χαίρων καρπαλίμως in line 905 with the *comes* εἰ καὶ μάλα τηλόθεν ἐσσὶ is found only twice in Homer, at *Od.* 6.312 and *Od.* 7.194, two closely related, context-bound passages. In both it is preceded by a different *dux*. *Od.* 6.312 (Nausicaa speaking to Odysseus):

τὸν παραμειψάμενος μητρὸς ποτὶ γούνασι χεῖρας
βάλλειν ἡμετέρης, ἵνα νόστιμον ἦμαρ ἴδηαι
χαίρων καρπαλίμως, εἰ καὶ μάλα τηλόθεν ἐσσί.

By-passing him [Alcinous], around the knees of my mother
throw your hands so as to see your homecoming day
speedily, with rejoicing, even though you are far off.

In the second example, *Od.* 7.194, Alcinous recommends that the Phaeacians speed Odysseus on his way so that

πομπῇ ἐφ' ἡμετέρῃ ἣν πατρίδα γαῖαν ἵκηται
χαίρων καρπαλίμως, εἰ καὶ μάλα τηλόθεν ἐσσί,

By our escort you might reach your ancestral land
speedily, with rejoicing, even though you are far off.

Note that although the first part of the *dux* in *Od.* 10.65 (used in Cento line 904 above) is different from *Od.* 7.193 (both however contain the verbal idea in πέμπ -), Eudocia preserves the end-line/beginning-line collocation, ἵκη(τ)αι / χαίρων . . . κ.τ.λ. of 7.193. To supply the destination (πατ–ρίδα), she adds *Od.* 10.66 in the next line. In Homer, the verb ἴδηαι at 6.311, a homophone and allomorph of ἵκη(τ)αι and sometimes found as a variant of that word in Homer (e.g., at *Od.* 17.448), may have brought χαίρων καρπαλίμως . . . κ.τ.λ. to the poet's mind.

We have seen this type of word-association already as a factor in Cento accommodation. Clark makes a similar observation about the oral poet's repeated association of words and phrases in his discussion of *semantic trigger*, which sets off a formulaic molecule in the poet's mind. The Homeric phrase βριθὺ μέγα στιβαρόν, for example, which occurs six times in the epics, always as a runover and in various environments, does so regularly in close proximity to the word ἔγχος (Clark 1994:107). Semantic triggers clearly fire off rounds of word- and phrase-association in Eudocia's mind, and thus are, more broadly

defined, crucial to the Cento technique. Take for example the formula
line ὄφρ᾽ εἴπω τά με θυμὸς ἐνὶ στήθεσσι κελεύει in Cento line 5 (= Il. 8.6):

Κέκλυτε, μυρία φῦλα περικτιόνων ᾽ἀνθρώπων᾽,	i 17.220 †
ὅσσοι νῦν βροτοί εἰσιν ἐπὶ χθονὶ σῖτον ἔδοντες	o 8.222
ἠμὲν ὅσοι ναίουσι πρὸς ἠῶ τ᾽ ἠέλιόν τε	o 13.240
ἠδ᾽ ὅσσοι μετόπισθε ποτὶ ζόφον ἠερόεντα	o 13.241
ὄφρ᾽ εἴπω τά με θυμὸς ἐνὶ στήθεσσι κελεύει	i 8.6
᾽ὡς᾽ εὖ γινώσκητ᾽ ἠμεν θεὸν ἠδὲ καὶ ἄνδρα	i 5.128 ✳ †

Hear me now, you countless tribes of men who inhabit this land—
all you who are mortal and eat food on the earth
and as many as dwell facing the east or the west,
and those dwelling towards the murky gloom—
when I say what my spirit in my breast bids me,
so that you might have sure knowledge of both God and man.

This line, an example of adding enjambement, occurs four times total
in the *Iliad* (8.6, 7.369, 7.349, 7.68), notably all with κέκλυτε (used in
Cento line 1) preceding. Similarly, a little further on in the same
passage (lines 14-17),

ἰχθῦς ὄρνιθάς τε φίλας ὅ τι χεῖρας ἵκοιτο	o 12.331 ✳
εἰναλίων τοῖσίν τε θαλάσσια ἔργα μέμηλεν	o 5.67 ✳
δελφῖνάς τε κύνας τε καὶ εἴ ποθι μεῖζον ᾽ἔνεστι᾽	o 12.96 †
κῆτος, ἃ μυρία βόσκει ἀγάστονος ᾽Αμφιτρίτη,	o 12.97

Fish and friendly birds, that which comes into the hands
of fishermen who make it their business to work the sea;
and dolphins and dogfish and, if there be anything greater therein,
the whale, which groaning Amphitrite feeds in great numbers,

line 15 (*Od.* 5.67), in adding enjambement, is preceded in Homer by
two lines (*Od.* 5.65-6) that, like Cento line 14 (*Od.* 12.331), mention
birds (ὄρινθες, ἵρηκες, κορῶναι). At Cento lines 238-9,

τοῦ δὴ νῦν γε μέγιστον ὑπουράνιον κλέος ἐστὶ	o 9.264
πάντας ἐπ᾽ ἀνθρώπους, καί οἱ δόσις ἔσσεται ἐσθλή	i 10.213

His reputation now is the greatest under heaven
among all men, and his gift will be good,

the phrase ὑπουράνιον κλέος in *Od.* 9.264 brings *Il.* 10.213 to mind because of the unexpressed verse, *Il.* 10.212, the only other place in both poems where the phrase occurs. Eudocia's use of theme words will be discussed in more detail in chapter 6. We see clearly enough here, however, that keywords and semantic clusters bring associations with them recalling various lines from similar contexts.

Oftentimes a semantic trigger helps Eudocia with an enjambement, as at 355-6 (a description of the infant Jesus):

καὶ γὰρ θαῦμ' ἐτέτυκτο πελώριον. οὐ 'γὰρ' ἐῴκει   o 9.190 †
ἀνδρός γε θνητοῦ πάϊς ἔμμεναι, ἀλλὰ θεοῖο.   i 24.259

For he was a marvelous thing to behold. He did not seem
to be the son of a mortal man, but of a god.

In this example, *Od.* 9.190 (which describes the Cyclops, thus used here with considerable *Verfremdung*) is followed in Homer by the dative ἀνδρὶ in line 191, but with a different *comes* (ἀνδρί γε σιτοφάγῳ, ἀλλὰ ῥίῳ ὑλήεντι); conversely, *Il.* 24.259 is preceded by οὐδὲ ἐῴκει at end-line in 24.258 with a different *dux* ("Εκτορά θ' ὅς θεὸς ἔσκε μετ' ἀνδράσιν, οὐδ' ἐῴκει). Eudocia takes some liberty with the personal construction of ἐῴκει, but it may be that the nonsemantic structure of the inappropriate verse *Od.* 9.190 suggested to her *Il.* 24.259, a verse of almost identical sentence structure (ἀνδρός γε . . . ἀλλὰ . . .) that *did* fit the context.

Another example is 2031-2 (the burial of Christ):

'τὸν δ' ἄρ' ἔπειθ' ὑποδύντε δύω ἐρίηρες ἑταῖροι,   i 8.332 †
κάτθεσαν ἐν λεχέεσσι· φίλοι δ' ἀμφέσταν ἑταῖροι   i 18.233
μυρόμενοι, θαλερὸν δὲ κατείβετο δάκρυ παρειῶν.   i 24.794

Two of his trusty companions shouldered him and
set him on a bier, and his friends, his companions, stood around
wailing, as a fresh tear wet their cheeks.

The μυρόμενοι . . . κ.τ.λ. here, from *Il.* 24.794, is preceded in Homer by ἕταροί τε at the end of 24.793 (with a completely different *dux*), and ἑταῖροι at end-line at *Il.* 18.233 is followed by a line beginning with an enjambed μυρόμενοι, but with an entirely different *comes*.

There are dozens of similar examples. I note here only two more,[3] each of which shows the fascinating effects of semantic trigger on Eudocia's movement from one line to the next.

1. Lines 910-11:

ἀχλὺν δ' αὖ τοι ἀπ' ὀφθαλμῶν ἕλεν, ἣ πρὶν ἐπῆεν,   i 5.127 ✲
θεσπεσίην· ὁ δ' ἔπειτα μέγ' ἔξιδεν ὀφθαλμοῖσιν   i 20.342

In response he took the <u>mist</u> from his eyes, which had settled upon them
    earlier,
<u>and was uncanny</u>; then he saw very clearly with his eyes.

In Homer, the lines used here by Eudocia to describe a blind man involve the displacement of a formula where ἀχλύν with ἀπ' ὀφθαλμῶν occupies verse-initial position at *Il.* 5.127 rather than the more frequent end-line position. Nontheless, Eudocia enjambs θεσπεσίην in agreement with it (though there is no such enjambement in Homer), no doubt because she freely associates it with the ἀχλὺν / θεσπεσίην collocation, which appears for example at *Il.* 20.341.

2. Lines 1008-9 (the description of the Woman with a Flow of Blood):

ἕλκος μὲν γὰρ ἔχω τόδε καρτερόν, οὐδέ μοι <u>αἷμα</u>   i 16.517 + 518
<u>τέρσεται</u>, 'ἀλλὰ μάλ'' ὦκα κατειβόμενον κελαρύζει.   i 21.261 †

You see I have this terrible wound: my <u>blood</u> does not
<u>coagulate,</u> but keeps flowing steadily and trickling down.

This example involves the conflation of two successive lines from a battle type-scene in the *Iliad*. The semantic trigger αἷμα sets off τέρσεται, although at *Il.* 21.261 the enjambed word is not that but ὀχλεῦνται Eudocia slips into the enjambement quite naturally because she remembers, or is prompted by, τερσῆναι in the unexpressed verse, *Il.* 16.519.

---

3. Other examples include lines 285-6 (= *Od.* 13.93 + *Il.* 5.6), 829-30 (*Il.* 23.75 + *Od.* 14.139), 941-2 (= *Od.* 18.99 + *Il.* 15.369), and 1183--4 (= *Il.* 17.446 followed by a series of lines from *Odyssey* Book 18 [*Od.* 18.131 = *Il.* 17.447, through to the caesura of *Od.* 18.137]).

According to Clark, runover in type-scenes is due to the fact that "Similar scenes naturally call forth similar phrasings which may then produce or protect embedded and orphan runovers" (Clark 1994:101). The question arises: "When we have repeated runover words in such cases, 'which unit is the unit of repetition—the runover, or the context in which the runover occurs?'" With Clark I would conclude it is the context.[4] Eudocia's "thinking in context" is the topic of part 3, an investigation of the morphological and semiotic reasons she chose the particular lines she did. But as we see here context certainly played a role in the actual process of stitching the lines together.

A final example gives us a glimpse of how, before Eudocia, archaic rhapsodes (or a later interpolator) could work in the Homeric manner of whole-line formulas. At Cento lines 578-81 (The Wedding at Cana), Eudocia uses an orphan runover cited by Clark: τερπόμενοι·μετὰ δέ σφιν ἐμέλπετο θεῖος ἀοιδὸς / φορμίζων. This line occurs twice in the *Odyssey*, at 4.17 *verbatim*, and 13.27 with Δημόδοκος as the runover instead of φορμίζων. The enjambed line also occurs in the vulgate text of *Il.* 18.603-5, although Allen brackets it in the Oxford text on the authority of Aristarchus. However, we find the orphan in Eudocia, followed by four more lines from *Iliad* Book 18 that precede the *dux*—*Il.* 18.603—in Cento line 578 (The Wedding at Cana):

πολλὸς δ᾽ ἱμερόεντα χορὸν περιίσταθ᾽ ὅμιλος	i 18.603
τερπόμενοι · μετὰ δέ σφιν ἐμέλπετο θεῖος ἀοιδὸς	o 4.17
φορμίζων · δοιὼ δὲ κυβιστητῆρε κατ᾽ αὐτοὺς	o 4.18
μολπῆς ἐξάρχοντες ἐδίνευον κατὰ μέσσους.	o 4.19
ἔνθα μὲν ἠίθεοι καὶ παρθένοι ἀλφεσίβοιαι	i 18.593
ὠρχεῦντ᾽, ἀλλήλων ἐπὶ καρπῷ χεῖρας ἔχοντες.	i 18.594
τῶν δ᾽ αἱ μὲν λεπτὰς ὀθόνας ἔχον, οἱ δὲ χιτῶνας	i 18.595
εἵατ᾽ ἐϋννήτους, ἦκα στίλβοντας ἐλαίῳ.	i 18.596

A great throng stood around the beautiful dance floor
and were enjoying themselves; in their midst a divine minstrel sang
strumming his harp. Two tumblers in the crowd
took up the dance-song, and whirled into the center.
Then bachelors and dowered maidens
began to dance, locked together hand in hand.

---

4. Clark (1994:105) also notes that "the process of composing in molecules increases the statistical occurence of runovers without increasing the difficulty of composing in performance."

The girls wore fine linen, the boys were dressed
in finely-woven attire, their bodies gleaming with oil.

It may be that in Eudocia's text of Homer that's where the lines
stood. Or it may be that she transposed two blocks of lines, *Il.*
18.603-6 and 18.593-6, omitting lines 597-602 (which describe a
sword-dance inappropriate to the context). Be that as it may, what
Clark says of the appearance of this orphan runover in the *Iliad*
applies exactly to Eudocia: "If it is in fact an interpolation, the
interpolator was completely conversant with Homeric technique."
However, in many other places Eudocia diverges from Homeric
practice in that she often separates an end-line/beginning-line
collocation. Compare again 475-6 (cited above):

πατρὸς δ' εἴμ' ἀγαθοῖο, θεὸς δέ με γείνατο 'πατὴρ'	i 21.109 ⁕ †
ἤπιος ὅς δή τοι παρέχει βρῶσίν τε πόσιν τε,	o 15.490 ⁕
ξείνιος, ὅς τε μάλιστα νεμεσσᾶται κακὰ ἔργα.	o 14.284 ⁕

I stem from a good father, and a god, my father, begat me;
gentle is he, who provides you with food and with drink,
a protector of strangers, who is sure to avenge evil deeds.

In Homer, there are only two occurrences of the form ξεινίο(υ) in
adding enjambement, one of which is *Od.* 14.284, the verse in grammatical accommodation here (the other is at *Il.* 13.625). Both times
ξεινίου refers (of course) to Zeus, but as in the *Odyssey* examples just
discussed, the wording of the *dux* (and *comes*) in each passage is rather
different:

Ζηνὸς ἐριβρεμέτεω χαλεπὴν ἐδείσατε μῆνιν
ξεινίου ὅς τέ ποτ' ὕμμι διαφθέρσει πόλιν αἰπυήν·
(*Il.* 13.624-5)

You did [not] fear thundering Zeus's terrible rage,
the protector of strangers, who will eventually crush our lofty city

ἀλλ' ἀπὸ κεῖνος ἔρυκε, Διὸς δ' ὠπίζετο μῆνιν
ξεινίου ὅς τε μάλιστα νεμεσσᾶται κακὰ ἔργα.
(*Od.* 14.283-4)

But he restrained them, for he respected the rage of Zeus,
the protector of strangers, who is sure to avenge evil deeds

The end-line/beginning-line collocation μῆνιν / ξεινίου in both Homeric passages is broken up by Eudocia with *Od.* 15.490, where ἠπίο(υ) is used by Odysseus of a guest-friend from Eumaeus's past and, interestingly, in a line that begins with an enjambed Ζεύς.

As is well known, many lines in Homer come in "clusters," and "couplets" (cf. Lord 1960:58; 1991:75), what Clark calls "formulaic molecules" (1994:99). Runovers within such molecules are said to be *embedded*. An example is the enjambed line at Cento lines 212 and 249—ἀδμήτην, ἥν οὔ πω ὑπὸ ζυγὸν ἤγαγεν ἀνήρ—which occurs in Homer only in a couplet and only at *Il.* 10.293 and *Od.* 3.383:

σοί δ᾽ αὖ ἐγὼ ῥέξω βοῦν ἦνιν εὐρυμέτωπον
<u>ἀδμήτην</u>, ἥν οὔπω ὑπὸ ζυγὸν ἤγαγεν ἀνήρ

I will sacrifice to you a broad-faced cow, one year of age,
<u>unbroken</u>, whom a man has not yet brought under his yoke.

This second line of this couplet is used twice by Eudocia in the Annunciation scene to describe the Virgin Mary (evoking, I would add, strange images of Io given the context):

1. At lines 211-3:

βῆ δ᾽ ἴμεν ἐς θάλαμον πολυδαίδαλον, ᾧ ἔνι κούρη	o 6.15
ἕζετ᾽ ἐνὶ κλισμῷ· ὑπὸ δὲ θρῆνυς ποσὶν ἦεν,	o 4.136 †
ἠλάκατα στρωφῶσ᾽ ἁλιπόρφυρα, θαῦμα ἰδέσθαι	o 6.306
<u>ἀδμήτη</u>, τὴν οὔ πω ὑπὸ ζυγὸν ἤγαγεν ἀνήρ.	i 10.293 ※

He [the angel] entered an elaborate room—there was the girl,
Sitting on a couch, a footstool supporting her feet
as she spun yarn into thread, a wonder to see.
<u>She was unbroken</u>: a man had not yet brought her under his yoke.

2. At lines 247-8 (Mary speaking):

ὦ φίλ᾽, ἐπεί 'δή' μοι καὶ ἀμείψασθαι θέμις ἐστί,	o 16.91 @
τίπτε με κεῖνος ἄνωγε μέγας θεός; αἰδέομαι δὲ	i 24.90
<u>ἀδμήτη</u>, ἥν οὔ πω ὑπὸ ζυγὸν ἤγαγεν ἀνήρ.	i 10.293 ※

Friend—since indeed it is right that I answer you back—
Why me? what is this that God the almighty commands? I am shamefast,

unbroken: a man has not yet brought me under his yoke.

Compare Cento lines 1473-14 (describing Judas at the betrayal):

κλίμακα δ' ὑψηλὴν κατεβήσατο τοῖο δόμοιο,   o 1.330 ⁂
'χωόμενος· μένεος δὲ μέγα φρένες ἀμφὶ μέλαιναι   i 1.103 †
πίμπλαντ· ὄσσε δέ οἱ πυρὶ λαμπετόωντι ἐΐκτην.   i 1.104

He climbed down the ladder in the house
full of rage, and fury about his black soul
swelled, and his eys burned as bright as fire

   In the Homeric passage in question the orphan runover ἀχνύμενος
occurs with its embedded partner πίμπλαντ'. . . κ.τ.λ. (see Clark 1994:
103). Here it is changed by Eudocia to the stronger χωόμενος. This is
either a slip of the poet's memory, or a creative substitution on
Eudocia's part to keep out any resonances of "grief" in the word
ἀχνύμενος. Perhaps she felt χωόμενος "full of rage" (which frequently
occurs in this position in Homer), better captured the villainy of
Judas.
   Though she freely departs from strict adherence to Homeric usage,
Eudocia is nonetheless an expert seamstress whose stitchings reveal a
poetic mind well versed in the Homeric and biblical texts. Take this
example of a brilliant but unhomeric use of enjambement in the
Crucifixion scene (1872-7):

ᾟμος δ' ἠέλιος μέσον οὐρανὸν ἀμφιβεβήκει,   i 8.68
δεξάμενοι δ' ἄρα τοί γε διαστάντες τανύουσι   i 17.391
'σταυροῖσιν πυκινοῖσι' διαμπερὲς ἔνθα καὶ ἔνθα   o 14.11 †
γυμνόν, ἀτάρ τοι εἵματ' ἐνὶ μεγάροισι κέοντο,   i 22.510 ⁂
ὀρθὸν ἐν ἱστοπέδη· ἐκ δ' αὐτοῦ πείρατ' 'ἀνῆψαν'   o 12.179 @
ὕψι μάλα μεγάλως· ἐπὶ δ' ἴαχε λαὸς ὄπισθε.   i 17.723

And when the sun had come 'round to mid-heaven
they took him, stood apart and stretched him out
with stake after stake, now here, now there, incessant,
and naked, since his clothes lay in the palace,
straight up at the foot of the mast-beam, then fastened cables around him
very high up in the air, while the mob was shouting behind him.

   As it is construed here, the adjective γυμνόν in 1875, referring to
Jesus, is the direct object of the verb τανύουσι in line 1873. Γυμνόν in

enjambement (separated from its verb by a whole line) is further qualified by the adjective ὀρθόν in 1876 in apposition to it. In Homer, γύμνον refers to Hector's corpse. The direct object of τανύουσι at *Il.* 17.391 is a bull's hide, in a simile that compares the struggle over the body of Patroclus to a procedure in the tanning of leather. Ὀρθόν at *Od.* 12.179 refers to Odysseus who has been tied to the mast in order to hear the song of the Sirens. Though Eudocia's syntax is "unhomeric" in that no expressed referent exists for γυμνόν and ὀρθόν, she skilfully organizes four consecutive enjambements (using lines taken from scenes of death) around an episode from the *Odyssey*, which for early Christians was pregnant with Crucifixion symbolism (Pépin 1982).

Another example: at lines 1236-9, where Jesus learns from Martha and Mary of his friend Lazarus's death, we read

πεύσεαι ἀγγελίης, ἢ μὴ ὤφελλε γενέσθαι,	i 18.19
<u>λυγρῆς</u> ἀγγελίης, ὅτι σοι φίλος ὤλεθ᾽ ἑταῖρος·	i 17.642 ※
<u>λυγρῆς</u>· ἤ τέ μοι αἰεὶ ἐνὶ στήθεσσι φίλον κῆρ	o 1.341
τείρει, ἐπεί με μάλιστα καθίκετο πένθος ἄλαστον.	o 1.342

You will hear a report which should not be reported,
a <u>grievous</u> report, that your beloved companion is dead;
<u>grievous</u> indeed: it oppresses the heart in my breast,
since now pain has descended on me and I cannot blot it out.

In this (unhomeric) example of hyperenjambement (with the genitive λυγρῆς repeated twice anaphorically in apposition), the poet lingers on what are two of the most grievous reports in Homer: the news of Patroclus's death, and Phemius's song about the *nostoi*, which for Penelope and Telemachus is tantamount to the death of a beloved husband and father (cf. *Od.* 1.354-5). Similarly, in the description of King Herod's Slaughter of the Innocents (307-12), Eudocia enjambs the word-root νήπιος twice in a row, playing with the Homeric words' literal and figurative meanings, "fool" and "infant" respectively:

πολλὰ δ᾽ ἀτάσθαλ᾽ ἔρεξε βίη καὶ κάρτεϊ εἴκων,	o 18.139
πάντων μὲν κρατέειν ἐθέλων, πάντεσσι δ᾽ ἀνάσσειν.	i 1.288 ※
<u>νήπιος</u>· ἤ τε πολέσσιν ἐπ᾽ αὐτῷ θυμὸν ἀπηύρα	i 17.236
<u>νηπιάχοις</u>· ξυνὸν δὲ κακὸν πολέεσσιν ῾ἔθηκε᾿	i 16.262 ※ †
κτείνας ἐπιστροφάδην· τῶν δὲ στόνος ὤρνυτ᾽ ἀεικὴς	i 10.483 ※
ἄορι θεινομένων, ἐρυθαίνετο δ᾽ αἵματι γαῖα.	i 10.484

He committed a very foolhardy mistake by yielding to violence and force,
out of a desire to control and rule over all,
the fool! Indeed, he robbed many of their lives for that reason—
and they were mere babes! He was the common cause of woe for many
    people
by killing one after another. The shocking cries of those being
slain by the sword resounded, and the earth was stained red with blood.

In a recent book on formal, but nonformulaic patterns of repetition
in Homer, one author observes of Homeric poetics that "the study of
patterns is, to a point, an investigation of *usage*. It emphasizes
reception and response rather than composition" (Kahane 1994:16).
Such are the limitations faced by all modern Homerists seeking to
describe the making of Homeric verse: the *Iliad* and *Odyssey* are the
culmination and refinement of a long poetic tradition that originated
in an oral milieu, yet, because they exist only as written texts, the
origin and generation of the poems in that milieu is accessible to us, if
at all, only through a textual medium (cf. Griffin 1980:xiii). Thus, on
this view, we can go no farther back in our investigations into the oral
tradition of Greek epic poetry than the reception of and response to
it in the works of Homer.

    Analogously, but at a second remove, reception and response are
what the Homeric Centos represent (cf. Smolak 1979:49; Stehlíková
1987). However, with Eudocia, unlike "Homer" himself, we can
observe the poet interacting with her repertoire and get that much
closer to the moment and manner of verse composition. In the
Centos, the processes of reading Homeric poetry (reception) and
composing with it (response) are complementary, even symbiotic,
and this is what makes them so intriguing.

    In chapters 2 and 3, it was argued that the Centos were composed
in a mode that presupposes a high degree of what Walter Ong calls
"residual orality," by which he means that a "manuscript culture . . .
[is] always marginally oral" (Ong 1982:157). To establish whether or
not some degree of orality is present in a given text, we must ask a
basic question: "How can one distinguish an oral-traditional text from
one of written literature?" (Lord 1991:25). To answer it, Albert Lord
offered some sound advice based on a lifetime of fieldwork.

First, "one must know what the specific characteristics of a given tradition are in order to tell whether they are present or not in the text under consideration" (cf. Miller 1982:26; Foley 1991:43). This has been the aim in writing a Cento poetics. Obviously, because the Centos are comprised entirely of Homeric lines and phrases, they would qualify as an oral-traditional text by virtue of that fact alone.[5] But we have also seen that the *process* of Cento composition has many features in common with the processes used by the oral poet(s), proto-poets, or later performers of the *Iliad* and *Odyssey*. In all types of Cento accommodation and enjambement, we see the large part played by homophony, allomorphism, and the spontaneous association of words and phrases. I have suggested that in many instances Eudocia, like an ancient bard, composed by analogy, adapting Homeric formulas in her word and phrase substitutions. Her frequent use of all types of enjambement is especially impressive given her concern to reproduce Homeric lines as accurately as possible. In sum, Eudocia proves to be fluent in Homer and the Homeric style.

Once the specific characteristics of a given tradition have been established, Lord suggests that a text be scrutinized using Milman Parry's three criteria for determining whether or not a text is oral-traditional: Does it contain formulas? Does it make use of themes? Is there frequent unperiodic enjambement? The Centos in fact satisfy all three criteria. We have dealt only with the use of formulas and enjambement so far. Themes, also fundamental to Cento composition, will be discussed fully in the next four chapters.

As to the criterion of formulas, Russo, following Notopoulos, has advanced the useful concept of the "structural formula," a nuanced development of Parry's notion of a formula-system that allows "any and all the members of a phrase to be variable and still count the phrase as formulaic, so long as it continue[s] to share similarities of rhythm, parts of speech, syntactic relationship, and . . . localization within the hexameter verse, with a series of other phrases that could be related to the same 'system'" (Russo 1976:32).

In an attempt at clarity and differentiation in this flexible approach to Homeric formularity, Russo has graded Homeric formulas

---

5. Although Stanley (1992:268-79) offers notable objections to Ong's criteria for orality and their applicability to Homer, I am still very much in agreement with Ong's basic premises.

into five basic levels according to how far removed a phrase is from exact repetition. From most concrete to most abstract, these are, (1) exact repetition, allowing for simple inflection of the elements, (2) formulas with only one variable element, (3) formulas with two or more variables, (4) the "single-term structural formula" (e.g., middle-passive participles at verse-initial position), and (5) the purely rhythmic formula, not corresponding to actual words at all, but to metrical *sedes* and the patterns of colometry in the Homeric line (Russo 1976:35-7).

In principle, Eudocia operates at each of these levels. In her very use of Homeric lines, line-formulas, and grammatical accommodation she operates at level 1. In her substitutions in semantic accommodation and her conflated and half-lines, she works at levels 2-5. Seen thus, we might say that Eudocia's use of Homer and the formula system is, in a modified form, an expression of the Parryan principles of economy and extension (on which see Hainsworth's excellent summary 1993:23-6). Extension, understood in terms of Cento poetics, is the hypothetical set of Homeric lines capable of appropriation (mostly those that do not contain proper names). Economy is at work in the particular use of those lines: for example in the use of periphrasis to identify the *dramatis personae*, in the repetition of other whole-line formulas, and in the semantic accommodations (intentional or otherwise) where she is consistent with Homeric practice elsewhere.

If Homeric Cento poetry is a *parole* re-generation of Homeric verse, then it must be, like the original generation of the verse by the bards of old, a line-by-line transaction *of thought* along the axes of selection and combination. This is a crucial point for a proper understanding of Homeric and Homeric Cento enjambement. I would like to dwell on it briefly here, for I believe Eudocia's pratice in this regard quickens our understanding of audience expectation and reader response, adding much to that understanding—by way of clarification—of how a Homeric poet's thought proceeds from line to line.

According to Higbie, the difference between Homeric enjambement types is "the degree of expectation of or grammatical need for what follows the verse end" (Higbie 1990:29). In her analysis, however, it turns out that "expectation" for Higbie *is* grammatical.[6] This misses what is best in the Parry-Lord tradition. In a seminal article on enjambement published in 1929, Parry noted how often in Homer's style "several *ideas* [are] added to one another . . . which could not be foreseen, were not even looked for, until each one was told" (emphasis added). Parry rightly understood that for a true poetics of enjambement and an accurate appraisal of Homer's oral style, the expectation of the audience during performance and the generation of the verse by the poet must be seen as a phrase-by-phrase, line-by-line transaction *of thought*.[7] However, as to the expression of thought in words, even Parry's notion of expectation becomes problematic.

Parry argued that the audience or reader gradually acquired "*a sense for the formula*. Meeting over and over the same group of words expressing the same idea, he comes to look on this group of words as a whole which has a fixed end." In short, "He reads by formulas." Thus, accorrding to Parry, the auditor's response to the enjambed line at *Iliad* 5.16 (Τυδεΐδεω δ᾽ ὑπὲρ ὦμον ἀριστερὸν ἤλυθ᾽ ἀκωκὴ / ἔγχεος) would be conditioned by his memory of the more usual and generic end-stopped versions of this formula, *Il.* 17.49 and *Il.* 22.327: ἀντικρὺ δ᾽

---

6. I cite only one of several examples of this tendency, her discussion of *Il.* 5.144-7 in which line 145 is classed as "clausal-external" enjambement because the verb πλῆξ in line 147 constitutes the previous two lines as a clause (Higbie 1990:30). But surely, based on any definition of expectation, lines 145 and 146 are also "adding-internal" in that they are explicative of the double object of the verb ἕλεν in line 144. Put another way, the sentence could happily end at 146 and πλῆξ᾽ in 147, though technically in "necessary" enjambement, is super-fluous.

7. Bakker's 1990 analysis of the hexameter line by "idea units" as opposed to grammatical units—that is, "from the point of view of the cognitive processes of the narrator, not from the point of view of the standards applied by a [modern] reader"—is truer to Parry's early insights on the question. Bakker's model of Homeric enjambement based on the "left and right dislocation" of elements in the Homeric sentence reveals that the varieties of Homeric enjambement involving the separation of verb, subject and/or object from the rest of their sentence by verse-end (so-called necessary enjambement) are not *categorically* different because the grammatical need is greater, as Higbie believes, but rather occupy a place on a manageable spectrum of oral discourse familiar to the poet and his or her audience.

ἁπαλοῖο δι᾽ αὐχένος ἤλυθε ἀκωκή (Parry 1929:258). However, if, as Parry believed, the *Iliad* was composed during performance, the original Homeric audience could not, strictly speaking, hone its expectations for Book 5 on Books 17 and 22 since those parts of the performance had yet to be realized. While I am in full agreement that any "cross-reference that we admire in our two-dimensional text did not just happen one time in one performance," and that "the resonances of Homeric cross-referencing must be appreciated within the larger context of a long history of repeated performances" (Nagy 1996b:82),[8] it is difficult, if not impossible, to prove which version of a given formula was the standard wherefrom the audience acquired its "sense."

So far as enjambement is concerned, however, by measuring Eudocia's practice against Homer's, we get a glimpse of what *her* expectations as a Homeric reader and poet were: we have already seen that she enjambs lines that are end-stopped in Homer and vice versa παρὰ προσδοκίαν. Parry's notion of expectation actually better suits the centonist Eudocia—a literate poet fully conversant in the Homeric *langue*, who composed in a culture still marked by oral residue—than it does the oral bard of primary orality.

In the final analysis I agree with Russo and others that "history has hidden Homer's methods of poetic creation from us. . . . All we have is his style; and all that can be put to the proof is our own capacity to respond to it" (Russo 1976:39). "The fundamental quality of such a style," Russo insists,

> is that it is one shaped by the ear. It is laden at every level with the devices that facilitate this process: the level of rhythmical metric [and] the level of "structural" patterning of language in formulaic moulds that may be filled in a variety of ways, and as such may be called "aural" formulas but not "oral" ones. . . . It is a style, and a poetry, organized at every level, from the acoustic to the sociolinguistic, to serve the needs of *rapport* and *communication* between the poet and his audience.

---

8. *Pace* Ong (1982:31-2), whose characterization of the spoken word in a primary oral culture as an "ephemeral event" runs the risk of undervaluing a long-standing, conventional poetic tradition.

Eudocia, we have seen, responded to this aural style by reproducing it—twelve-hundred years later in a very different milieu—and used Homer's poetry as a vehicle for communicating the Christian story. Fluent in the texts of the *Iliad* and *Odyssey*, her poetic idiom, Eudocia manipulated the inner workings of the Homeric system to stitch together a new ἀοιδή out of Homer.

Part Three

Cento Semiotics and Aesthetics

5

Themes and Intertextuality

In or about the year 400 C.E., a bishop in northern Asia Minor named Asterius commented on the high fashion of his day: "The more religious among rich men and women," he complained before his congregation, "have carded through the Gospel story and handed it over to the weavers." In the streets of fifth-century Constantinople, Antioch, or Alexandria, Asterius informs us, you could find "Christ and his disciples" woven into the fine garments of these religious rich, "and each of the miracles, as the story goes (ὡς ἡ διήγησις ἔχει): the wedding in Galilee with the water jars; the paralytic carrying his bed on his back; the blind man healed with clay; the woman with the flow of blood seizing the hem of Jesus' cloak; the sinful woman falling at his feet; Lazarus coming back to life from the grave" (Migne *PG* 40:168; Mango 1972:51; cf. Maguire 1995:52-9).

It is no surprise that Eudocia embroidered these same biblical scenes into her literary textile. Christ's miracles were favorite themes for all arts and crafts in late antiquity. They are commonly found on Christian sarcophagi, diptychs, wall-paintings, and mosaics, often presented paratactically in successive registers (Matthews 1993:54-91). Eudocia's choice and treatment of her subject matter shows her general sympathy with the tastes of the period, much as Homer's treatment of his themes can be fruitfully compared to Geometric pottery and the "Dipylon Style" (Whitman 1958:87-101; Hurwit 1985:93-106). Of course, unlike Homer, Eudocia knew her themes from texts, or from lectionary readings and sermons based on those texts. And yet Eudocia's choice and treatment of her themes, like her selection and combination of Homeric verses, reveals that she was not directly dependent upon texts, much less any single text, in composing the Centos.

Of the scenes mentioned by Asterius, for example, the Wedding at

Cana (Cento lines 528-627) and the raising of Lazarus (1228-99) are
story-traditions unique to the Gospel of John. The Annunciation
(203-68) appears only in Luke; the Visit of the Magi (294-300) only
in Matthew. The story of Christ's descent to Hades (lines 2105-48),
on the other hand, is not told in the canonical Gospels. That episode,
perhaps implied in a few New Testament passages and mentioned
briefly in early patristic writings, is first narrated only in the fourth-
century *Gospel of Nicodemus* (Schneemelcher 1991:I.501-36; Ferguson 1990:411-12). The heavenly conversation between Christ and
"God the Father" (88-201) has no narrative source at all, but is a
purely imaginative dialogue modeled, it seems, after the familiar
Homeric council-of-gods scene (cf. Smolak 1979:32), and based on
theological speculation about Christ's preexistence—speculation that
stretches back to the earliest Messianic and Christological interpretations of biblical passages like Psalm 110:1 ("The LORD says to
my Lord . . .") and Genesis 1:26 ("Let *us* make man in our image").
    As we see from the diverse nature of her sources, Eudocia does not
approach her theme material like a biblical metaphrast, whose
primary objective is to turn the prose text of a "stylistically simple
original" into poetry that "typically involve[s] a great deal of
rhetorical embellishment" (Roberts 1985:58). Like her contemporary
Nonnus, who wrote a hexameter poem of this sort based on the
Gospel of John, Eudocia was certainly capable of the rhetorical
paraphrase, as can be seen from her own hexameter version of the
prose *Life of St. Cyprian*. Photius in fact praises Eudocia (notoriously,
the only poet he discusses at all in the *Bibliotheca*) for being
particularly good at sticking close to the text of the original in her
lost paraphrases of the Octoteuch and Daniel (*Bibl.* Codd. 183-4).
However, Eudocia faced a rather different task in composing the
Centos: she was not working with a fixed *text*, but rather with a *story*
that had been spun over time from various themes, themes drawn
from various spheres of Christian discourse—narrative, theological,
even iconographic.[1]
    To comprehend themes in the Homeric Centos, we must go below
the poetic surface of the Centos and venture into the areas of
context, referentiality, and meaning. At this semantic level of the

---

1. On the role of story in early Christian culture, see Sykes 1987 with Averil
Cameron 1991:13.

poem the Homeric verses used by Eudocia must constantly be related to the biblical or biblically derived theme material. Todorov calls this a relationship *in absentia*: "A certain signifier *signifies* a certain signified, a certain phenomenon *evokes* another, a certain episode *symbolizes* an idea, another *illustrates* a psychology" (Todorov 1973: 14). In the Centos there is an additional twist in that the signs of one system have been appropriated to express the signifieds of another. Consequently, in discussing the use and function of themes in the Homeric Centos, we face the whole question of intertextuality and its effects.

In spite of this apparent complexity, my fundamental thesis here is simple and straightforward. As was stated for Homer by Bernard Fenik in his landmark study of Homeric battle type-scenes: Cento "verse-building and action narrative . . . represent two aspects of basically the same compositional technique" (Fenik 1968: Summary). That is, traditional themes, like the free association of words and phrases in all types of accommodation and enjambement, play a major role in the Cento poet's cognitive processes of selection and combination, and thus contribute to the generation of the poem.

This chapter attempts to provide an explanatory model for Eudocia's use of themes in both their generative and aesthetic dimensions. "Aesthetics," as understood here, is not the study of beauty *per se* but of perception, and it is primarily the eye of the beholder that fixes our attention throughout. While Eudocia's generation of Cento verse may have been facilitated by thematic structures built into and shared between the Homeric and biblical narratives, her choice and handling of this material was also a reader's response, that is, an aesthetic judgment. Our task, then, is twofold: first, to state what that choice entailed. This I do by demonstrating how Eudocia, taking her cues from Homer, composed her poem by theme. Second, I state what her choice of material implies, semantically and artistically: this through an analysis and interpretation of Cento intertextuality. Before we delve into Eudocia's use of Homeric themes and type-scenes, however, we must introduce and define some terms.

Themes and Type-scenes

The Homeric "type-scene," a phrase coined by Walter Arend in 1933, is a recurrent block of narrative in either the *Iliad* or the

Odyssey, whose elements consistently appear in the same order. Type-scenes express the customary, everyday activities and etiquettes of the Homeric age (departing, arriving, eating, entertaining, sleeping, sailing, holding assembly, etc.), and thus, by their frequency and regularity, reflect and preserve fundamental Homeric values (cf. Foley 1991:34-5).

Homeric type-scenes fall into five basic categories: battle, social intercourse, travel, ritual, and speech and deliberation, each of which has various subspecies (so Edwards 1992). To construct a given episode, Homer draws from several of these categories at once (cf. Arend 1933:35). The hospitality scene, or *xenia*, for example, crucial to the composition of the Centos, utilizes type-scenes belonging to the spheres of social intercourse, ritual, and speech and deliberation (cf. Reece 1993:5-39). On the larger level, as has been demonstrated by Mark Edwards, "the whole of Homeric narrative can be analyzed into type-scenes" and typical motifs (Edwards 1992:287; cf. Edwards 1991:11-12; Kirk 1990:16-18).

Inevitably, every Cento episode draws on Homeric type-scenes or other recurrent motifs. In fact, each of the above categories is represented. Lines from Homeric scenes of feasting and sacrifice, for example, abound in the Wedding at Cana episode (528-627), the Feeding of the Five Thousand (1153ff), and the Last Supper (1385ff). Homeric lines describing the wounding of warriors are used repeatedly to describe the blind, sick, bleeding, crippled, and lame persons healed by Christ (628-1045). The healings themselves use various lines describing the divine enabling of Homeric heroes. At Christ's burial (2030-86), lines taken from Homeric burial and mourning scenes flow freely.

"Theme" is Albert Lord's term for these recurrent blocks of narrative in oral poetry, which, as he defines it in *Singer of Tales*, "is not any fixed set of words but a grouping of ideas" (Lord 1960:69; 1938:73).[2] V. V. Radlov, a pioneer in the study of themes in oral poetry, used the apt term *Bildtheile*, "idea-parts", to describe the

---

2. In using Lord's now standard phrase "composition by theme" (Lord 1951), I have this definition in mind. As Edwards notes (1992:286), however, Lord's later definition of theme and its character in Serbo-Croatian poetry as "a repeated passage rather than a repeated subject" (Lord 1991:27) is not well suited to the great verbal and structural variety found in the Homeric type-scene.

phenomenon (Foley 1988:12). Taking a given theme as a whole (e.g., "hospitality") the type-scene (e.g., "sacrifice") is the smaller narrative unit. But whether Homer elaborates a type-scene, as in the case of Nestor's sacrifice at *Od.* 3.418-76, or uses type-scene shorthand as at *Od.* 13.26, the notion of "sacrifice" is common to both treatments. A theme, then, is what any typical recurrent passage in Homer "is about." "The theme (what is being said in a work) unites the separate elements of the work. The work as a whole has a theme, and its individual parts also have themes" (Tomashevsky in Lemon and Reis 1965:63).

Theme Activation

Themes and type-scenes are the building blocks of Homeric narrative. An oral poet, as Lord observed of the Serbo-Croatian *guslari*, knows the whole song by theme before he sings it. However, "when he reaches key points in the performance of the song, he finds that he is drawn in one direction or another by the similarities with related groups [of songs] at those points" (Lord 1960:123). In the act of composition, in other words, there is always "an explicit awareness . . . of the existence of the possibilities that could become other songs" (Slatkin 1996:228). Eudocia realized these "possibilities" in an extreme fashion by using Homeric verses to express a completely different "song" from a completely different tradition. She was drawn in that direction, as we shall see, by perceived similarities between the Homeric and biblical stories as she moved from one verse to the next.

Although Eudocia was composing in a literate society, the Centos, like the Homeric poems, presuppose, even depend upon, a thematic knowledge of the Christian story on the part of both poet and audience. Eudocia's re-generation of Homeric verse thus entails what Egbert Bakker calls theme "activation and preservation" (Bakker 1993). Bakker suggests that in order to understand the place of Homeric poetry in its oral or residually oral tradition, we must move away from the modern idea that the primary function of texts and language in society is to transmit information, *new* information in particular. With special reference to the interdependence of text and performance, Bakker argues that the ancient Greek poet and/or writer of texts

> is concerned not with the transmission of messages to readers
> (the text being a container for these contents), but with the
> fixation, and thereby the *preservation*, of what binds container
> and content together into an indissoluble whole, that is,
> speech. Similarly, "reading" a text that is meant to represent
> . . . speech is nothing other than the *re-enactment* of it, or
> better its reactivation.

Following a hint provided by the Greek verb "to read,"
ἀναγιγνώσκω, Bakker suggests that

> if speaking is a matter of cognition, of the activation of ideas
> in one's consciousness . . . then reading is a matter of the "*re-
> cognition*" and reactivation of these same ideas, both in the
> reader's and the listeners' consciousness. Writing and reading,
> in short, are related to each other as performance and re-
> performance. (Bakker 1993:16)

This notion of theme activation and preservation, which sees content
and container as an "indissoluble whole" representing original speech,
is especially important for us as it accounts for both the orality of an
original performance and the aural dimension of texts like the Centos,
which were composed by a literate poet in a residually oral culture.

Intertextuality

Although Eudocia activates her themes with Homeric lines, the
themes themselves, of course, are not Homeric but biblical. Cento
composition by theme therefore involves applying the Homeric sign
system and the conventions and compositional techniques associated
with it to themes taken from a completely different system. Thus, as
a concatenation of Homeric verses expressing biblical themes, the
Homeric Centos are a perfect instance of intertextuality: the condition or quality of being poised between texts. Intertextuality, as I
understand it here, embraces not only the intertext in question, but
the poet and audience as well. Indeed, with Eudocia, the poet, as
reader, is a member of the audience. To cast this mutual relationship
in terms of Cento theme activation in a generative system: "Each
occurrence of a theme (on the level of content) or of a formula (on
the level of form) in a given composition-in-performance refers not

only to its immediate context but also to . . . other analogous contexts remembered by the performer or by any member of the audience" (Nagy 1996a:50).[3]

Intertexts themselves, according to a recent semiotic formulation by Heinrich Plett, "consist of signs. Signs are part of codes. Codes have two components: signs and rules. The signs represent the material, the rules the structural aspect of the code" (Plett 1991:13). Intertextuality in Plett's model may be "material," "structural," or based on a combination of the two. Material intertextuality corresponds to the quotation, the repetition of signs. Structural intertextuality consists in the repetition of narrative rules. Both types are fully operative in the Homeric Centos, which use the repetition of signs (Homeric verses) to reproduce biblical narrative according to narrative rules that both codes share. Although the signs of the Homeric and biblical codes are often at variance, the two texts can be assimilated in the reader's response because on the narrative plane their signifieds, or themes, share structural, that is, morphological elements.

Functions and Attributes

The "rules" of narrative are nowhere better explained than in Propp's *Morphology of the Folktale*, and a brief overview is necessary here, for Propp's work is of the greatest importance for a clear understanding of Cento intertextuality. In the *Morphology*, Propp rejected the classification of tales by subject matter and along with it the view

---

3. Zumthor justly describes this phenomenon as "intervocality." In speaking of texts and intertextuality in a generative system, we must keep in mind that "Chaque texte enregistré par l'ecriture, tel que nous le lisons, occupa néanmoins un lieu précis dans un ensemble de relations mobiles et dans une série de productions multiples, au sein d'un concert d'échos réciproques: d'une intervocalité, comme l' 'intertextualité' dont on parle tôt depuis quelques années, et que je considère ici sous son aspect d'échange de paroles et de connivence sonore; polyphonie perçue par les destinataires d'une poésie qui leur est communiquée—quelles qu'en soient les modalités et le style performanciel—exclusivement par la voix. Ces relations intervocales, dans l'univers des contacts personnels et des sensations, tiennent de celles qui s'instaurent (avec moins de chaleur!) dans notre pratique moderne entre le texte original et son commentaire ou sa traduction" (Zumthor 1987:161).

(espoused by Stith Thompson) that each simple sentence of a tale comprises a motif, as in "a dragon kidnaps the tsar's daughter," and that this motif is the basic narrative unit. Propp showed to the contrary that this and most sentence-motifs are in fact divisible into four component parts, "each of which in its own right can vary." The dragon, for instance, is often replaced by a whirlwind, a devil, falcon, or magician; abduction can be effected by vampirism or some other method resulting in disappearance; the daughter may become a sister, bride, wife, or mother, and the tsar a prince, priest, or peasant (Propp 1928:12-13; cf. Bremond 1993:51).

Given these variables, Propp saw the need to isolate the stable elements in a narrative. He did so by maintaining that the function of a character is the stable, constant element in the tale, "independent of how and by whom it is fulfilled." Although "the actual means of the realization of functions can vary," he notes, "the function as such is a constant" (Propp 1928:21). Propp further observed that the sequence of functions in the Russian fairy tale is also constant (1928:22), and that although "all tales do not contain all functions, the absence of certain functions does not affect the sequence of the rest": "the number of functions is extremely small, whereas the number of personages is extremely large" (Propp 1928:20), a factor that explains "the two-fold quality of tale: its amazing multiformity, picturesqueness, and color; and on the other hand, its no less striking uniformity, its repetition" (Propp 1928:20-1).[4]

Independently of Propp, Arend, the father of Homeric type-scene scholarship, established the importance of sequence for the Homeric type-scene.[5] As to the "two-fold quality of the tale, its amazing multiformity, picturesqueness, and color; and . . . its no less striking uniformity [and] repetition," this has long been recognized as a defining characteristic of Homeric poetry, attributable to its origin in a preliterate culture. As Arend observed in reference to the Homeric

---

4. These two claims have occasioned some criticism, much of which is based, I think, on misunderstandings (e.g., Nathhorst 1970:16-29; Lévi-Strauss 1960). Propp's claim about the limited number of functions is not important here, though he made it only for the limited body of material he studied (Propp 1928:23-4), and primarily for the purposes of classification.

5. A glance at his charts conveys this best (Arend 1933; see especialy Plate 5, Chart 9, "Landung," with discussion on 79-81).

type-scene:

> All variation . . . preserves the fixed form. Such is the source
> of the peculiar and unique quality of Homeric art—the inter-
> play between the fixed form and the various embellishments,
> between what is formally required and what arises serendi-
> pitously, between the typical and the particular, between
> repetition and variation.[6]

Propp's emphasis on the narrative function of a character, irrespective of his attributes, is his great contribution to narratology.[7] Given the clash of sign-systems in the Homeric Centos, the distinction between function and attribute is especially important. As we have seen already in chapter 3, the cento poet's use of grammatical accommodation often makes such attributes as the person, number, and gender of a character a matter of indifference. A character's other attributes, too, though they be uncongenial to the correspoding biblical character's, are also often ignored, or seemingly so.

---

6. "Alle Variation . . . hat die feste Form nicht aufgelöst. So entsteht das Eigenartige und Einzigartige der homerischen Kunst, der Wechsel von fester Form und verschiedener Ausschmückung, von Notwendigem und Zufälligem, von Typischem und Individuellem, von Wiederholung und Variation" (Arend 1933:27).

7. Propp's many successors in the morphological approach to narrative have adapted his work to accommodate other modes of structuralist thought. Notable among these is A. J. Greimas, who took the concept of the binary opposition of phonemes developed in the work of Saussure and Jakobson and applied it to Propp's morphology with the result that Propp's seven general spheres of character action are resolved into three pairs of opposed "actants" (Greimas 1966:197-207; Hawkes 1977:87-95). At first sight this is a simplification of Propp, but Greimas's nuanced scheme, I find, adds more terminology than substance and is too complicated to be useful here. Moreover, as Propp himself realized (completely independently of Greimas's work), binarily opposed functions are performed by different characters in the story, and are fulfilled at different points in the narrative sequence, "Therefore, in the study of composition, that is, of the sequence of functions, reduction of the binary elements to a single one will not reveal the laws that govern the development of the plot" (Propp 1966:75).

Consider Eudocia's version of the Annunciation (202-68):

καὶ τότ᾽ ἄρ᾽ ἄγγελον ἦκεν, ὃς ἀγγείλειε γυναικὶ	o 15.458 ✳
βουλήν, ἥ ῥα ᾿τότε σφιν᾽ ἐφήνδανε μητιόωσι.	i 7.45 †
αὐτὰρ ὃ βῆ, μέγα γάρ ῥα θεοῦ ὤτρυνεν ἐφετμή,	i 21.299 ✳
ἀντία δεσποίνης φάσθαι καὶ ἕκαστα πυθέσθαι.	o 15.377
καρπαλίμως δ᾽ ἤϊξεν ἐπὶ χθόνα πουλυβότειραν	i 11.118+619
οὐρανόθεν καταβὰς διὰ αἰθέρος ἀτρυγέτοιο,	i 11.184+17.425
νύμφη εὐπλοκάμῳ εἰπεῖν νημερτέα βουλήν.	o 5.30
βῆ δ᾽ ἴμεν ἐς θάλαμον πολυδαίδαλον, ᾧ ἔνι κούρη	o 6.15
᾿ἕζετ᾽ ἐνὶ᾽ κλισμῷ· ὑπὸ δὲ θρῆνυς ποσὶν ἦεν,	o 4.136 †
ἠλάκατα στρωφῶσ᾽ ἁλιπόρφυρα, θαῦμα ἰδέσθαι	o 6.306
ἀδμήτη, τὴν οὔ πω ὑπὸ ζυγὸν ἤγαγεν ἀνήρ.	i 10.293 ✳
τήνδε τότ᾽ ἐν μεγάροισι πάτηρ καὶ πότνια μήτηρ	i 9.561
ἀνδρὶ φίλῳ ᾿ἔπορον᾽· ὁ δέ μιν πρόφρων ὑπέδεκτο	i 14.504+9.480 ✳
οὔτ᾽ εὐνῆς πρόφασιν κεχρημένος, οὔτέ τευ ἄλλου,	i 19.262
ἀλλ᾽ ἔμεν᾽ ἀπροτίμαστος ἐνὶ κλισίησιν ἑῇσιν.	i 19.263
οὔ τι γάμου τόσσον κεχρημένος οὐδὲ χατίζων,	o 22.50
ἀλλ᾽ ἄλλα φρονέων, τά οἱ οὐκ ᾿ἀτέλεστα γένοντο᾽.	o 22.51 †
ἤ τι ὀϊσσάμενός γ᾽ ἢ καὶ θεὸς ὣς ἐκελεύσεν,	o 9.339
μή ποτε τῆς εὐνῆς ἐπιβήμεναι ἠδὲ μιγῆναι,	i 9.133
ἢ θέμις ἀνθρώπων πέλει, ἀνδρῶν ἠδὲ γυναικῶν.	i 9.134
δέσποιναν μὲν πρῶτα κιχήσατο ἐν μεγάροισιν.	o 7.53 ✳
στῆ δ᾽ αὐτῆς προπάροιθεν ἔπος τ᾽ ἔφατ᾽ ἔκ τ᾽ ὀνόμαζε	i 14.297
κήρυξ πεισήνωρ, πεπνυμένα μήδεα εἰδώς,	o 2.38
τυτθὸν φθεγξάμενος· τὴν δὲ τρόμος ἔλλαβε γυῖα.	i 24.170 ✳
"θάρσει ᾿ὦ γύναι χαρίεσσα,᾽ μηδέ τι τάρβει·	i 24.171 †
νῦν ᾿δ᾽ ἐμέθεν ξύνες ὦκα· ᾿θεοῦ᾽ δέ τοι ἄγγελος εἰμί,	*i 24.133 †*
᾿ὅς κέν με᾽ προέηκε τεῒν τάδε μυθήσασθαι.	i 11.201 †
χαῖρε μοι, ὦ βασίλεια, διαμπερές, εἰς ὅ κεν ᾿ἔλθοι᾽	o 13.59 †
ἀνδράσιν ἠδὲ γυναιξὶν ᾿ἐπὶ᾽ χθόνα πουλυβότειραν	o 19.408 †
᾿γῆρας᾽ καὶ θάνατος, τά τ᾽ ἐπ᾽ ἀνθρώποισι πέλονται.	o 13.60 †
σὸν δ᾽ ἤτοι κλέος ἔσται ὅσον τ᾽ ἐπικίδναται ἠώς.	i 7.458
τοῖς οἳ νῦν γεγάασι καὶ οἳ μετόπισθεν ἔσονται.	o 24.84
χαῖρε, γύναι ᾿χαρίεσσα᾽· περιπλομένου δ᾽ ἐνιαυτοῦ	o 11.248 †
ἐκφανεῖ, ὃς πάντεσσι περικτιόνεσσιν ἀνάσσει	i 19.104 ✳
τῶν ἀνδρῶν οἳ σῆς ἐξ αἵματός εἰσι γενέθλης.	i 19.111
νημετερὲς γάρ τοι μυθήσομαι, οὐδ᾽ ἐπικεύσω,	*o 19.269 ✳*
τοῦ δὴ νῦν γε μέγιστον ὑπουράνιον κλέος ἐστὶ	o 9.264
πάντας ἐπ᾽ ἀνθρώπους, καί οἱ δόσις ἔσσεται ἐσθλή."	i 10.213
ὣς φάτο· τῆς δ᾽ αὐτοῦ λύτο γούνατα καὶ φίλον ἦτορ.	*o 4.703*
ἡ δ᾽ οὔτ᾽ ἀθρῆσαι δύνατ᾽ ἀντίη οὔτε νοῆσαι,	o 19.478
καί ῥ᾽ ἀκέουσα καθῆστο, ἐπιγνάμψασα φίλον κῆρ.	i 1.569

τὴν δ᾽ ἅμα χάρμα καὶ ἄλγος ἕλε φρένα, τὼ δέ οἱ ὄσσε   o 19.471
δακρύοφιν πλῆσθεν, θαλερὴ δέ οἱ ἔσχατο φωνή.   o 4.705
ὀρθαὶ δὲ τρίχες ἔσταν ἐνὶ γναμπτοῖσι μέλεσσι.   i 24.359
ὀψὲ δὲ δή μιν ἔπεσσιν ἀμειβομένη προσέειπε·   o 4.706
   "ὦ φίλ᾽, ἐπεί ᾽δή᾽ μοι καὶ ἀμείψασθαι θέμις ἐστί,   o 16.91 @
τίπτε με κεῖνος ἄνωγε μέγας θεός; αἰδέομαι δὲ   i 24.90
ἀδμήτη, ἣν οὔ πω ὑπὸ ζυγὸν ἤγαγεν ἀνήρ.   i 10.293 ✳
ἀλλὰ τί κεν ῥέξαιμι; θεὸς διὰ πάντα τελευτᾷ,   i 19.90
ὅππως κεν ἐθέλῃσιν· ὃ γὰρ κάρτιστος ἁπάντων.   i 20.243
τοῦτο μὲν οὕτω δὴ ἔστω ἔπος, ᾽ὡς εἴρηκας᾽,   o 11.348 ✳ †
αὐτὰρ ᾽μὴ᾽ νῦν μοι τόδε χώεο μηδὲ νεμέσσα   o 23.213
οὕνεκά σ᾽ οὐ τὸ πρῶτον, ἐπεὶ ἴδον, ὧδ᾽ ἀγάπησα.   o 23.214
αἰεὶ γάρ μοι θυμὸς ἐνὶ στήθεσσι φίλοισιν   o 23.215
ἐρρίγει, μή τίς με βροτῶν ἀπάφοιτ᾽ ἐπέεσσιν   o 23.216
ἐλθών. πολλοὶ γὰρ κακὰ ᾽κήδεα βουλεύονται᾽."   o 23.217 † ✳
τὴν δ᾽ ἀπαμειβόμενος προσέφη κήρυξ πεισήνωρ,   cf. o 2.38
   "καὶ δέ σοι ὧδ᾽ αὐτῇ πολὺ κάλλιον, ὦ βασίλεια,   o 17.583
οἵην πρὸς ξεῖνον φάσθαι ἔπος ἠδ᾽ ἐπακοῦσαι.   o 17.584
θάρσει ᾽μοι᾽· ἐπεὶ οὔ ᾽τι᾽ ἄνευ θεοῦ ἥδε γε βουλή.   o 2.372 †
σίγα καὶ κατὰ σὸν νόον ἴσχανε μηδ᾽ ἐρέεινε·   o 19.42
ἀλλ᾽ ἔχε σιγῇ μῦθον, ἐπίτρεψον δὲ ᾽θεῷ᾽ περ.   o 19.502 ✳
αὐτὰρ ἐγὼ νέομαι· σὺ δὲ τέρπεο τῷδ᾽ ἐνὶ ᾽χώρῳ᾽.   o 13.61 †
εἶμι μέν, οὐδ᾽ ἅλιον ἔπος ἔσσεται, ὅττι κεν εἴπῃ.   i 24.92
ἀργαλέον, βασίλεια, διηνεκέως ἀγορεῦσαι."   o 7.241
   αὐτὰρ ἐπεὶ δὴ πᾶσαν ἐφημοσύνην ἀπέειπε,   o 16.340 ✳
χάλκεον οὐρανὸν ἷκε δι᾽ αἰθέρος ἀτρυγέτοιο.   i 17.425

At that time he sent a herald to inform the woman
of the plan, since it pleased them who devised it.
He went, for God's great authority moved him
to speak before the queen and make several requests.
He shot swiftly over the nourishing earth,
descending from heaven through fallow air
to tell the fair-haired bride about the sure plan.
He entered an elaborate room—there was the girl,
Sitting on a couch, a footstool supporting her feet
as she spun yarn into thread, a wonder to see.
She was unbroken: a man had not yet brought her under his yoke.
This girl once lived in the house of a noble mother and father;
they had given her to a dear husband, who took her in good faith,
neither using her for his bed, nor for anything else;
she remained untouched, uncaressed in his tents.
He did not enjoy the stuff of marriage, he had no desire to,

For he had other things on his mind which for him did not go unfulfilled.
Either it was his own idea, or God himself gave the command
that he not make her mount that bed or mingle in love,
though such is proper for human husbands and wives.
The queen was the first person the herald met in the house.
He stood before her, named her and spoke,
Persuasive this herald, inspired with knowledge,
Softly intoning. Nonetheless, fear seized her limbs.
  "Courage, woman of grace, do not be afraid.
Hear me now: I am God's messenger
He sent me to you to with the following message:
'Hail to you queen, for all time, until there comes
upon the women and men of the nourishing earth
old age and death, which things are their lot.
Indeed your fame will spread as far as dawn scatters its dew
on men living today and on those born tomorrow.
Hail, woman of grace! and when the time is come round
there will appear a man to rule those who dwell upon earth,
over all men who are of your race and your blood.
What I will say is true. I shall not mislead you.
His fame now will be greatest of all under heaven;
he will be over all mankind, and noble his gift.'"
  Those were his words, and her knees and heart sank.
She was unable to look at him straight, nor could she think,
but sat down in silence, bending her heart to his will.
Then pain mixed with joy snatched her breath away, and her eyes
Flooded with tears, her lovely voice stuck in her throat;
the hair on her shapely arms stood on end,
and she answered him back with these words:
  "Friend—since indeed it is right that I answer you back—
Why me? what is this that God the almighty commands? I am shamefast,
Unbroken: a man has not brought me under his yoke.
But what can I do? God brings all to completion
however he wants. For he is the strongest of all.
Let your word be as you say.
But do not be angry at me over this, nor find fault
Because I did not welcome you the instant I saw you.
For the spirit in my breast is always afraid
that some mortal man will come and seduce me with words.
As you know there are many men with evil intent."
  In reply the persuasive herald addressed her:
"Surely, my queen, it is much better for you to speak
as you did with a stranger in private and to hear him out.

Courage! this plan is not without God's approval.
Quiet now, check your thoughts, ask no more questions,
Don't tell a soul, but turn your thoughts toward God.
As for me, I am going away. You enjoy yourself here.
I'm off. The story he tells is not meant to trick you.
Continual talk, queen, is a difficult work."
 And when he had conveyed the whole message,
he passed through fallow air to a heaven of bronze.

The Virgin Mary is equated in this scene—by means of direct quotation of Homeric lines (i.e., material intertextuality)—with a motley crew of Homeric characters. Among them are: a Sidonian slave girl (202), Calypso (208), Nausicaa (209), Helen (210), Arete (211, 222, 229), Briseis (213, 220-1), Priam (225-6, 245), Tyro (234), Penelope (240, 241, 243, 244, 246, 253-7, 259-60), Hera (242), Thetis (248), and Eurycleia (261, 262, 263).

Obviously, Mary has attributes in common with many of these characters, even where they do not consistently share the same attributes with one another. Like Nausicaa she is a young virgin; like Penelope and Arete a mother and queen (the latter through a theological development that by Eudocia's time was well established; Graef 1963:133-8 with Plate 2); like the Sidonian slave girl, Eurycleia, and Briseis, she is a servant (cf. Lk 1:38 and 48). But what of King Priam?

It could be argued that Mary shares with Priam, if not gender, the attribute of bereavement, for she, like him, loses a son to a violent, ignominious death. The assimilation of Mary and Priam at this early juncture of the narrative might then be taken to foreshadow the event described at Cento lines 2030ff, comprised largely of material drawn from *Iliad* Books 22 and 24, where Christ is represented as the dead and dying Hector. A detail from Eudocia's biblical theme may have suggested a comparison with Priam, for according to the Gospel of Luke, Jesus' death is foreshadowed in his infancy in the Presentation in the Temple episode, where the prophet Simeon warns Mary that the boy will be "a sign that shall be spoken against," adding, in reference to her son's eventual death: "Yea, a sword will pierce through your own soul also" (Lk 2:34). Such *intra*-Cento referentiality, if that is what this represents, is just one of the many intricacies of Cento intertextuality. But there is something much more basic at stake in this passage.

Stripped of all attributes, the biblical theme in the Annunciation scene consists of the reception of a visitor (the angel Gabriel sent by God). In the Homeric *langue*, visitation is realized as a type-scene. Thus, although the Homeric lines Eudocia uses refer to distinct epic characters, they come to mind because the vast majority of these lines are taken from Homeric type-scenes involving the arrival and reception of a stranger or herald (Arend 1933:28-63; Edwards 1992:304-6; 308-9; Reece 1993:5-46). Mary is equated with these several Homeric characters—just as the angel, the other *dramatis persona* in this episode, is equated with Hermes, Athena, and other human heralds (lines 202, 204, 206, 207, 209, 224, 237, etc.)— because their function in their respective contexts in Homer corresponds to her function in the biblical story. The two narratives here are linked by structural intertextuality.

Interpretants, Icons, Symbols

To begin to understand Cento intertextuality, we must analyze Cento episodes, as Propp did for the Russian material, "by structural, interior features, and not by features which are external and changeable." This does not mean that external or attributive features are not important. Certainly the virginity of Nausicaa, the compassionate motherhood of Thetis, and the queenly stature of Penelope and Arete apply to Mary; perhaps too the bereavement of Priam. These are attributes she possesses in Christian discourse. However, other characters in this scene possess attributes, the semantic effects of which are difficult to imagine the poet intending, but which nonetheless demand resolution if we are to comprehend this poem in all its facets.

For example, in Homer, the Sidonian slave girl to whom Cento line 202 refers (in a tale told by Eumaeus) is seduced by a Phoenician trader, and makes love to him in the hollow of his ship (μίγη κοίλῃ παρὰ νηΐ / εὐνῇ καὶ φιλότητι). Her pleasure and complicity in this sexual encounter are perfectly *un*ambiguous: τά τε φρένα ἠπεροπεύει / θηλυτέρῃσι γυναιξί (*Od.* 15.420-2). Obviously, if attribute is the point of comparison here, it plays havoc with the Christian doctrine of the Virgin Birth, effectively undoing four hundred years of Mariology, and implicitly turns God into a philandering Phoenician pirate. This case confirms Propp's view and our proposition that the Homeric characters' narrative *function* (in this case as receivers of guests) takes priority in the compositional process.

The semiotic impasse in line 202 is precipitated by the fact that, unavoidably, lines appropriated from Homer in the Homeric Centos always resonate with their original Homeric context, even if this is in conflict with the biblical or theological context. On the level of meaning as opposed to morphology—of *product* as opposed to *process*—such appropriation inevitably compromises the integrity of all parties involved, Homeric and biblical, leading to *Verfremdung*. And yet we also find many instances in the Centos where function and attribute seem to coincide; that is, a biblical character happens to share both narrative function and character attribute with his Homeric counterpart, as we saw in Mary's relationship in the Annunciation scene to Thetis and Nausicaa. Furthermore, many other Cento character assimilations based on attributes do not involve the damaging associations brought on by Homer's Sidonian slave girl; these assimilations are based on something other than simple narrative function and must be taken into account. Cento line 242, where Mary reacts to God's plan as Hera does to the βουλή of Zeus in *Iliad* 1.569, provides a good example.

The Homeric context of this line does not involve the herald-theme as do most of the lines in the Annunciation, but the line *does* capture Mary's biblical response to the events surrounding the birth of Jesus with Homeric imagination. In Luke's Gospel, Mary "kept all the things the angel told her and pondered them in her heart" (πάντα συνετήρει τὰ ῥήματα ταῦτα συμβάλλουσα ἐν τῇ καρδίᾳ αὐτῆς Lk 2:19); whereas Hera, rebuked in front of all the gods by Zeus, "took her seat in silence, bending her heart to his will" (καί ῥ' ἀκέουσα καθῆστο, ἐπι-γνάμψασα φίλον κῆρ). Read in light of Homer, there is some *Verfrem-dung* in the appropriation of this line, which suggests that the Centos' Mary is not unequivocally St. Luke's obedient "handmaid of the Lord," but also, like Homer's Hera, the recalcitrant bride of an Almighty. The scenes, however, *are* linked—not by function, but by the attributive word/idea "heart" (Homer's ἐπιγναμψασα <u>κῆρ</u>; Luke's συμβάλλουσα ἐν <u>καρδίη</u>). Both characters' hearts figure prominently in their response to divine injunction.

Clearly, then, both function *and* attribute—in that order—are important in the generation and appreciation of Homeric Cento verse. Whether there is a satisfying congruence or a startling discrepancy, characters' attributes nuance every Cento episode. They are, as it were, adjectival elements in the narrative syntax; as such they are telling of the reader's aesthetic response to both texts, and cannot be neglected.

The logic of Eudocia's handling of character attributes in Cento intertextuality is, we have said, particularly amenable to semiotic analysis. The semiotic model of thought expounded by the founder of the discipline, C. S. Peirce, provides the basic tools and terminology for understanding such relationships. I give only the necessary details here.[8]

Peirce saw all thought as a signifying process involving three essential elements: an *object*, a *sign*, and an *interpretant*. In the processes of thought and signification, a sign always stands for something (an object) to something else (its interpretant) (Peirce 1955:99). To apply Peirce's model to the Centos (speaking in the broadest terms): the *object* is the biblical, or biblically derived theme or themes, the *sign* is the Homeric verse or verses used to convey it, and the *interpretant* is the poet, or to put it more abstractly, a "second thought," which interprets a first thought initiated by the sign. This abstract notion of the interpretant is preferable to simply equating it with the poet since, as Peirce is careful to point out, "throughout this process, *introspection* is not resorted to. Nothing is assumed respecting the subjective elements of consciousness which cannot be securely inferrred from the objective elements" (Peirce 1867:26). For our analysis of Cento intertextuality as a generative system, the interpretant is the most important element of the semiotic triad. How it mediates between sign and object is of primary concern.

In making comparisons (as between a Homeric and biblical character or episode), the interpretant, according to Peirce, "cannot comprehend an agreement of two things, except as an agreement in some *respect*" (Peirce 1867:27). The respect in which two things are related by the interpretant is called by Peirce its *ground*. Of the three types of ground identified by Peirce, two are relevant to our analysis here: the *iconic* and the *symbolic* grounds.

---

8. For a summary of Peirce's thought, terminology, and relationship to other semiotic systems, see Nöth 1990:39-47; 115-21, with ample bibliography, and recently Deledalle 1995.

In iconic relations, object and sign participate in some quality or characteristic. Icons are in some way like their objects—representationally, like a painting; relationally, as a diagram or algebraic equation is to a logical or mathematical proposition; or analogically, as is the case when "I surmise that zebras are likely to be obstinate, or otherwise disagreeable animals, because they seem to have a general resemblence to donkeys, and donkeys are self-willed" (Peirce 1955: 106).

In symbolic relations, unlike iconic relations, "the sign would lose the character which renders it a sign if there were no interpretant. Such is any utterance of speech which signifies what it does only by virtue of its being understood to have that signification." In other words, a symbol is "a conventional sign, or one depending upon habit (acquired or inborn)" (Peirce 1955:104, 113). In Cento intertextuality, a symbol's full significance, unlike an iconic sign, demands that we import information from outside of the two texts or passages at hand; the symbolic relationship between sign and object is conventional or (less accurately) arbitrary, and at the level of meaning, is independent of shared qualities or characteristics.

From these "objective elements" of the signifying process, namely the morphological relationships between biblical and Homeric themes, and the iconic and symbolic grounds that connect particular characters or events, we can identify with some confidence the one or more interpretants behind any instance of Cento intertextuality. I think we can even distinguish between the interpretant that was foremost "in Eudocia's mind," and the interpretant that may be present in the thoughts of a third-party reader. Of course, it is not impossible that both thoughts occurred to the poet herself, one in composition and one, as it were, as an afterthought, and I would like to keep that possibility in play throughout this discussion. In either case, it is important to emphasize here that, as an object of analysis, Peirce's interpretant, or "second thought," yields information about *signification*. An author's intention is of course embedded in this process, but need not be invoked in our analysis. I offer the customary apologies now if in what follows I occasionally attribute a particular meaning to "Eudocia."

❖

In 1697 Marius D'Assigny, an English clergyman and scholar of French Huguenot extraction, published a short treatise for aspiring preachers entitled *The Art of Memory*.[9] In it he offers six "Rules to be observed to help our Remembrance of things that we desire to preserve in Mind." D'Assigny's rules epitomize Propp's morphology and Peirce's semiotics with an elegance the latter both lack. To the extent that the cento is connected with the art of declamation, especially in the need to internalize the laws of a generative system, I think these rules convey something of the cognitive and aesthetic dynamics involved in Cento composition. Trusting the reader to the heuristic power of conceits, I offer D'Assigny's mnemonic rules here, prefatory to the following chapters, for they show a keen awareness of character attribute and character function as separate, but related grounds for intertextuality, Cento or otherwise. The rules are (D'Assigny 1697:78-80):

> (1) Mind the Order in which those things were first entered into our Memories; for things that precede will oblige us to think upon those that followed and the Consequences of things will refresh in our Fancies that which went before. It becomes us therefore to record them in order with a Connexion and a mutual Dependence.

> (2) For the better remembering of things, we ought to compare them with those things with which we are familiar or best acquainted, and that have a Resemblance with them, either in Syllables, in Quantity, in Office, Employment &c. for this Similitude will certainly imprint the Thing or Person so in our Mind.

> (3) We may imprint in our Minds, and fix Things in Memory, by thinking upon their Contraries or Opposites; and we may by the same means better remember Things that are almost blotted out of our Imagination. For Example, he that remembers an *Hector*, cannot forget *Achilles*; he that thinks upon a *Goliah*, will also mind a *David*.

---

9. Much of D'Assigny's work is an abridgement of Gulielmus Gratarolus's *De Memoria Reparanda* (1553) (DePorte 1985:v). On ancient and medieval mnemonics generally, see Carruthers 1990.

(4) If we desire to mind Things of Importance, we ought to imprint all the Circumstances in our Memories of Time, Place, Persons, Causes, &c. because these Circumstances being always in our Fancy, will also keep there the things that we intend to preserve from Oblivion.

(5) We may think upon Things, and remember them by their Properties, and Qualifications. For Example; if we desire to remember a gross and fat Man, we may think upon King Dionysius, of whom an Author tells us, that he grew so fat that he could scarce see, and that at last his Eyes were closed up with Fat.

(6) If we desire to remember any thing, let us mind that Circumstance that is belonging to it, most admirable, remarkable, or sutable [sic] to our Genius, Temper, or Interest; for this will fix it in our Memories in such a manner that it will not easily be forgotten.

D'Assigny's rule 1 may be understood as Propp's rule of sequence, rule 4 as that of morphological function. Rules 2, 3, and 5 represent three varieties of Peirce's iconic ground.[10] Rules 3 and 5 are a binarily opposed pair.[11] Rule 5 makes a positive comparison. Rule 3 is

---

10. In choosing which Homeric lines to use to express her biblical themes, Eudocia is always motivated by an icon. As Peirce himself observed, "Anything whatever, be it quality, existent individual, or law, is an Icon of anything in so far as it is like that thing and used as a sign of it" (Peirce 1955:102). Thus, the Proppian rules of function and sequence (1 and 4) are iconic to the extent that intertextuality based on either rule is based on a perceived similarity between texts or stories at the level of narrative structure. Symbolic relationships between biblical theme and Homeric sign (rule 6) are intelligibile primarily because symbols themselves participate in iconicity. The capaciousness of the icon has prompted some, particularly Eco, to criticise its utility. The problem is well put by W. J. T. Mitchell: "Everything in the world is similar to everything else in some respects, if we look hard enough" (Mitchell 1986:56-7). In using D'Assigny's rules I have intentionally limited the application of the term icon here.

11. Peirce was well aware that iconic similarity between object and sign requires that iconic difference or contrast be a ground for an interpretant as well: "if a drunken man is exhibited in order to show, by contrast, the excellence of

dependent on rule 5 in so far as it presupposes that an identity or assimilation has already been established (based on rule 5), which, once remembered, sets off contrasting associations of character and/or quality. This is what the words "Contraries" and "Opposites" in D'Assigny's seventeenth-century English mean, as his example shows. "He that remembers an *Hector*, cannot forget Achilles": only one sign needs to be present in order to evoke the other. In Cento intertextuality, the antagonist of rule 3—not necessarily an adversary—is present *in absentia* via the Homeric context of a given line or passage.

Rule 2 I take to refer to the linguistic devices discussed in the previous chapters that help the poet link one line to another; this rule also applies to verbal or semantic resemblances between Homeric and biblical signs (as opposed to codes). These iconic devices, for example the κῆρ-καρδίη connection between Mary and Hera in the Annunciation scene, also serve as mnemonic aids in the generation of the verse.

Rule 6, which corresponds to Peirce's symbolic ground, is by definition the most subjective of the six criteria ("sutable to [one's] own Genius, Temper, or Interest"), and consequently the most fascinating, yet difficult, of the criteria to apply in our analysis, for it often involves a gross misreading of the Homeric (and biblical) text. However, assimilations based on this ground can and will be explained and defended with reference to late antique discourse and culture at large, for "Interpretants are the testable and describable correspondents associated by public agreement to another sign" (Eco 1976:1471).

---

temperance, this is certainly an icon, but whether it is a likeness or not may be doubted" (Peirce 1955:107). The way in which such contrasts may lead to defamiliarization in the Centos is suggested by D'Assigny's younger contemporary, Alexander Pope, commenting on the comparison of Odysseus's bow to a lyre at *Od.* 21.404-23: "When similitudes are borrow'd from an object entirely different from the subject which they are brought to illustrate, they give us a double satisfaction, as they surprize us by shewing an agreement between such things in which there seems to be the greatest disagreement" (G. Steiner 1996:102).

6

Composition by Theme

Οὔτε γὰρ μέτρον οὔτε τρόπος οὔτε λέξεως ὄγκος οὔτ᾽
εὐκαιρία μεταφορᾶς οὔθ᾽ ἁρμονία καὶ σύνθεσις ἔχει τοσ–
οῦτον αἱμιλίας καὶ χάριτος ὅσον εὖ πεπλεγμένη διάθεσις
μυθολογίας.

—Plutarch, *How to Study Poetry*

The tale's the thing.

—A. B. Lord

Having established a working model that can account for both the
narrative function and attributes of characters in the story, let us look
closely at some particular examples of the use of Homeric themes in
the Centos.

This chapter contains a general discussion of the character, scope,
and techniques of Cento composition by theme and its basis in
Homer. In chapter 7, I discuss Eudocia's realization of the Homeric
hospitality type-scene, a theme particularly associated with the *Odyssey*. In chapter 8, we turn our attention to the realization of themes
typical of the *Iliad* through an analysis of Eudocia's use of Homeric
similes. This is not an exhaustive treatment. I have sought to provide
enough evidence, however, to illustrate most aspects of Cento intertextuality and the general utility of the approach advocated in the
previous chapter. Every episode in the Homeric Centos deserves the
close attention I give select passages in chapters 7 and 8. I would be
gratified if my efforts here reveal the need for further research on this
amazing poem and spur the reader on to seek greater clarification.

Because of the interdependence of form and content in a
generative system, it is difficult to discuss structural elements and

compositional techniques without calling attention to the iconic and symbolic grounds upon which the realization of those elements are simultaneously based. All of D'Assigny's rules, in other words, work together toward the realization of a Cento episode, even if one rule is dominant in a given assimilation. Moreover, as we have seen, Homeric characters may share both function and attribute with their biblical counterpart. Conscious of this, I nevertheless confine my remarks here to observations relating to the Proppian rules of sequence and function, and to the intertextual law of verbal resemblance (D'Assigny's rules 1, 2 and 4). The semiotics of Cento intertextuality come into full play in the next two chapters.

The Feeding of the Five Thousand episode (1153-1227) illustrates several features characteristic of Eudocia's handling of themes and type-scenes. Morphologically, this biblical scene is a combination of a Homeric assembly and meal type-scene. The basic narrative sequence in the Gospels is (1) a great crowd gathers on the shore where Jesus and the disciples have landed (Mk 6:30-4); (2) Jesus teaches them (v. 34), (3) performs the miracle with loaves and fishes (vv. 35-44), and (4) dismisses the crowd (v. 45). The same basic sequence applies to the doublet of this scene at Mark 8:1-10, and in the other Gospel accounts as well (Mt 14:13-21; Lk 9:10-17; Jn 6:1-13)—an example, incidently, of structural intertextuality among the Gospels.

Items (1), (2) and (4) correspond to the Homeric assembly scene; item (3) to the meal scene. As realized in the Centos, the sequence of elements in each section corresponds to the proper Homeric sequence. For the assembly scene, this is *assembly* (lines 1153-74, cited and translated below), *speech* (1176-1204, cited, translated and discussed in chapter 7), and *dismissal* (1222-3 = *Il.* 23.58 + 61); for the meal: *preparation*, including prayer and hand-washing (1211-16 = *Od.* 17.343 + *Il.* 19.255 + *Od.* 3.58 + *Il.* 7.177 + *Od.* 10.181-2), *consumption* of the food and drink (1217-21 = *Od.* 14.453 + *Il.* 23.55-6 + *Od.* 5.201 + *Od.* 6.250), *satiety* (1226-7 = *Il.* 9.705-6) and after-dinner *entertainment* (1224 = *Il.* 1.472) (Edwards 1992:311).

Eudocia's replication of narrative function and sequence here preserves conventions of the Homeric type-scene even when this introduces elements not present in the Gospels. Jesus' speech, for example, mentioned only in passing in the Gospels, is a major intrusion, added no doubt because no Homeric assembly scene is complete without one. In the meal preparation, which begins with a shorter version of an assembly scene (1206-9 = *Od.* 8.16 + *Il.* 2.144 + *Il.* 2.99 + *Od.* 3.7), elements such as hand-washing (1216 = *Od.* 10.182), the mention of beverages (1220 = *Od.* 5.201), and a dance-propitiation of the god (1224 = *Il.* 1.472) are intruded for the same reasons.

Eudocia's realization of the Wedding at Cana episode as a feast type-scene goes equally far beyond the biblical details. Lines from Homeric feast-scenes at Ithaca, Pylos, Sparta, Scheria, and from the description of Achilles' shield crowd the scene. Eudocia "reads into" the biblical passage full contingents of dancing κοῦροι and νύμφαι, bachelors and maidens (582 = *Il.* 18.593), a minstrel (548-9 = *Il.* 18.569-70), acrobats (580-1 = *Od.* 4.18-9), and large-scale animal sacrifices (550-1 = *Od.* 10.104 + *Il.* 8.545; 556-9 = *Il.* 23.30-3), none of which is present in the Gospel, each of which is attributable to the pressure exerted by the conventions of the Homeric type-scene. One senses that conventional elements of contemporary wedding feasts may also be intruding themselves.

Several structural features in the assembly portion of the feeding episode call for comment (1153-74):

Ἀλλ' ὅτε δή ῥ' ἐκίχανε πολὺν καθ' ὅμιλον ὀπάζων,	i 5.334
βῆ ῥ' ἀν' ὁδὸν μεμαώς· τὸν δὲ φράσατο προσιόντα	i 10.339
πληθύς, ὡς ὁπότε 'Ζέφυρος νέφεα' στυφελίξῃ,	i 11.305 ✳ @
ὅσσαι ἀριστήων ἄλοχοι ἔσαν ἠδὲ θύγατρες,	o 11.227
νύμφαι τ' ἠΐθεοί τε πολύτλητοί τε γέροντες·	o 11.38
χωλοί τε ῥυσσοί τε παραβλῶπές τ' 'ὀφθαλμῶν'.	i 9.503 @
ἀλλ' οὔ πω τοιόνδε τοσόνδε τε λαὸν ὄπωπα·	i 2.799
λίην γὰρ φύλλοισιν ἐοικότες ἢ ψαμάθοισιν	i 2.800
ἠϊόνος προπάροιθε βαθείης ἐστιχόωντο	i 2.92
ἠχῇ, ὡς ὅτε κῦμα πολυφλοίσβοιο θαλάσσης	i 2.209
αἰγιαλῷ μεγάλῳ βρέμεται, σμαραγεῖ δέ τε πόντος.	i 2.210
οὐ γὰρ πάντων ἦεν ὁμὸς θρόος οὐδ' ἴα γῆρυς,	i 4.437
ἀλλὰ γλῶσσα μέμικτο, πολύκλητοι δ' ἔσαν ἄνδρες.	i 4.438
τῶν δ' ἄλλων τίς κεν 'ᾗσι' φρεσὶν οὐνόματ' εἴπῃ;	i 17.260 ✳ †
ὡς ἄρα τῶν ὑπὸ ποσσὶ μέγα στεναχίζετο γαῖα	i 2.784
ἐρχομένων· μάλα δ' ὦκα διέπρησσον πεδίοιο,	i 2.785
ἠΰτε ἔθνεα εἶσι μελισσάων ἀδινάων	i 2.87
πέτρης ἐκ γλαφυρῆς αἰεὶ νέον ἐρχομενάων·	i 2.88
βοτρυδόν 'τε' πέτονται ἐπ' ἄνθεσιν εἰαρινοῖσιν,	i 2.89 †
αἱ μέν τ' ἔνθα ἅλις πεποτήαται, αἱ δέ τε ἔνθα.	i 2.90
ὡς τῶν ἔθνεα πολλὰ νεῶν ἄπο καὶ κλισιάων	i 2.91

ἠϊόνος προπάροιθε βαθείης   ἐστιχόωντα   i 2.92

And when he reached the crowd, leading them in train,
he eagerly took to the road. As he approached, the mob
pointed him out; as when Zephyrus pummels the clouds,
that's how many people there were: the wives and daughters of nobles,
bachelors, maidens, old experienced men,
the lame, the shrivelled, the blind.
To this day I have not seen an army of people of that size or type.
Like so many leaves, or as the sands
facing the widening shore they fell into line.
And the noise of it was as when the waves of the sonorous sea
roar against the vast strand and the waters crash.
Everyone's language was not the same; they were not of identical speech,
but tongues were confused, for they were called from many a land.
Who with all his heart could mention the names of the rest?
Oh, how the earth groaned under their feet
as they advanced, and made their way swiftly over the plain:
they travel like tribes of swarming bees
darting constantly out from the crevices found in a rock,
in clusters they hover over spring flowers,
in a group some fly persistently here, and some there—
just so those tribes piled out from the cabins and ships, and
facing the widening shore, they fell into line.

The considerable *Verfremdung* of this passage aside, notice how
Eudocia frames her type-scene here by repeating line 1161 (= *Il.*
2.92) at 1174. One finds such framing techniques throughout the
Centos. In Christ's conversation with the blind man, for example, line
887 (= *Od.* 13.332) is repeated at 898 to close one thought before the
speaker moves on to another. An even more pervasive framing technique, however, is the intercalation of thematically related material.
Eudocia frequently takes a line or a block of lines from one place in
Homer, continues with another line or lines from somewhere else, and
then returns to the Homeric passage with which she began.[1]
    Lines 1154-59 of the feeding scene also serve as an excellent

---

1. Among dozens of examples of this Cento phenomenon compare 538-43 (=
Il. 18.492-3 + *Od.* 23.147+146 + *Il.* 18.494-5); 331-7 (= *Il.* 5.406-8 + two
miscellaneous lines + *Il.* 5.687-8); 500-506 (= *Od.* 19.332-4 + 329 + *Il.* 512 +
Od. 19.330-1).

example of how theme-based repetition within the Centos combines with semantic trigger to help Eudocia with enjambement. At Cento line 741, for example, the first word of the Homeric reading, μύριοι, is changed by Eudocia to πληθὺς in the line 'πληθὺς', ὅσσά τε φύλλα καὶ ἄνθεα γίγνεται ὥρῃ (= *Il*. 2.468); at 1155 a different line beginning with πληθὺς without accommodation (*Il*. 11.305) is bound to the same line, *Il*. 10.339 (= 1154), in a similar context. Contrast line 1268 where *Il*. 2.468, referring to the crowd that has gathered to watch the raising of Lazarus, is repeated unchanged (bound to *Il*. 12.251). As is the case with Homer, realizing the same scene several times in the poem/ performance produces slight variations in organization and diction (cf. Edwards 1991:13).

The feeding episode further shows how within the Centos themselves Eudocia repeats lines in similar contexts. The cluster of lines at 1154-59, and line 1179, for example, are repeated from Cento lines 740-744, which describe a different crowd gathered to witness the Healing of the Centurion's Daughter. Many of these same lines, or formula lines close to them thematically, also occur in the description of the crowd following Jesus at the beginning of his ministry (lines 512-27). All told, 99 out of 1223 whole-lines from the *Odyssey* and 87 of 1070 from the *Iliad*, roughly 10 percent, are repeated one or more times elsewhere in the Centos. Many such lines are taken from Homeric type-scenes. Most of the repeated lines not from type-scenes are gnomic or, as noted in chapter 3, periphrases for biblical characters' names, or one-line formulas introducing speeches.

Here are some typical examples of intra-Cento repetition: suppliants in two different healing scenes use the line εἰ μὲν δὴ θεὸς ἐσσι θεοῖό τ' ἔκλυες αὐδῆς (*Od*. 4.831 at Cento lines 704 and 860) in their address to Jesus, both expressing their initial doubts about his divine status. At 1894 the same line is spoken by the mocking thief on the cross; at 1946 by a heckling bystander, both at the Crucifixion scene. Similarly, *Od*. 21.327—ἄλλος δ᾽ αὖτις πτωχὸς ἀνὴρ ἀλαλημένος ἐλθών—is repeated at 852 and 924, both in healing scenes introducing a cripple. *Odyssey* 7.135—καρπαλίμως ὑπὲρ οὐδὸν ἐβήσετο δώματος εἴσω—is used three times to describe a character entering a house (534, 775, 1301); *Odyssey* 8.16—καρπαλίμως δ᾽ ἔπληντο βροτῶν ἀγοραί τε καὶ ἕδραι— describes a gathering crowd at 374, 1146, and 1206. *Iliad* 15.369— χεῖρας ἀνίσχοντες μεγάλ᾽ εὐχετόωντο ἕκαστος—is used in prayer scenes at

694 and 942. And, a final example, *Il.* 17.466—οὔδει ἐνισκίμψαντε
καρήατα· δάκρυα δέ σφι (the line describing the weeping horses of
Achilles)—is used of the Samaritan woman's penitent supplication
(1072), and of two disciples mourning over the body of Jesus (2103).[2]

Such repetition is a strong indication that Eudocia, taking her cue
from Homer, was actually *composing* by theme, that is, that she was
reusing lines in typical scenes under similar narrative conditions.
However, such thematic economy is not limited to the verbatim
repetition of Homeric verses. Another help in verse generation is the
use of thematic keywords, which serve to link related material in the
poet's mind as she scans the axis of selection. This is one of
Eudocia's favorite tricks.[3]

Marcel Jousse, an early and careful observer of the "mnemo-
technics of the oral style," recognized that "the prior knowledge of
just one single word of an oral recitative has [the] power to conjure up
an entire block" for the performing poet or cantor (Jousse 1925:211-
25; cf. Rubin 1995:31-35). With copious examples, many drawn from
Homer and the biblical and rabbinic traditions, Jousse demonstrated
that such words can appear anywhere in a stich or strophe. In the
Centos we find combinations of keywords at the beginning-, middle-
and end-line positions, as in the Visit of the Magi episode (294-300),
a gift-giving scene, where the keywords are δῶρα and δεξάμεν–:

δεξάμενοι δ᾽ ἄρα παῖδες ἀμύμονες 'ἀγνοτόκοιο᾽	o 8.419 †
δῶρα, τά οἱ φέρον ἀστέρα δερκόμενοι ἀντολίηθεν,	?
μητρὶ παρ᾽ ἀιδοίῃ ἔθεσαν περικαλλέα δῶρα.	o 8.420
τέρπετο δ᾽ ἐν χείρεσσιν 'ἔχουσά περ᾽ ἀγλαὰ δῶρα	i 19.18 ⁂ †

---

2. For other repetitions involving type-scene or related formula lines
compare, from the *Odyssey*: 5.450 (842, 1246), 8.551 (517, 1099), 10.105 (39,
1052), 17.343 (1211, 1387), 23.20 (1904, 1949), 24.320 (437, 1665), 24.441
(1283, 1747); from the *Iliad*: 7.108 (668, 2303).

3. The use of keywords to link related material is a compositional technique
also used in *catena* commentaries, a literary form originating in late antiquity
and probably invented by Eudocia's near contemporary and fellow Homer
enthusiast, Procopius of Gaza (Wilson 1983:32-3). Japanese renga poetry of the
fifteenth and sixteenth centuries operates on similar principles, where a given
stanza is linked semantically to the preceding and successive stanzas (Miner
1979:ix). Keyword techniques are characteristic of the troubadours' *sestina* form
as well (Preminger and Brogan 1993:1146-7).

μήτηρ, ἥ μιν ἔτικτε καὶ ἔτρεφε τυτθὸν ἐόντα   o 23.325 ※
χρυσοῦ δοιὰ τάλαντα· φύλασσε ʽδὲ ταῦτ᾽ ἐνὶ οἴκῳʼ   o 4.526 †
δεξαμένη, καὶ πάντα ἑῷ θηήσατο θυμῷ.   o 15.132 ※

The blameless children of the Chastizer <u>took</u>
the <u>gifts</u> which they brought with them, observing the star from the east,
and placed the beautiful <u>gifts</u> before the shamefast mother.
And she was happy to take the shining <u>gifts</u> in her hands,
that mother who bore him and nourished him when he was young:
two talents of gold; and she <u>took</u> them and kept them in her house,
and looked upon them all with wonder in her heart.

Similarly, a vignette from the Wedding at Cana episode (571-7) is replete with lines containing the words δαιν– / δαιτ– taken from Homeric feast and sacrifice scenes:

οἱ δ᾽ ἧος μὲν σῖτον ἔχον καὶ οἶνον ἐρυθρὸν   o 12.327 †
<u>δαίνυντ᾽</u>· οὐδέ τι θυμὸς ἐδεύετο <u>δαιτὸς</u> ἐΐσης.   i 1.468 ※
<u>δαιτυμόνες</u> δ᾽ ἀνὰ δώματ᾽ ἀκουάζονται ἀοιδοῦ,   o 9.7
πίνοντες καὶ ἔδοντες· ἐπηετανὸν γὰρ ἔχεσκον   o 7.99
<u>δαίνυνθ᾽</u> ἑζόμενοι· ἐπὶ δ᾽ ἀνέρες ἐσθλοὶ ὄροντο   o 3.471
οἶνον οἰνοχοεῦντες ἐνὶ χρυσέοις δεπάεσσιν.   o 3.472

These others meanwhile partook of food, and on red wine
were <u>feasting</u>. Not a soul lacked an equal share of the <u>feast</u>.
They <u>feasted</u> throughout the halls and they listened to the bard,
all the while eating and drinking, for they had a constant supply.
They sat and they <u>feasted</u>. And then good men rose up
to pour the wine in golden cups.

Compare further this string of lines linked by the words παιδ– and τέκνον at 2043-58 (translated and discussed in chapter 8):

ἐκπάγλως γὰρ <u>παιδὸς</u> ὀδύρετο οἰχομένοιο.   o 15.355 ※
ὀξὺ δὲ κωκύσασα κάρη λάβε <u>παιδὸς</u> ἑοῖο.   i 18.71
ἀμβρόσιαι δ᾽ ἄρα χαῖται ἐπερρώσαντο ἄνακτος.   i 1.529
τὴν δὲ κατ᾽ ὀφθαλμῶν ἐρεβεννὴ νὺξ ἐκάλυψεν.   i 22.466
ἀλλ᾽ ὅτε δή ῥ᾽ ʽἄμπνυτοʼ καὶ ἐς φρένα θυμὸς ἀγέρθη, o 5.458 @
καί ῥ᾽ ὀλοφυρομένη ἔπεα πτερόεντα προσηύδα·   i 18.72
"<u>Τέκνον</u> ἐμόν, πῶς ἦλθες ὑπὸ ζόφον ἠερόεντα   o 11.155
ζωὸς ἐών; χαλεπὸν δὲ τόδε ζωοῖσιν ὁρᾶσθαι.   o 11.156 ※
οἴ μοι, <u>τέκνον</u> ἐμόν, περὶ πάντων κάμμορε φωτῶν,   o 11.216
πῶς ἂν ἔπειτ᾽ ἄπο σεῖο, φίλον <u>τέκος</u>, αὖθι λιποίμην; i 9.437

πῇ γὰρ ἐγώ, φίλε <u>τέκνον</u>, ἴω; τεῦ δώμαθ' ἵκωμαι;   o 15.509
πῶς ἔτλης ᾿Αϊδόσδε κατελθέμεν, ἔνθά τε νεκροί;"   o 11.475
ἀμφὶ δὲ παιδὶ φίλῳ βάλε πήχεε 'δάκρυ χέουσα'·   o 17.38 †
κύσσε δέ μιν κεφαλήν τε καὶ ἄμφω φάεα καλά,   o 17.39
χεῖρας τ' ἀμφοτέρας· θαλερὸν δέ οἱ ἔκπεσε δάκρυ.   o 16.16
"᾿ <u>Τέκνον</u>᾿, ἐμοί γε μάλιστα λελείψεται ἄλγεα λυγρά."   i 24.742 †

Similarly, the Woman with a Flow of Blood scene (993-1029), too long to quote here, is organized around lines containing the keywords ἕλκος, αἷμα and various synonyms. Consider, however, this clever concatenation of lines that describe the healing of the lame man with a withered hand (843-51); "feet," "hands," and "knees" are made suddenly strong as the cripple gambols off like a colt:

"Κλῦθι, 'ἄναξ᾿, ἀγαθός μοι ἐπίρροθος ἐλθὲ <u>ποδοῖιν</u>.   i 23.770 ✳ †
οὐ μὲν γὰρ μεῖζον κλέος ἀνέρος ὄφρα κεν ᾖσιν   o 8.147
ἢ ὅ τι <u>ποσσίν</u> τε ῥέξῃ καὶ <u>χερσὶν</u> ἐῇσιν."   o 8.148
῍Ως φάτο· τοῦ δ' ἔκλυε μέγας θεὸς εὐξαμένοιο.   cf. i 1.453
ἄλθετο <u>χεὶρ</u>, ὀδύναι δὲ κατηπιόωντο βαρεῖαι.   i 5.417
<u>γούνατα</u> δ' ἐρρώσαντο, <u>πόδες</u> δ' ὑπερικταίνοντο.   o 23.3
ὡς 'δ᾿ ἄρ ὅ κεν᾿ λαιψηρὰ <u>πόδας</u> καὶ <u>γούνατ᾿</u> ἐνώμα,   i 15.269 †
ὡς ὅτε τίς στατὸς ἵππος, ἀποστήσας ἐπὶ φάτνῃ,   i 15.263
ἤϊξεν πεδίοιο <u>ποσὶ</u> κραιπνοῖσι πέτεσθαι.   i 21.247

"Hear me, lord; come, be a good help to my <u>feet</u>.
For there is no greater glory for a man as long as he lives
than to accomplish something with his <u>hands</u> or his <u>feet</u>."
   So he spoke, and the great God heard his prayer:
his <u>hand</u> was restored, and his heavy load of pain was lifted.
His <u>knees</u> were strengthened and he began to hobble onto his <u>feet</u>.
Thus he swiftly set his <u>feet</u> and <u>knees</u> in motion,
As when a penned horse escapes his stall,
And leaping, shoots over the plain at a break-neck <u>pace</u>.

The Centos are full of similar repetitions at close intervals on a smaller scale (e.g., θάρσει at 225 and 261, 890 and 891, and 1253 and 1256, ὦ γύναι at 1250 and 1251, εἰπέ at 1104 and 1105, σπεῖος at 1270 and 1271, etc.). As D. Gary Miller notes, "repetition within short spaces"—found in Homer at both the thematic and formular levels—"is a fact of cognitive operation. Use of a motif, formula, or unusual word restores it to active memory and any subsequent elaboration is apt to contain one or more recurrences of it" (Miller 1982:45). Nor is

Eudocia's concatenation of theme-words limited to the repetition of the same word. Often it involves synonyms or synonymous expressions, such as φωνή in 926 and αὔτει in 928. Eudocia's use of thematic keywords is similar to the cues provided by semantic trigger to join verses together in enjambement. The theme-word even seems to suggest semantic accommodations in cases where the poet must avoid inappropriate material, for example, a Homeric name in direct address (e.g., lines 1073, 1078, 1086, 1112, 1113, 2258, etc.).

Like semantic trigger, thematic keywords play a role in Homeric verse generation as well. Compare the *Odyssey* poet's treatment of a gift-giving scene (15.113-5), which uses keywords related to each other by *figura etymologica* (Fehling 1969:153-62; cf. Louden 1995:28-9):

δώρων δ' ὅσσ' ἐν ἐμῷ οἴκῳ κειμήλια κεῖται,
δώσω ὃ κάλλιστον καὶ τιμήεστατόν ἐστι.
δώσω τοι κρητῆρα τετυγμένον.

and of gifts, as much treasure as lies in my house
I will give; that which is the finest and most honorable,
I will give you a finished mixing bowl.

In Homer the technique is particularly associated with gnomic lines. Ahrens cites several examples of such "gnomic chains," where keywords, often in anaphora, bind successive lines together thematically (Ahrens 1937:54, citing e.g. *Il.* 14.394-9 and 23.315-8). Compare the gnomic chain bound by the keyword "stranger" at *Odyssey* 14.56-8:

ξεῖν,' οὔ μοι θέμις ἔστ ' οὐδ ' εἰ κακίων σέθεν ἔλθοι,
ξεῖνον ἀτιμῆσαι· πρὸς γὰρ Διὸς εἰσιν ἅπαντες
ξεῖνοί τε πτωχοί τε·

Stranger, it is not right for me, not even if someone worse than you should come,
to mistreat a stranger. For all people are, in Zeus' presence,
strangers and beggars.

Correspondingly, in the Centos we find in the Samaritan woman's speech (1100-103) a famous proverbial line from *Odyssey* 19.163 expanded by three thematically related gnomic lines from *Odyssey* 8 (cf. Ahrens 1937:64) with anaphoric repetition of οὐ:

οὐ γὰρ ἀπὸ δρυός ἐσσι παλαιφάτου οὐδ᾽ ἀπὸ πέτρης.   o 19.163
οὐ μὲν γάρ τις πάμπαν ἀνώνυμός ἐστ᾽ ἀνθρώπων,   o 8.552
οὐ κακὸς οὐδέ μὲν ἐσθλός, ἐπὴν τὰ πρῶτα γένηται,   o 8.553
ἀλλ᾽ ἐπὶ πᾶσι τίθενται, ἐπεί κε τέκωσι, τοκῆες.   o 8.554

For you are not sprung from an ancient oak, nor from a stone.
No human being is completely nameless,
neither gentleman, nor rogue, when first he's born,
For all parents name their children when they're born.

The result of this mnemonic technique in the Centos is the heaping up of lines that express virtually the same idea. Such redundancy, already characteristic of Homer's oral style (cf. Fehling 1969:164), is even more pervasive in the Centos. For example, at lines 1137-38 a line from *Odyssey* Book 16 follows immediately upon a synonymous one from 6.201:

οὐκ ἔσθ᾽ οὗτος ἀνὴρ διερὸς βροτὸς οὐδὲ γένηται.   o 6.201
οὐ γάρ πως ἂν θνητὸς ἀνὴρ τάδε μηχανόωτο   o 16.196

This is not your average mortal man, nor could he be.
For a human man could never do these things

Tautologies like this one abound in the Centos. Compare, for example, line 1093 (ἀλλ᾽ ἄγε μοι τόδε εἰπέ, καὶ ἀτρεκέως κατάλεξον = *Il.* 10.384), where the same thought is reiterated with no appreciable semantic gain at 1095 (καί μοι τοῦτ᾽ ἀγόρευσον ἐτήτυμον, ὄφρ᾽ ἐὺ εἰδῶ = *Od.* 1.174).

In all these instances Eudocia utilizes and builds upon features already present in the Homeric *langue*: she combines type-scenes to construct a larger episode; she structures scenes internally by the intercalation of thematically related material; she repeats lines or blocks of lines elsewhere in the poem under similar narrative conditions; she stitches lines together with keywords. The cumulative force of these techniques is a glossomatic redundancy typical of Homer's adding style. Each item enumerated here is a characteristic feature of oral poetry. Because she is working from within a closed system consisting of the orally derived texts of Homer, Eudocia's activation of biblical themes and her re-generation of Homeric verse are two aspects of the same phenomenon. Cento form and content work together in an indissoluble whole. It remains now to look closely at the content.

7

Themes from the *Odyssey*

'πάντων' δ' ἀνθρώπων ἴδεν ἄστεα καὶ νόον ἔγνω.

—*Od.* 1.3 = Cento line 387

As a rule, Eudocia tends to draw heavily from certain Homeric books, or a certain episode within a given book, to construct a given Cento scene. We may take such favoritism as an indicator of Eudocia's intercontextual thinking (if I may use that word), and from her tendencies to associate a particular Homeric scene or scenes with a given biblical episode, we may—by discerning the morphological and semiotic links between the passages in question—establish the motivation or ground behind a given comparison.

In the Samaritan Woman at the Well scene (1046-1152), for example, lines from the *Odyssey* predominate. Lines from Books 6, 8, 17, and 23 comprise 60 of 106 total lines. Lines from these books are favored in this scene because their themes are particularly compatible—at several levels—with the narrative structure and details of the biblical episode.

The biblical scene begins with Christ's and his disciples' encounter with the woman who is drawing water at Jacob's well (Jn 4:6-7). The Homeric lines used to express this encounter in the Centos are taken from the description of Eumaeus's and Odysseus's meeting with Melanthius near the spring in Ithaca (*Od.* 17.204-9 = 1047-51), and the Companions' encounter with the Laestrygonian king's daughter at the spring Artakia (*Od.* 10.105; 107-8 = 1052-4):

῏Ημος δ' ἠέλιος μέσον οὐρανὸν ἀμφιβεβήκει,	i 8.68
'καὶ τότε' δὴ στείχοντες ὁδὸν κάτα παιπαλόεσσαν,	o 17.204 †
ἄστεος ἔγγυς ἔσαν καὶ ἐπὶ κρήνην ἀφίκοντο	o 17.205
τυκτὴν καλλίροον, ὅθεν ὑδρεύοντο πολῖται.	o 17.206

ἀμφὶ δ' ἄρ' αἰγείρων ὑδατοτρεφέων ἦν ἄλσος,   o 17.208
πάντοσε κυκλοτερές, κατὰ δὲ ψυχρὸν ῥέεν ὕδωρ·   o 17.209
κούρῃ δὲ ξύμβλητο πρὸ ἄστεος ὑδευούσῃ,   o 10.105 ✳
ἡ μὲν ἄρ' ἐς κρήνην κατεβήσατο καλλιρέεθρον   o 10.107
Ἀρτακίην· ἔνθεν γὰρ ὕδωρ προτὶ ἄστυ φέρεσκεν.   o 10.108 ✳

When the sun had made its way 'round to mid-heaven,
they were walking along the rocky road
and soon came near to the town and its spring—
built up as a well, beautifully flowing—from which the citizens drew water.
And what a grove of watered poplars surrounded it!
forming a circle on all sides, and fresh water trickled down.
They met a girl drawing water in front of the town.
She was headed toward to the fine-flowing spring
the one called Close-moving; it is from there that she usually brought the
    water to town.

Eight times in the *Odyssey* a stranger meets with either a maiden
drawing water at a well, fountain, or river, or with a youth by the
roadside before being directed to his destination in town. This motif,
when present, is always the first element in the Homeric hospitality
scene (Reece 1993:12). So it is here. As it happens, the Bible shares
with Homer this universal folk motif; but the sequence of elements
continues to follow the Homeric norm throughout this scene, for the
Cento treatment of the first element also dispenses with the next two
elements of a *xenia* scene, *arrival* at the destination (II) and a *description* of the surroundings and the activities of the person sought
(III).[1] Element VI, *supplication*, occurs at line 1072:

οὔδει ἐνισκίμψασα καρήατα· αἴδετο γάρ ‘μιν’.   i 17.437 ✳ + o 6.329 †

She placed her head in the dirt, for she respected him.

Elements VII and IX, *reception* and *feast*, are implied in the
woman's speech (1081-89):

ἄστυ δέ τοι δείξω, ἐρέω δέ τοι οὔνομα λαῶν.   o 6.194
εἰμ', ἵνα θαρσύνω θ' ἑτάρους εἴπω τε ἕκαστα.   o 3.361

---

1. In enumerating the conventions of Homeric *xenia* here, I follow the
numbering and headings of Reece 1993:6-39.

ἔρχεο· ἶσον γάρ σε θεῷ τείσουσιν 'ἅπαντες',   i 9.603 †
ξεῖν', ἐπεὶ οὐκ ἀχάριστα μεθ' ἡμῖν ταῦτ' ἀγορεύεις,   o 8.236
ἀλλ' ἐθέλεις ἀρετὴν σὴν φαινέμεν, ἥ τοι ὀπηδεῖ.   o 8.237
'ξεῖν', ἐπεὶ ἡμετέρην τε πόλιν καὶ γαῖαν ἱκάνεις,   o 6.191 †
οὔτ' οὖν 'ἐσθῆτος' δευήσεαι οὔτε 'ποτῆτος'.   o 6.192 †
ἐν δ' ἄνδρες ναίουσι πολύρρηνες πολυβοῦται,   i 9.154
οἵ κέ σε δωτίνῃσι θεὸν ὣς τιμήσουσι.   i 9.155

I shall show you the city and tell the name of its people.
I am going to encourage my comrades and tell them everything.
Come with me, for they will honor you on par with a god,
Stranger, since you speak pleasingly in our midst,
and are ready to display the skill which attends you.
Stranger, when you come to our land and town
you will lack neither food nor drink.
Many strong men, rich in cattle, live there
and they will honor you with gifts like a god.

Next comes Element XI, *identification* (1093-98):

ἀλλ' ἄγε μοι τόδε εἰπὲ καὶ ἀτρεκέως κατάλεξον,   i 10.384
ξεῖν', ἐπεὶ οὔτε κακῷ οὔτ' ἄφρονι φωτὶ ἔοικας.   o 6.187
καί μοι τοῦτ' ἀγόρευσον ἐτήτυμον, ὄφρ' ἐὺ εἰδῶ·   o 1.174
τίς πόθεν εἰς ἀνδρῶν πόθι τοι πόλις ἠδὲ τοκῆες   o 1.170
τρισμάκαρες μὲν σοί γε πατὴρ καὶ πότνια μήτηρ.   o 6.154
εἴπ' ὄνομ' ὅττι σε κεῖθι κάλεον 'μήτηρ τε πατήρ τε',   o 8.550 †

But come now, tell me this and tell truly
Stranger, since you don't seem to be a mean or foolish man.
Tell me this truly, so that I may be sure:
What kind of man are you? where is your city and parents?
Thrice blessed indeed are your father and noble mother.
Tell me the name your mother and father call you by where you're from.

There follows Element XII, an *exchange of information* in which
the woman introduces Jesus to her people as the offspring of Paieon
(1128 = *Od.* 4.232), the physician of the gods (cf. *Il.* 5.401; 899), an
immortal who has disguised himself so as to seem a man (1133-44):

αὐτὸν δ' οὐ σάφα οἶδα, πόθεν γένος εὔχεται εἶναι.   o 17.373
νῦν 'δέ γε' κάλλιόν ἐστι μεταλλῆσαι καὶ ἔρεσθαι   o 3.69 †
ὁππόθεν οὗτος ἀνὴρ, ποίης δ' ἐξ εὔχεται εἶναι   o 1.406

γαίης, ποῦ δέ νύ οἱ γενεὴ καὶ πατρὶς ἄρουρα.	o 1.407
οὐκ ἔσθ᾽ οὗτος ἀνὴρ διερὸς βροτὸς οὐδὲ γένηται.	o 6.201
οὐ γάρ πως ἂν θνητὸς ἀνὴρ τάδε μηχανόῳτο	o 16.196
ᾧ αὐτοῦ ᾽γε νόῳ᾽, ὅτε μὴ θεὸς αὐτὸς ἐπελθών	o 16.197 †
ῥηϊδίως ἐθέλων θείη νέον ἠδὲ γέροντα.	o 16.198
ὥς τέ μοι ἀθάνατός γ᾽ ἰνδάλλεται εἰσοράασθαι	o 3.246
ἄλλῳ δ᾽ αὐτὸν φωτὶ κατακρύπτων ἤϊσκε.	o 4.247
ἀλλὰ ἴδεσθε καὶ ὔμμες ἀνασταδόν· οὐ γὰρ ἔγωγε	i 23.469
εὖ διαγιγνώσκω· δοκέει δέ μοι ἔμμεναι ἀνήρ.	i 23.470

I do not know him well, or his origin.
But it is surely better to inquire and ask
where this man is from, from what land he claims to come,
the source of his family and his fatherland.
For he is not your ordinary man, nor could he be,
for no mortal could devise these things
by his own intelligence except a god himself come upon him,
who, when he wishes, easily makes him a young or old man.
He looks like an immortal to me.
Secretly he has likened himself to a common mortal.
But stand forth and see for yourselves, for I am
far from certain. He looks to me like a man.

The scene closes with throngs of Shechemites rushing from their porches, calling their neighbors, to welcome the woman and her strange godlike guest (1145-52).

This Cento episode is typical of Eudocia's construction of Cento episodes in general, and of her treatment of Homeric type-scenes in particular. We note first that the majority of lines used to construct this episode is taken from Homeric hospitality scenes, and that most elements of the typical Homeric *xenia* scene are present, with only three out of place:[2] (1) the seating of the visitor (Element VIII), which in the Centos comes immediately upon arrival (1055), reflecting a biblical detail (Jn 4:6: ὁ οὖν᾽ Ἰησοῦς . . . ἐκαθέζετο . . . ἐπὶ τῇ

---

2. "Out of place" is perhaps the wrong phrase here, for as Edwards concludes in his comparison of Homer's treatment of funeral type-scenes: "Not only does he change the order of the elements of the type-scene . . . he uses regular elements and themes with greatly enhanced emotional significance" (Edwards 1986:90). On Vergil's displacement of elements of the Homeric type-scene in the *Aeneid*, see Krischer 1979:143-7.

πηγῆ); (2) the giving of guest-gifts (Element XX), which is mentioned at 1089, after reference to feasting; and (3) the host's taking the visitor by the hand (Element VIIf), which occurs at 1148. Eudocia's basic repetition of the narrative rules of the Homeric type-scene, however, is obvious, and accords with the principle of structural intertextuality and with the rules of function and sequence.

Second, we notice that two Homeric episodes in particular are favored in this scene's construction: (1) Odysseus's encounter with Nausicaa on the beach and his subsequent stay at Scheria (from *Odyssey* Books 6 and 8); and (2) Odysseus's two prerecognition encounters with Penelope in Ithaca (from *Odyssey* Books 17 and 23). Like the biblical episode, each of these Homeric books contains a private interview between a man and a woman. In each Homeric scene, moreover, Odysseus is a stranger (ξεῖνος) to his host: to Nausicaa by virtue of his having washed up on shore in Scheria, and to Penelope because of his beggar's disguise. This iconic trait is reinforced verbally by Eudocia's repeated use of the keyword ξεῖν-, which occurs anaphorically in the initial colon of the line nine times in this scene (1073, 1084, 1086, 1092, 1094, 1108, 1112, 1114, 1129), four times with semantic accommodation.

In terms of morphology, the scene involving Jesus and the Woman at the Well is a Cento version of the *xenia* theme. However, nonstructural elements have also influenced Eudocia's preference for lines from *Odyssey* Books 6, 8, 17, 23, and the interviews and stranger-motif they contain. While the biblical theme and Homeric signs are functionally compatible, lines spoken by Odysseus are not simply assigned to Jesus, nor lines spoken by Nausicaa/Penelope to the Samaritan woman. Moreover, at both functional and attributival levels, Homeric roles are reversed, and biblical details are contravened or elaborated. Such is the result of the complicated interaction of iconic and symbolic grounds in Cento intertextuality, to which we must now turn.

First, at the morphological level, there is the reversal of roles. This confirms Propp's dictum that "an action cannot be defined apart from its place in the course of narration." Consequently, we find that according to a morphological description of narrative "identical acts

can have different meanings, and vice versa."[3] Thus, at line 1072 it is
the host who supplicates the visitor (with an *Iliad* line describing the
weeping horses of Achilles), and though gifts are promised by the
woman (1088-90), they are actually given by Jesus in the form of a
ransom (ζωάγρια) at 1109, where the verb ὀφέλλεις, which in the
Odyssey passage means "you owe," is used somewhat catachrestically
to mean "you provide." That this is the proper translation here is
clear from line 1111 where the woman utters to Jesus the words of
Odysseus to Nausicaa, and a clever grammatical accommodation of
Homer's vocative to an accusative in apposition to the pronoun με
makes the woman the beneficiary (as opposed to Homer where it is
Odysseus who "owes" Nausicaa "the ransom" of his life). The Cento
passage runs thus:

χαῖρε, ξεῖν᾽, ἵνα καί ποτ᾽ ἐὼν ἐν πατρίδι γαίῃ,	ο 8.461
μνήσῃ ἐμεῖ᾽, ὅτι μοι πρώτῃ ζωάγρι᾽ ὀφέλλεις.	ο 8.462
τῶ κέν τοι καὶ κεῖθι θεῷ ὣς εὐχετοώμην	ο 8.467
αἰεὶ ἤματα πάντα· σὺ γάρ μ᾽ ἐβιώσαο κούρην.	ο 8.468 ※

Farewell, stranger. Be sure to remember me when you reach
Your father's land. I was, after all, the first woman you ransomed.
That's why I'll pray to you there as a god
All the days of my life. For you have given this girl life.

The intense *Verfremdung* of this and other role-reversals in this scene
is not softened by the coherent structural intertextuality of the larger
episode, as I hope the following analysis of the whole dialogue will
show.

The conversation begins with Jesus' words at 1057-65, which
consist of lines spoken by three different characters in Homer:

1. By Telemachus to Penelope (1057-8; 1062-4)

τίφθ᾽ οὕτω ῾ἀνδρὸς᾽ νοσφίζεαι, οὐδέ παρ᾽ αὐτὸν	ο 23.98 †
ἑζομένη μύθοισιν ἀνείρεαι ῾ἠδὲ᾽ μεταλλᾷς;	ο 23.99 @
. . .	

---

3. Hence Propp's formal definition: "*Function is an act of character,
defined from the point of view of its significance for the course of the action*"
(Propp 1928:21).

οὐ μέν κ' ἄλλη γ' ὧδε γυνὴ τετλήοτι θυμῷ   ο 23.100
ἀνδρὸς ἀποσταίη, ὅς τοι κακὰ πόλλ' ἐμόγησε.   ο 23.101 ※
σοὶ δ' αἰεὶ κραδίη στερεωτέρη ἐστὶ λίθοιο.   ο 23.103

2. By Nausicaa to herself (1059-61)

καὶ δ' 'ἄλλην' νεμεσῶ, ἥ τις τοιαῦτά γε ῥέζοι·   ο 6.286 @
ἥ τ' ἀέκητι φίλων πατρὸς καὶ μητρὸς ἐόντων,   ο 6.287
ἀνδράσι μίσγηται πρίν γ' ἀμφάδιον γάμον ἐλθεῖν.   ο 6.288

3. By the suitor Amphimedon about Penelope (1065)

ἡ δ' οὔτ' ἠρνεῖτο στυγερὸν γάμον οὔτε τελεύτα.   ο 24.126

These Homeric lines are used by Eudocia to express Jesus'
disapproval of the woman's improper relationship to her husband. In
(1) Telemachus reproaches his mother Penelope for her slowness in
recognizing her husband: "Why are you keeping yourself in this way
from your husband? You refuse to sit near him or engage him in
conversation. . . . No other woman of steadfast heart would keep
aloof as you do from her husband when he has suffered so much." In
(3) Amphimedon faults her stalling duplicity in courtship: "She says
neither 'no' nor 'yes.'" Of special note in Jesus' speech is (2), *Od.* 6.
286-8, which in Homer expresses the self-doubts of Nausicaa about
her sexual attraction to Odysseus: "I (would) find fault with any other
woman who would have intercourse with men against her parents'
will, before she was lawfully wed." These Homeric lines convey the
information in Jn 4:16-8:

> Jesus said to her, "Go, call your husband and come here."
> The woman answered him, "I have no husband." Jesus said to
> her, "You are right in saying 'I have no husband;' for you
> have had five husbands, and he whom you have now is not
> your husband; this you said truly."

Christ's intuition provokes a series of responses in the woman.
First there is embarrassment: In words used to describe Nausicaa's
reaction to her father's teasing her about marriage (*Od.* 6.66-7 =
1066-7), the woman "felt ashamed at the mention of lovely marriage
before her husband" (αἴδετο γὰρ θαλερὸν γάμον ἐξονομῆναι /
'ἀνδρὶ' φίλῳ). Then, taken aback by the stranger's knowledge of her situation, her

next response is wonder and trepidation, this time conveyed in Homer's memorable words describing Penelope's response to Odysseus in the couple's recognition scene (1069-70):

ἡ δ' ἄνεω δὴν ἧστο, τάφος δέ οἱ ἧτορ ἵκανεν·   o 23.93
ὄψει δ' ἄλλοτε μέν μιν ἐνωπαδίως ἐσίδεσκεν.   o 23.94

She sat speechless, amazed; but now and again
With a glance she would look him straight in the face.

The Samaritan woman then elaborates on her reaction at 1073-75 with lines from the same Homeric scene, but spoken this time by Penelope to Telemachus:

'ξεῖνε, ἐπεὶ' θυμός μοι ἐνὶ στήθεσσι τέθηπεν,   o 23.105 †
οὐδέ τι προσφάσθαι δύναμαι ἔπος οὐδ' ἐρέεσθαι   o 23.106
οὐδ' εἰς ὦπα ἰδέσθαι ἐναντίον· 'αἰδέομαι γάρ'.   o 23.107 †

Stranger, the heart in my chest is struck with wonder.
I can neither address, nor question you,
Nor look you in the eyes. I feel ashamed.

At 1086-89, as we have seen, the woman finally responds to Christ's request at 1068 for a drink and an escort to town with the words of Nausicaa, assuring him of the gifts and entertainment he will receive from her people, then adds, *in the words of Odysseus* (1090-1):

κεῖνος δ' αὖ περὶ κῆρι μακάρτατος ἔξοχον ἄλλων,   o 6.158
ὅς κέ 'σε ἔδνοισι' βρίσας οἰκόνδ' ἀγάγηται.   o 6.159 @

Blessed beyond compare is the man
Who loads you up with bridal gifts and takes you home to wed.

The *Verfremdung* here is particularly strong. While the use of marital imagery to describe the Christian's relationship to Christ is a topos in Christian discourse (originating from New Testament passages like Mt 25:1-13, Mk 2:19, Jn 3:29, 2 Cor 11:2, Eph 5:23-32. See Cameron 1991:68), usually it is the church or individual devotee who is the bride and Christ the bride*groom*. Here however the woman's use of Odysseus's words to Nausicaa makes Christ, as it were, the woman's bride, for ἔεδνα, "bridal gifts," are presented by a suitor to the bride's father, as if to purchase her, what anthropologists call a bride price.[4]

The appropriation of all these *Odyssey* lines precipitates the kinds of attributival conflicts that we have seen already with the Sidonian slave girl and Mary. Although they each involve some degree of *Verfremdung*, all the lines used in the exchange are nonetheless related to each other in that they are situtated in a larger Homeric context where marriage (real or imagined) is somehow at stake. And yet, marital imagery is not developed in the biblical Woman at the Well scene beyond Jesus' short mention of the woman's adultery, even if we concede that sexual tension (arising from Jesus' and the woman's disregard for the social mores of ancient Palestine) colors the whole scene. Conversely, Jesus' lectures in the Gospel about possessing "living water" and "food ye know not of"—what are clearly the theological focal points of the Johannine scene—are completely elided in Eudocia's treatment. What, we might ask, was she thinking?

A proper understanding and appreciation of the exchange between the woman and Jesus—indeed the interpretation of the entire episode—requires that we understand the iconic and symbolic relationships between signs and their various objects. From the Gospel of John, the basic information that Eudocia represents in this scene is (1) that the Samaritan woman is improperly related to her husband, Jesus' knowledge of which she takes as a sign of his prophetic skills (cf. Jn 4:19), and relatedly, (2) her recognition of Jesus as a god (cf. Jn 4:25-6; 39-42). Both (1) and (2) are key ingredients in the biblical scene, but they are realized quite differently in the Centos.

As noted above, (1) is realized primarily with the words of Telemachus to his mother Penelope regarding her reluctance to recognize Odysseus, her husband. The recognition of Jesus' godhood, (2), is realized within the conventions of the *xenia* scene with a farrago of lines (most of them in the woman's speech), taken from both the *Iliad* and the *Odyssey*, which compare mortals to im-

---

4. The V Scholion on this line glosses ἔδνοισι as τοῖς πρὸ γάμου δώροις, μνήστροις (Dindorf 1855:I,307). We have seen a similar reversal of marriage roles elsewhere in the Centos in the repeated use of lines from the *Odyssey* that describe the disciples as "suitors of Christ."

mortals.[5] Two of these passages stand out in that they are themselves taken from Homeric recognition scenes. In the first (1138-40 = *Od.* 16.196-8), Telemachus is slow to recognize that it is truly his father behind the beggar's disguise. As he explains:

οὐ γάρ πως ἂμ θνητὸς ἀνὴρ τάδε μηχανόῳτο
ᾧ αὐτοῦ 'γε νόῳ', ὅτε μὴ θεὸς αὐτὸς ἐπελθών,
ῥηϊδίως ἐθέλων θείη νέον ἠδὲ γέροντα.

No mortal could devise these things [i.e., a change of appearance]
by his own intelligence except a god himself come upon him,
who, when he wishes, easily makes him a young or old man.

These words are uttered by the woman to her Samaritan neighbors (though the τάδε in the Centos refers not only to Jesus' appearance but to his foreknowledge of her past activities as well; cf. 1131-2). The second instance (1120 = *Od.* 1.323), also spoken by the woman to her neighbors, is a single line from a scene in the *Odyssey* which evokes its larger Homeric context, namely Athena's visit to Telemachus in Ithaca disguised as Mentes (*Od.* 1.319-23):

ἡ μὲν ἄρ' ὣς εἰπουσ' ἀπέβη γλαυκῶπις Ἀθήνη
ὄρνις δ' ὣς ἀνοπαῖα διέπτατο· τῷ δ' ἐνὶ θυμῷ
θῆκε μένος καὶ θάρσος, ὑπέμνησέν τέ ἑ πατρὸς
μᾶλλον ἔτ' ἢ τὸ πάροιθεν. ὁ δὲ φρεσὶν ᾗσι νοήσας
θάμβησεν κατὰ θυμόν. ὀΐσατο γὰρ θεὸν εἶναι.

Grey-eyed Athena spoke and departed.
Like a bird she soared high in the air. In Telemachus' heart
she planted courage and strength, and he remembered his
father—more now than before. So he stood there amazed,
pierced to the heart by the realization, for he knew it was a god.

An interpretation of this Cento episode inheres in both the iconic qualities of the Homeric material itself, specifically in the Homeric recognition scenes where marriage is at issue, and in the symbolic relationship that obtains between Homeric sign and biblical theme in Christian discourse. In no uncertain terms: *the "husband" Jesus asks the woman not to draw back from, but recognize, is himself.* Through

---

5. 1083 = *Il.* 9.603; 1088-9 = *Il.* 9.154-5; 1094 = *Od.* 6.187; 1106-7 = *Od.* 6.160-1; 1120 = *Od.* 1.323; 1137 = *Od.* 6.201; 1138-40 = *Od.* 16.196-8.

a semiotic chain of images, referents, signs, themes, symbolic and iconic grounds, Eudocia's Woman at the Well episode, realized morphologically in the Homeric *langue* as a *xenia* scene, emerges in the end as a recognition scene—symbolically between husband and wife.[6] This interpretation can be established in several ways, beginning with the Homeric material.

The referent of the Homeric sign in Telemachus's reproach (changed by Eudocia from "father," πατρὸς, to "husband," ἀνδρός) is Odysseus. As a stranger in the Homeric scenes in question, he shares an iconic bond to Jesus in the biblical scene. At 1063 the "husband who has suffered so much" is also Odysseus. Suffering is an iconic quality both characters share as well. Given that Odysseus is the referent of the ἀνδρὸς at 1057, 1063 can also be taken as a reference to Jesus, a man of sorrows in his own right; in fact, in Homer, Telemachus's lines (= *Od.* 23.100-1) are repeated *verbatim* by Odysseus himself (*Od.* 23.168-9). Two other details confirm this: the metaphor at 1109, where the woman refers to the ransom (ζωάγρια) provided her by Jesus, referring proleptically to his own death, and the grammatical accommodation of the third-person pronoun οἱ to the second-person form τοι in 1063.

The "ransom theory" of redemption (ἀπολύτρωσις or λύτρον) was a topos among Christian teachers and theologians. Origen speaks of Jesus making an exchange of his own life with the Devil for the souls of men and women, a bargain that the Devil was unable to enforce (Kelly 1977:185-6). In explaining why the Devil would agree to such a deal in the first place Gregory of Nyssa puts his finger on the symbolism of recognition and disguise in the Cento scene. As J. N. D. Kelly paraphrases Gregory's argument (Kelly 1977:382):

> Since the Fall placed man in the power of the Devil . . . the
> Devil had a right to adequate compensation if he were to
> surrender him, and for God to have exercised *force majeure*
> would have been unfair and tyrannical. So He offered him the
> man Jesus as a ransom. When Satan saw Him, born as He was
> of a virgin and renowned as a worker of miracles, he decided
> that the exchange was to his advantage. What he failed to
> realize was that the outward covering of human flesh concealed

---

6. Cf. M. L. Lord: "The theme of the maiden at the well is usually associated with finding a husband" (1967:245).

the immortal Godhead.[7]

Like the appropriation of the line spoken by the suitor Amphimedon, these assimilations of Jesus to Odysseus on these particular grounds cast the woman momentarily in the part of Penelope. The biblical woman does not have an iconic connection with Penelope (as the wedded wife of the protagonist). Rather, the woman's relationship to Christ is grounded symbolically, and depends upon the topos in Christian discourse that joins Christian and Christ in a conjugal bond (though, as noted, Eudocia's symbolic realization of the topos stretches the metaphor considerably by reversing the roles). This symbolic link is in turn reinforced by Odysseus's iconic attributes in Homer as husband (ἀνήρ) and stranger (ξεῖνος).[8]

Homeric commentators have called attention to the peculiar use of the word ξεῖνος to describe the beggar Odysseus in the later books of the *Odyssey*, where it means "stranger" or "outsider" rather than possessing "its more favorable meaning of an artisocratic 'guest' whose rank would entitle him to guest-gifts" (Russo 1992:4). In the Cento scene, as surely in Homer also, there is ambiguity in the repeated use of this word: Jesus, as a Jew, is a stranger to the Samaritan woman, but paradoxically he is, as a god, also a guest of status, supplicated as such by the woman and offered gifts. Eudocia seems to have been aware of this paradox, for she exploits it in this scene, especially in the morphological inversion of the roles of supplication and gift-giving.

One can easily find in Christian discourse statements that attribute to Jesus himself the iconicity of a beggar-ξεῖνος. "Foxes have holes, and birds of the air have nests; but the Son of man has nowhere to lay his head," is Jesus' answer in the Gospels to a rich young ruler eager to enter the religious life (Mt 8:20 and pars.). With reference to this biblical passage, a sermon attributed to Epiphanius of Salamis on the humility of Joseph of Arimathea emphasizes these same qualities:

---

7. In Greek, the last sentence reads: ἀλλὰ μὴν ἀμήχανον ἦν γυμνῇ προσβλέψαι τῇ τοῦ θεοῦ φαντασίᾳ, μὴ σαρκός τινα μοῖραν ἐν αὐτῷ θεω–ρήσαντα, ἥν ἤδη διὰ τῆς ἀρματίας κεχείρωτο. διὰ τοῦτο περικεκάλυπται τῇ σαρκὶ ἡ θεότης (Migne *PG* 45:60-4).

8. Note especially Eurycleia's appeal to Penelope to recognize her husband at *Od.* 23.28, where Odysseus is still (for Penelope) ὁ ξεῖνος, "that stranger."

"Give me the corpse of Jesus of Nazareth," the preacher imagines Joseph to say to Pilate,

> the man you condemned, Jesus the beggar (ὁ πτωχός), the homeless (ὁ ἄοικος) . . . the naked (ὁ γυμνός) . . . the stranger (ὁ ξένος). . . . Yes, give me this stranger. For he came from a distant land to save strangers like himself. . . . Give me this man who had nowhere to lay his head (Migne *PG* 43:445).

The Christian doctrine of Christ's κένωσις or "emptying" of himself at the Incarnation to take a lowly human form strengthened this topos, and served as a paradigm for Christian behavior:

> Have this mind among yourselves which is yours in Christ Jesus, who, though he was in the form of God, did not count equality with God a thing to be grasped, but emptied himself, taking the form of a servant (μορφὴν δούλου λαβών), being born in the likeness (ὁμοιώματι) of men, and found in human form (σχήματι εὑρεθεὶς ὡς ἄνθρωπος). (Phil 2:5-7)

With such thoughts in mind, John Chrysostom explains our Samaritan woman's willingness to entertain Christ, whom she (as a Samaritan and a woman) had every reason not to greet, as attributable to Jesus' "disguise": "Christ took upon himself a disguise (σχῆμα) so plain and ordinary," John notes in a sermon on this episode, "that even Samaritan women, harlots and publicans had the confidence to approach him with boldness and engage him in conversation."[9] In Eudocia's treatment of the scene, however, the σχῆμα of Christ, like the disguise of Odysseus, makes identification and full recognition difficult. In this she follows the *Odyssey* more closely than the Bible. To the typical questions about identity posed by a host to his or her guest—τίς πόθεν εἰς ἀνδρῶν, πόθι τοι πόλις ἠδὲ τοκῆες *Od.* 1.170 = 1096; εἴπ' ὄνομ' ὅττι σε κεῖθι κάλεον μήτηρ τε πατήρ τε *Od.* 8.550 = 1098; εἰπὲ δέ μοι γαῖάν τε τεὴν δῆμόν τε πόλιν τε *Od.* 8.555 = 1104—Jesus gives no answer in the Centos, quite unlike in the Gospel of John where he responds to the Samaritan woman's suggestion that he is the Messiah

---

9. Οὕτω γὰρ εὐτελὴς περιέκειτο σχῆμα καὶ κοινὸν ἅπασιν ὁ Χριστός, ὡς καὶ Σαμαρείτιδας γυναῖκας καὶ πόρνας, καὶ τελώνας μετὰ πολλῆς τῆς ἀδείας θαρρεῖν αὐτῷ προσιέναι καὶ διαλέγεσθαι (Migne *PG* 59:89).

with an emphatic ἐγώ εἰμι (Jn 4:26). Mysterious already in the Gospel, Christ is more so in the Centos.

Who is this man? For the woman who receives him he is a healing god who looks like a man or perhaps a man with godlike abilities (cf. 1143-4 = *Il.* 23.469-70). Behind this ambivalence lurk larger theological themes current in the Christological controversies of the fourth and fifth centuries, the dominant discourse of Eudocia's age. Such debates over the nature and status of Christ gave rise to the Christological paradoxes of the Ecumenical Councils, for example Chalcedon (451), where Christ is professed as "truly god and truly man" (θεὸς ἀληθῶς καὶ ἄνθρωπος ἀληθῶς Schaff 1919:62). Homeric hospitality and recognition scenes, as realized within the parameters of Cento intertextuality, stand to Eudocia as icons and symbols for the intellectual and cultural property of her own time.

We noted at the outset of this analysis that the Woman at the Well episode is typical of Cento intertextuality in general. All six of D'Assigny's rules work toward the generation and interpretation of this scene. Homeric *xenia* scenes (and their symbolic transformations into recognition scenes) play a role in the generation of many other Cento episodes, for the arrival and reception of Christ in various places under various circumstances with varying results is the narrative backbone of the Gospel story, especially as Eudocia read it. It is tempting, in fact, to read the entire poem as a *theoxeny* ("the hospitality shown to a god"). This theme, present already in the *Odyssey*, is even more conspicuous in the Homeric Hymns, for example, those to Demeter and Dionysus, where reception and recognition of the god by mortals is a central theme. As the Gospel of John puts it, Christ "came unto his own and his own knew him not. But to those who received him . . . he gave power to become children of God" (Jn 1:11-2).

In the Gospel according to Eudocia, steeped as she is in the Homeric *langue*, this theological and narrative theme takes on a distinctively Homeric quality. One consequence of the Fall, for example, in Athena's words of warning to Odysseus about the Phaeacians, is that "these people do not much tolerate strangers" (115 = *Od.* 7.32: οὐ γὰρ ξείνους οἵδε μάλ᾿ ἀνθρώπους ἀνέχονται). This lack of *philoxenia* is part of God's rationale (βουλή 203; cf. 195, 199) for sending his son from heaven, to cure this social malaise. That hospitality is the "will of God" in the Centos, and not just a template for Cento intertextuality, is clear from Christ's teaching at lines 475-6 (= *Od.* 15.490 + *Od.* 14.284) about the nature of his Father: "He is gentle, and provides you with food and with drink." Like Zeus, he is "a patron of strangers, who is sure to avenge misdeeds" (ἤπιος, ὅς δή τοι παρέχει βρῶσίν τε πόσιν τε / ξείνιος, ὅς τε μάλιστα νεμεσσᾶται κακὰ ἔργα). Christ's sermon at 1176-1204 is emphatic about the treatment of strangers. This speech, which follows immediately upon the Woman at the Well episode, is delivered to a diverse gathering of people—"wives, mothers, maidens, bachelors, old men, the lame, the crippled, the blind" (1156-8)—who have assembled for a feeding miracle:

Ὑμῶν ἀνδρὶ ἑκάστῳ ἐφιέμενος τάδε εἴρω,	ο 13.7
ὡς ἂν 'καὶ' τιμὴν μεγάλην καὶ κῦδος ἄρησθε,	i 16.84 † ✳
τιμήν, ἥ τ' ἄλλων περ ἐπιγνάμπτει νόον ἐσθλῶν·	i 9.514
πολλοὶ δὴ ξεῖνοι ταλαπείριοι ἐνθάδ' ἵκοντο,	ο 19.379
καὶ μάλα τειρόμενοί περ· ἀναγκαίη γὰρ ἐπείγει·	i 6.85
τοὺς νῦν χρὴ κομέειν. πρὸς γὰρ 'θεοῦ' εἰσὶν ἅπαντες	ο 6.207 ✳ †
ξεῖνοί τε πτῶχοί τε· δόσις δ' ὀλίγη τε φίλη τε.	ο 6.208
οὐ μὲν γάρ τι που ἐστὶν ὀϊζυρώτερον ἀνδρὸς	i 17.446
πάντων ὅσσα τε γαῖαν ἔπι πνείει τε καὶ ἕρπει.	ο 18.131
οὐ μὲν γὰρ ποτέ φησι κακὸν πείσεσθαι ὀπίσσω,	ο 18.132
ὄφρ' ἀρετὴν παρέχῃσι θεὸς καὶ γούνατ' ὀρώρῃ·	ο 18.133 ✳
ἀλλ' ὅτε δὴ καὶ λυγρὰ θεὸς μάκαρ ἐκτελέῃσι,	ο 18.134 ✳
καὶ τὰ φέρει ἀεκαζόμενος τετληότι θυμῷ.	ο 18.135
τοῖος γὰρ νόος ἐστὶν ἐπιχθονίων ἀνθρώπων	ο 18.136
οἷον ἐπ' ἦμαρ ἄγῃσι θεὸς πάντεσσιν ἀνάσσων.	ο 18.137+cf. i 1.288
πάντες μὲν στυγεροὶ θάνατοι δειλοῖσι βροτοῖσι,	ο 12.341
λιμῷ δ' οἴκτιστον θανέειν καὶ πότμον ἐπισπεῖν.	ο 12.342
οὐδὲν ἀκιδνότερον γαῖα τρέφει ἀνθρώποιο.	ο 18.130
αἶψα γὰρ ἐν κακότητι βροτοὶ καταγηράσκουσιν.	ο 19.360
οἵη περ φύλλων γενεή, τοιή δὲ καὶ ἀνδρῶν.	i 6.146
χρὴ ξεῖνον παρεόντα φιλεῖν, ἐθέλοντα δὲ πέμπειν.	ο 15.74
τοῦ γάρ τε ξεῖνος μιμνήσκεται ἤματα πάντα	ο 15.54
ἀνδρὸς ξεινοδόκου, ὅς κεν φιλότητα παράσχῃ.	ο 15.55
ἶσόν τοι κακόν ἐσθ', ὅς τ' οὐκ ἐθέλοντα νέεσθαι	ο 15.72
ξεῖνον ἐποτρύνει καὶ ὃς ἐσσύμενον κατερύκει.	ο 15.73
ἀλλ' ἄγεθ', ὡς ἂν ἐγὼ εἴπω, πειθώμεθα πάντες·	i 2.139
μοίρας δασσάμενοι δαίνυσθ' ἐρικυδέα δαῖτα.	ο 3.66
δήμῳ καί κε τότ' ἀντήσαιτο δεῦρο μολόντες·	cf. ο 3.44
μεῖζόν κε κλέος εἴη ἐμὸν καὶ κάλλιον οὕτως.	ο 18.255

I give the following commands to each man among you
if you would gain great honor and glory,
an honor which influences the minds of other important men.
Many wretched strangers have come here
and they are very tired, for necessity compels them.
You must look after these, for in the presence of God all
are strangers and beggars. Even a small gift is precious.
There is nothing more pitiful than man—
of all the creatures that breathe and creep on the earth.
For he says he will never experience harm
So long as God gives him skill and his knees are strong.
And when blessed God brings dire fortune his way,
this too he endures, reluctantly, but with a patient heart.
Such is the mindset of men who inhabit the earth.
God, the ruler of all, drives them to a day such as this.
All deaths are despicable to sorry mortals.
To die of hunger and to meet one's fate is the sorriest thing of all.
The earth rears nothing more worthless than man.
For mortals grow old in wickedness.
As the race of leaves, so is the race of men.
You should treat a stranger kindly when he's with you, but
send him on his way when he wants to go.
A stranger will remember all of his days
the host who offers him kindness.
Of course you know it is just as bad to dismiss
one who doesn't want to leave, as it is to detain one who is eager to depart.
But come now, let us all believe what I say,
Divide up the portions and dine upon a lavish meal.
Then they would come here and meet in the country.
In this way my reputation may become greater and more excellent still.

We find here in Christ's discourse on *xenia* the same iconic grounds for comparison that we saw in the Woman at the Well scene. Lines 1196-1200, bound together by the appropriate theme-word, are the words of the swineherd Eumaeus to his ξεῖνος, Odysseus. Likewise, the gnomic lines 1184-90, from Odysseus's speech to the suitor Amphinomus in Book 18 (*Od.* 18.131-7), are spoken by the beggar-hero himself, after he has overcome the rival beggar, Irus, in a beggars' duel. Eudocia's intercontextual thinking—her composition by "idea-parts"—is evident in Cento line 1184 (= *Od.* 18.131), the first of seven consecutive lines from this *Odyssey* scene. *Od.* 18.131

is identical to *Il.* 17.447, which in Homer follows *Il.* 17.446 (= Cento line 1183). *Od.* 18.130, the line in the series from the Iros scene that the poet suppresses (using the thematically similar line from *Il.* 17.446), actually surfaces at line 1193.

Pagans and Christians alike knew that the gods were hard to recognize, and that it was better to err on the side of caution than to mistreat a stranger.[10] The author of the New Testament Epistle to the Hebrews, drawing on a rich Old Testament tradition of angelic visitations, encourages his readers "not to forget about hospitality to strangers (φιλοξενίας), for thereby some have entertained (ξενίσαντες) angels unawares" (Heb 13:1). Eudocia's treatment of Jesus' encounter with the Woman and the Well as a *xenia* scene—in all its facets— shows that Homer continued to be a Bible for Greek-speaking Christians.

10. Cf. *Od.* 16.161: οὐ γάρ πως πάντεσσι θεοὶ φαίνονται ἐναργεῖς, and *Hom. Hymn Dem.* 111: χαλεποὶ δὲ θεοὶ θνητοῖσιν ὁρᾶσθαι. Robin Lane Fox fruitfully compares the story of Baucis and Philemon (Ovid, *Met.* 8.625ff.), where Zeus and Hermes come down to earth as mortals, to that of Paul and Barnabas at Acts 14:8ff, where the apostles are received and worshipped as Zeus and Hermes come down from heaven (Lane Fox 1989:99-101; and on late antique theoxeny and divine epiphany in general 102-67).

8

Themes from the *Iliad*

ἐπέων δὲ πολὺς νομὸς ἔνθα καὶ ἔνθα (*Iliad* 20.249)

There is a great range of epics from place to place.

—Nagy 1990:24

It is well known that a fundamental difference between the narrative strategies of the *Iliad* and the *Odyssey* is seen in each poem's use of similes. In the *Iliad* the simile is the chief means of expanding, embellishing, or punctuating the narrative. The "outstanding characteristic of the similes in the *Iliad* is their concentration in battle contexts. Over three-fourths of the developed comparisons occur in scenes of fighting" (Moulton 1977:50).

The Centos contain twelve Homeric similes of the "long," prepositioned *Wie-stück-So-stück* type (Fränkel 1921:4; Edwards 1991:26-8). Eleven of these come in the final scenes of the poem, which recount the betrayal, death, burial, and resurrection of Jesus. Nine of these eleven are taken from the *Iliad*. It is not accidental that the distribution and concentration of Homeric similes in the Centos correspond to the increasingly violent themes toward the end of the poem. The Centos' concentration of Homeric similes in the "Iliadic" second-half of the poem is an example of structural intertextuality vaguely reminiscent of Vergil's treatment of Homeric themes in the *Aeneid*. This intertextual pattern in the Centos is based on iconicity in its broadest application: as the theme becomes violent, the poet scans the axis of selection for the appropriate signs, and finds them most readily in the *Iliad*. Such intertextuality is also a factor on a smaller scale in several other episodes. In the Slaughter of the Innocents (301-39), for example, with its violent, even martial theme, thirty-two of thirty-nine total lines come from the *Iliad*.

Cento similes provide the perfect opportunity for discussing Eudocia's activation of Iliadic themes and the iconic and symbolic grounds on which they are based. The simile presents an interesting case, for it is iconic by definition: it makes a comparison between two or more objects or situations based on a perceived similarity. The use of Homeric similes in the Centos adds as a third point of comparison the Homeric context in which the simile occurs which contains its own object of comparison. That Homeric context with its object stand together (at one remove) as an icon to Eudocia and can serve as an intertextual ground for a symbol. Thus, the Homeric similes in the Centos contain within them the grounds for their appropriation *from* Homer and, *in absentia*, their points of reference *in* Homer. The semiotic process thickens. Consider these examples:

1. At 1519-21, Judas enters the upper room for the Last Supper and is indirectly compared to Sarpedon storming the Achaean wall:

βῆ δ᾽ ἴμεν ὥς τε λέων ὀρεσίτροφος, ὅς τ᾽ ἐπιδευὴς	i 12.299
δηρὸν ἔῃ κρειῶν, κέλεται δέ ἑ θυμὸς ἀγήνωρ	i 12.300
μήλων πειρήσοντα καὶ ἐς πυκινὸν δόμον ἐλθεῖν.	i 12.301

He came on like a mountain lion when he's gone
without meat for a spell and his strong heart compels
him to make an attempt on the sheep and go for the sheepfold.

2. Judas is indirectly compared to Hector standing his ground against Achilles at Jesus' arrest in the Garden of Gethsemane (1643-16):

ὡς δὲ δράκων ἐπὶ χειῇ ὀρέστερος ἄνδρα μένῃσι,	i 22.93
βεβρωκὼς κακὰ φάρμακ᾽, ἔδυ δέ τέ μιν χόλος αἰνός,	i 22.94
σμερδαλέον δὲ δέδορκεν ἑλισσόμενος περὶ χειῇ·	i 22.95
ὡς ᾽ἄρ᾽ ὅ γ᾽᾽ ἄσβεστον ἔχων μένος οὐχ ὑπεχώρει.	i 22.96 †

You've seen a snake from the mountains wait for a man near his hole,
glutted with poison, who, when fury comes dreadful upon him,
stares at you horribly, coiling himself around his lair:
just so, with inexhaustable nerve, he held firm to his ground.

3. At Jesus' arrest, Judas is further compared to Ajax in his rush against the Trojans to retrieve the body of Patroclus (1658-60):

ἴθυσεν δὲ διὰ προμάχων συῒ εἴκελος ἀλκὴν   i 17.281
καπρίῳ, ὅς τ᾽ ἐν ὄρεσσι κύνας θαλερούς τ᾽ αἰζηοὺς   i 17.282
ῥηϊδίως ἐκέδασσεν, ᾽ἀλυξάμενος᾽ διὰ βήσσας.   i 17.283 †

He shot through the front lines, like a wild boar
in his strength, who scatters sleek, vigorous dogs
with no trouble at all, and escapes through the ravines.

In using these similes to describe the villain Judas, Eudocia disregards the fact that in their original context the comparisons serve to enoble brave, heroic actions. In her disregard, she is no respector of persons, but predicates the martial fury of both Achaeans and Trojans to the traitor Judas without partiality.

Iconically, these similes are related to each other: each occurs in a scene of violence, and makes a comparison between man and beast. The wild animals with which the Homeric heroes are compared—lion, snake, and boar—carry largely negative symbolic connotations in Christian discourse. The Devil "prowls about like a roaring lion" (1 Pe 5:8) and deceives the first man and woman in the form of a serpent (Gen 3:1). Pigs are fit only for demonic possession (cf. Mk 5:11-3; Cento lines 960-72). Thus, the identification of Judas with these animals implies that his behavior is demonic. That this is Eudocia's interpretant here is suggested by Cento line 36 (from the Fall of Adam and Eve episode) where the Devil himself, the δράκων of *Il.* 2.308 (= line 34), is identified with a Cento periphrasis used elsewhere only of Judas: ὅς κακὰ πόλλ᾽ ἔρδεσκεν ὅσ᾽ οὐ σύμπαντες οἱ ἄλλοι (*Il.* 22.380). The biblical theme provided further grounds of its own for the assimilation, for the Gospel of Luke explicitly states that Satan "entered" Judas at the Last Supper (Lk 22.3). In these Cento similes we see the interpretant processing Homeric icons (i.e., similes) as symbols for something larger than the similes themselves. As Peirce saw so well, "Symbols grow. They come into being by development out of other signs, particularly from icons, or from mixed signs partaking of the nature of icons and symbols" (Peirce 1955:115).

Eudocia's symbolic use of animal similes extends once to Christ. At the Crucifixion—predictably—Jesus is compared to a ram (ἀρνειός) with a two-line simile spoken by Priam of Odysseus in the *Teichoscopia* (for Christ as an ἀμνός see e.g. Jn 1:29 and 36, as ἄρνιον see the Book of Revelation *passim*). Those lines are followed, with considerable *Verfremdung*, by a line from *Odyssey* Book 9 describing the Cyclops' favorite sheep (under which, suggestively, Odysseus is hid). These three lines in turn come straight on the heels of a short simile comparing the Roman soldiers to wolves (1862-6):

ʽδρηστῆρεςʼ δ᾽ ἑτέρωθεν ὁμόκλεον ἐν μεγάροισι.	o 22.211 †
ἴθυσαν δὲ ʼλύκοισινʼ ἐοικότες ὠμοφάγοισιν.	i 17.725+5.782 †
ἀρνειῷ μιν ἔγωγε ἐίσκω πηγεσιμάλλῳ,	i 3.197
ὅς τ᾽ ὀιῶν μέγα πῶϋ διέρχεται ἀργεννάων	i 3.198
ἀρνειὸς γὰρ ἔην μήλων ὄχ᾽ ἄριστος ἁπάντων.	o 9.432

On both sides of the palace, the perpetrators urged themselves on.
They sprang forth like carnivorous wolves.
And so I would liken him to a fleecy ram,
who passes through a large flock of white sheep;
he was, after all, by far the finest ram in the flock.

In accordance with D'Assigny's rule 3, the semantic accommodation of *Il.* 17.725 from "dogs" to "wolves" suggests its "Contrary" or "Opposite," the lamb; that in turn stands to the interpretant as a symbol for Christ, the paschal Lamb of God in Christian discourse.

In contrast to these examples of animal similes used as symbols, other Cento similes, although transformed by their new context, retain their original iconic qualities. For example,

1. As they seize Jesus and whip him, Roman soldiers are compared to the Myrmidons joining the fray (1820-3):

αὐτίκα δὲ σφήκεσσιν ἐοικότες ἐξεχέοντο	i 16.259
εἰνοδίοις, οὓς παῖδες ἐριδμαίνωσιν ἔθοντες,	i 16.260
αἰεὶ κερτομέοντες, ὁδῷ ἔπι οἰκί᾽ ʽἔχοντεςʼ,	i 16.261 @
νηπίαχοι· ξυνὸν δὲ κακὸν πολέεσσι τιθεῖσι.	i 16.262

Suddenly they poured out like hornets
At the wayside, which children enrage, as children do,
Constantly provoking them in their roadway nest,
The fools, causing a public nuisance for many.

2. At 2154-60, the soldiers guarding the tomb wake from sleep before dawn with a simile describing the Achaean sentries in the *Doloneia*:

ὡς δὲ κύνες περὶ μῆλα δυσωρήσωνται ἐν αὐλῇ	i 10.183

θηρὸς ἀκούσαντες κρατερόφρονος, ὅς τε καθ᾽ ὕλην   i 10.184
ἔρχηται δι᾽ ὄρεσφι· πολὺς δ᾽ ὀρυμαγδὸς ἐπ᾽ αὐτῷ   i 10.185
ἀνδρῶν ἠδὲ κυνῶν, ἀπό τέ σφισιν ὕπνος ὄλωλεν.   i 10.186
ὣς τῶν νήδυμος ὕπνος ἀπὸ βλεφάροιιν ὀλώλει.   i 10.187

As dogs keep a hard watch over sheep in the yard
When they hear a dangerous beast clamber through the woods
And mountains, and there's a loud noise
Of both dogs and men over it, and their sleep is ruined—
That's how sweet sleep died in their eyes.

3. In a piquant simile from the *Odyssey*, Peter is compared to Odysseus camped out on the porch of his palace in Ithaca (1808-11). These lines describe Peter's remorse over his denial of Christ:

ὡς δ᾽ ὅτε γαστέρ᾽ ἀνὴρ πολέος πυρὸς αἰθομένοιο   o 20.25
ἐμπλείην κνίσης τε καὶ αἵματος, ἔνθα καὶ ἔνθα   o 20.26
αἰόλλῃ, μάλα δ᾽ ὦκα λιλαίεται ὀπτηθῆναι,   o 20.27
ὣς ἄρ᾽ ὅ γ᾽ ἔνθα καὶ ἔνθα ἑλίσσετο μερμηρίζων.   o 20.28

You know how a man rotates a haggis,
Stuffed with blood and with fat, over a blazing bonfire
Back and forth, anxious for it to be roasted quickly:
That's how he tossed, turning things over in his mind.

In Homer the comparison of Myrmidon troops to hornets (exhibit 1 above) conveys the quality of their movement and demeanor as they disembark from their ships: "This image of angry wasps makes an impact on almost every level of the senses—audible, visual, tactile, and kinesthetic" (Hofmeister 1995:311). Although here, as in Homer, the simile is predicated of soldiers, the quality of the comparison has changed, acquiring its significance from its new context: the hornets' "sting" is suggestive of the pain of flogging that Jesus is enduring in this scene at the hands of the swarming soldiers (1825 = *Il.* 23.363; cf. Mk 15:17-9; Lk 22:63-5); the children who have provoked them suggest a reference by analogy to the mob and their jeering condemnation of Jesus (cf. Lk 23:23; Mt 27:24).

In exhibit 2 the guards the Pharisees have had stationed at Christ's tomb (Mt 27:63-6) are positively compared to vigilant dogs. The point of this simile appears to be to dispel rumors recorded in the Gospel of Matthew that the "elders and chief priests," upon learning that Christ's body was missing, bribed the soldiers to say that his disciples had stolen the corpse while they had fallen asleep on the watch (Mt 28:11-3; explicitly stated at Cento lines 2088-99 = *Il.* 24.71 + *Il.* 24.436). They were not in fact sleeping (οὐδὲ γὰρ εὔδοντες φυλάκων ἡγήτορες ἔσσαν 2154 = *Il.* 10.181), the simile informs us, but were wide awake, when Jesus "easily escaped their notice" (ῥεῖα λαθὼν φύλακάς τ' ἄνδρας δμῷάς τε ἄπαντας 2153 = *Il.* 9.477).

Underlying this apparently polemical intent, however, is a keen iconic awareness of context and detail. The simile is introduced in the Centos by *Il.* 9.477, which describes Phoenix's predawn escape from the house of his father Amyntor, where he was kept under guard (φύλακας ἔχον) by his kinsmen for nine nights after a quarrel over his father's mistress (*Il.* 9.470-1). Like Phoenix, Christ too is held captive by guards (φύλακες) for a set period of time ("two days and two nights" 2163-4 = *Od.* 9.74 + *Il.* 16.414). The noise of wild beast, men, and dogs in the simile suggests by analogy the ruckus caused by the great earthquake attending the Resurrection (Mt 28:2).

In using *Od.* 20.25-8 (exhibit 3) to describe Peter's remorse, Eudocia displays a deep Homeric awareness of human psychology. In Homer these lines describe Odysseus's rage at the disloyalty of his serving women who go out nightly to sleep with the suitors. In the simile he is both the haggis and the man who roasts it as he wrestles with whether he should kill them on the spot, or keep to his comprehensive plan for revenge (*Od.* 20.10-3). "Disloyalty" is also the point of the biblical theme—of which the protagonist himself is guilty; thus, instead of indignant rage, we have remorse. The simile is used in the Centos as an icon for the nausea associated with remorse: the churning and burning of a stomach (γαστέρα) "filled with blood and with fat."

As in (2), other iconic details link this biblical theme and the Homeric context: the presence of serving women (a παιδίσκη interrogates Peter at Lk 22:56), the time (after dark), and the setting (both scenes take place on the porch or forecourt of a palace: ἐν προδόμῳ *Od.* 20.1; Jn 18:16 πρὸς τῇ θύρᾳ ἔξω; Lk 22:55 ἐν μέσῳ τῆς αὐλῆς). Place, occasion, physiological symptom: not only is Peter's remorse "like" a sizzling haggis and the man who impatiently waits to see it done with (i.e., "cooked"), his larger situation is "like" the one Odysseus faces in Ithaca. In fact, the whole Cento scene is introduced by the opening verses of *Odyssey* Book 20 (verses 6-7, 9, 10, and 13 at Cento lines 1768-70 and 1789-90). As recent empirical studies of the role of context in human faculties of memory-recall attest, "what is remembered is not a word, but an experience" (Baddeley 1990:285). For Eudocia this is the experience of reading; the fruit of her experience here is a brilliant transformation of an already ingenious simile.[1]

At Christ's death and burial the use of similes is more involved:

1. The soldiers presiding over the Crucifixion are compared to a mass of Achaeans who crowd over Sarpedon's body as the Trojans try to recover it (1936-8):

οἱ δ᾽ αἰεὶ περὶ νεκρὸν ὁμίλεον, ὡς ὅτε μυῖαι	i 16.641
σταθμῷ ῾ἔπι᾿ βρομέωσι περιγλαγέας κατὰ πέλλας	i 16.642 †
ὥρῃ ἐν εἰαρινῇ, ὅτε γλάγος ἄγγεα δεύει.	i 16.643

They were gathered around the corpse like flies
In a barn, buzzing over the milk pails
In springtime, when the milk splashes in buckets.

2. In bringing the body of Jesus to burial, the disciples are compared to the Danaans carrying the body of Patroclus away from the battle line (2077-81):

οἱ δ᾽ ὥς θ᾽ ἡμίονοι κρατερὸν μένος ἀμφιβαλόντες	i 17.742
ἕλκωσ᾽ ἐξ ὄρεος κατὰ παιπαλόεσσαν ἀταρπὸν	i 17.743
ἢ δοκὸν ἠὲ δόρυ μέγα νήϊον ἐν δέ τε θυμὸς	i 17.744
τείρεθ᾽ ὁμοῦ καμάτῳ τε καὶ ἱδρῷ σπευδόντεσσιν·	i 17.745
ὡς οἵ γ᾽ ἐμμεμαῶτε νέκυν φέρον. αὐτὰρ ῾ὕπερθεν᾿	i 17.746 †

As mules clothed in their full strength

---

1. With the foregoing examples of Eudocia's reuse of Homeric similes in the Centos, compare Pope's comments on the two similes describing Ajax's retreat from battle at *Iliad* 11.548-62: "He compares him first to the Lion for his Undauntedness in Fighting, and then to the Ass for his stubborn Slowness in retreating; tho' in the latter Comparison there are many other Points of Likeness that enliven the Image: The Havock he makes in the Field is represented by the tearing and trampling down the Harvests; and we see the Bulk, Strength, and Obstinacy of the Hero, when the *Trojans* in respect to him are compared but to Troops of Boys that impotently endeavour to drive him away" (G. Steiner 1996:85).

Haul a beam or a huge plank for a ship
Down a rugged mountain path, and their hearts
Fail as they hasten with the toil and sweat of the work,
So did the two of them strain to carry the corpse.

Here, unlike the animal similes discussed above, the context is respected. The first simile equates Jesus with Sarpedon—in spite of the fact that Judas had just been compared to him at 1519-21. The context and perspective, however, have changed and with it the character's iconic potential: Sarpedon is now noble in death where he once was (symbolically) a demon in life. The dead Sarpedon has other iconic qualities to recommend him as well: the beloved of Zeus, over whom he weeps tears of blood (*Il.* 16.459), Sarpedon is saved from the shame of death (though not actual death) and whisked away to Lycia for an honorable burial (*Il.* 16.667-83). In fact, when Zeus sees that the warrior's fate is near in his duel with Patroclus, he is tempted to save him, like Jesus, from death altogether, though Hera dissuades him from this unprecedented course of action (*Il.* 16.440-58).

The simile involving Patroclus (exhibit 2) brings the scene of Christ's death and burial (2030-86) to a close, yet, like a hypertext link, opens up other windows connected by images of death. This vignette of Homeric *Pietà* deserves our closest attention.

The episode begins with three lines describing how two disciples haul Jesus' body from the cross like a fallen soldier from battle (2030 of Teucer; 2031 of Patroclus):

῾τόνδ᾽ ἄρ᾽ ἔπειθ᾽ ὑποδύντε δύω ἐρίηρες ἑταῖροι,	i 8.332 †
κάτθεσαν ἐν λεχέεσσι· φίλοι δ᾽ ἀμφέσταν ἑταῖροι	i 18.233
μυρόμενοι, θαλερὸν δὲ κατείβετο δάκρυ παρειῶν.	i 24.794

And then, supporting him, two faithful companions
placed him on the bier, while his companions, his friends, stood around
grieving; and a fresh tear fell from their cheeks.

Structurally, this episode unfolds as a Homeric burial type-scene (see Edwards 1986:84). Eudocia's book- and episode-favoritism points specifically to the deaths and burials of Patroclus and Hector, where the intertextual connections between Homeric sign and biblical theme are particularly strong. A series of fitting verses are taken from *Iliad* Books 18, 19, and 24 (2033-2039) which describe the preparation of the bodies of Hector and Patroclus for burial and their magical preservation from the rot of worms and flies:

ἀμφὶ δὲ μιν φᾶρος καλὸν βάλον ἠδὲ χιτῶνα.	i 24.588
ἐν λεχέεσσι δὲ θέντες ἑανῷ λιτὶ κάλυψαν	i 18.352
ἐς πόδας ἐκ κεφαλῆς, καθύπερθε δὲ φάρεϊ λευκῷ.	i 18.353
ἐν δ᾽ ὠτειλὰς πλῆσαν ἀλείφατος ἐννεώροιο.	i 18.351
'ἀλλὰ γὰρ᾽ οὐδέ τί οἱ χρὼς σήπετο, οὐδέ μιν εὐλαὶ	i 24.414 ※ †
ἔσθουσ᾽, αἵ ῥά τε φῶτας ἀρηϊφάτους κατέδουσιν.	i 24.415
αἰεὶ τῷδ᾽ ἔσται χρὼς ἔμπεδον, ἢ καὶ ἄρειον.	i 19.33 ※

And they tossed a fine cloak and tunic around him,
set him out on a bier, and covered him with soft linen
from head to foot, with a clean cloak underneath.
Then they stopped the wounds with an oil aged for nine years.
His flesh, however, saw no decay, nor did the worms
consume it, who are otherwise wont to devour men slain in battle.
This man's flesh will always be intact—even firmer than before.

Like Sarpedon, Hector is a Judas in actual battle, but becomes a powerful icon for Jesus in death: his feet are pierced (*Il.* 22.396-7) and his corpse is stabbed with spears (*Il.* 22.371; cf. Jn 19:34 and Cento lines 1951-5 = *Il.* 21.60-3). The connection between the two characters is explicit at 1930-1 where Christ gives up the ghost in lines describing the death of Hector, the breaker of horses (*Il.* 22.361-2). Both heroes die naked (1875 = *Il.* 22.510) and taunted to the last (1956 = *Il.* 22.375).

In Homer, the bodies of Hector and Patroclus are miraculously preserved, by Hermes and Thetis respectively. In Eudocia's activation of this theme, lines referring to both Homeric scenes come to mind, one after the other (2037-9). At one level, the lines are used here as an icon for the "natural" consequence and intended purpose of the wraps, herbs, perfumes and oils used by the women in the preparation of Jesus' body (Lk 24:1; Jn 19:39-40; Mk 16:1). However, given the preternatural quality of their preservation in Homer and the interpretant's grounding in Christian discourse, there is surely also a symbolic reference to the belief that Jesus' body did not decay, in fulfillment of several Old Testament prophecies, for example, LXX Psalm 16:110, quoted as a Christian prooftext at Acts 2:27 and 13:35: "For thou wilt not abandon my soul to Hades, nor let thy Holy One see corruption (διαφθοράν)." In the Centos this theme foreshadows the Resurrection, as the retention of the future tense ἔσται at 2039 suggests.

Mary's lament over her dead son (2040ff) continues the structural intertextuality of the larger scene, and builds on the comparison of Christ with Hector and Patroclus in accordance with D'Assigny's rule of Contraries and Opposites: she embraces and addresses him as Briseis does Patroclus (2041-2; 2064), weeps for him as Thetis for Achilles (2044, 2048), faints, recovers, and pronounces a moving elegy like Andromache at Hector's funeral (2046; 2058-61; 2065-7), and mourns her son's trip to Hades as Anticleia does Odysseus's (2049-51; 2062-3). The passage runs thus:

μήτηρ δ᾽, ἥ μιν ἔτικτε καὶ ἔτρεφε τυτθὸν ἐόντα,	o 23.325 ✳
ἀμφ᾽ αὐτῷ χυμένη λίγ᾽ ἐκώκυε, χερσὶ δ᾽ ἄμυσσε	i 19.284
στήθεά τ᾽ ἠδ᾽ ἁπαλὴν δειρὴν ἰδὲ καλὰ πρόσωπα.	i 19.285
ἐκπάγλως γὰρ παιδὸς ὀδύρετο οἰχομένοιο.	o 15.355 ✳
ὀξὺ δὲ κωκύσασα κάρη λάβε παιδὸς ἑοῖο.	i 18.71
ἀμβρόσιαι δ᾽ ἄρα χαῖται ἐπερρώσαντο ἄνακτος.	i 1.529
τὴν δὲ κατ᾽ ὀφθαλμῶν ἐρεβεννὴ νὺξ ἐκάλυψεν.	i 22.466
ἀλλ᾽ ὅτε δή ῥ᾽ 'ἄμπνυτο' καὶ ἐς φρένα θυμὸς ἀγέρθη,	o 5.458 @
καί ῥ᾽ ὀλοφυρομένη ἔπεα πτερόεντα προσηύδα·	i 18.72
"Τέκνον ἐμόν, πῶς ἦλθες ὑπὸ ζόφον ἠερόεντα	o 11.155
ζωὸς ἐών; χαλεπὸν δὲ τόδε ζωοῖσιν ὁρᾶσθαι.	o 11.156 ✳
οἴ μοι, τέκνον ἐμόν, περὶ πάντων κάμμορε φωτῶν,	o 11.216
πῶς ἂν ἔπειτ᾽ ἀπὸ σεῖο, φίλον τέκος, αὖθι λιποίμην;	i 9.437
πῆ γὰρ ἐγώ, φίλε τέκνον, ἴω; τεῦ δώμαθ᾽ ἵκωμαι;	o 15.509
πῶς ἔτλης "Αϊδόσδε κατελθέμεν, ἔνθά τε νεκροί;"	o 11.475
ἀμφὶ δὲ παιδὶ φίλῳ βάλε πήχεε 'δάκρυ χέουσα'·	o 17.38 †
κύσσε δέ μιν κεφαλήν τε καὶ ἄμφω φάεα καλά,	o 17.39
χεῖρας τ᾽ ἀμφοτέρας· θαλερὸν δέ οἱ ἔκπεσε δάκρυ.	o 16.16
"Τέκνον', ἐμοί γε μάλιστα λελείψεται ἄλγεα λυγρά.	i 24.742 †
οὐ γάρ μοι θνήσκων λεχέων ἐκ χεῖρας ὄρεξας.	i 24.743
οὐδέ τί μοι εἶπες πυκινὸν ἔπος, οὗ τέ κεν αἰεὶ	i 24.744
μεμνήμην νύκτάς τε καὶ ἤματα δάκρυ χέουσα.	i 24.745
ἀλλά με σός τε πόθος σά τε μήδεα, 'φαίδιμε υἱέ',	o 11.202 †
σή τ᾽ ἀγανοφροσύνη μελιηδέα θυμὸν ἀπηύρα.	o 11.203
τώ σ᾽ ἄμοτον κλαίω τεθνηότα, μείλιχον αἰεί.	i 19.300
νῦν δὲ σὺ μέν 'ῥ' Ἀΐδαο δόμους ὑπὸ κεύθεσι γαίης	i 22.482 @
ἔρχεαι, αὐτὰρ ἐμὲ στυγερῷ ἐνὶ πένθεϊ λείπεις."	i 22.483

The mother who bore him and nursed him when he was young,
pouring all over him, raised a sharp cry of lament, and with her hands she

tore
at her breast, her supple neck, and lovely face,
for she was struck with grief over her departed son.
She wailed bitterly as she took hold of her son's head,
while the ambrosial locks of the Lord flowed down.
A night as dark as Erebus covered her eyes—
but once she regained consciousness, and her spirit returned to her chest,
she uttered winged words, afflicted with grief:
   "O my child, how can you have gone down to the nether gloom
and still be alive? This is a difficult thing for the living to see.
Oh my child! more fated than all mortal men.
How can I possibly remain, separated from you?
Where will I go, my dear child? to whose home?
How have you dared go down to Hades, where the corpses are?"
   She threw her arms around her dear son, weeping,
and kissed his head, the area around his handsome eyes,
and his two hands. A fresh tear fell:
   "Child, for me grievous woe remains.
For in death you do not reach out to me from the bier.
You did not utter a pithy saying that I could always
remember, as I weep night and day.
But my longing for you, your counsels, shining son,
and your gentle manner has begun to steal my sweet life away.
I mourn you, motionless, dead and forever mild.
But now to Hades' home, in the recesses of earth,
you go and leave me here in awful pain."

The comparison of Mary with Briseis and Andromache follows from the intitial comparisons of Christ with Patroclus and Hector. With Thetis and Anticleia, Mary shares the additional attribute "mother" and the iconic quality "grief." The former comparison implies "child" or "son," and this in turn generates several miscellaneous lines with that icon: 2043 = *Od.* 15.355 (of Laertes' grief over his son Odysseus), 2052 = *Il.* 9.437 (Phoenix pleading with Achilles), 2057 = *Od.* 16.16 (Eumaeus embracing Telemachus "as a father does a son"), 2071 = *Od.* 16.220 (describing the joy of Odysseus and Telemachus as they are united as father and son). All these appropriations depend upon the rule of Contraries and Opposites, and, as seen in chapter 6, are linked together by the keywords τέκνον and παῖς.[2]

Cento similes reveal Eudocia's intercontextual thinking as she processes signs from the *Iliad en bloc*. However, her use of *Iliad* lines is by no means limited to similes. Many scenes are realized with individual lines or series of lines from the Poem of Force. Cento healing episodes especially are populated with lines taken from Homeric battle type-scenes. The sick are described as wounded heroes; Christ and his patients are consistently compared to warriors locked in battle. In Jesus' encounter with the demoniac of Gerasa, to cite but one example, the possessed man is portrayed with lines describing the furious fighting of Ajax (926; 935-7), Athena's entry into battle (927-8), Bellerophontes' mad wandering (929-30), Hector foaming at the mouth (932), and Achilles ignited to fury by the sight of his new armor (933). This depiction of demonic possession reflects biblical details (foaming at the mouth; unusual gait) and clearly has been influenced by accounts of possession from other sources as well (e.g., wild hair; fiery eyes; sweating; heavy breathing) (cf. Makris 1995):

φοίτα ʽδὲʼ μακρὰ βιβάς, φωνὴ δέ οἱ αἰθέρ᾽ ἵκανεν.	i 15.686 †
στὰς δ᾽ ὅτε μὲν παρὰ τάφρον ὀρυκτὴν τείχεος ἐκτός,	i 20.49 ✳
ἄλλοτ᾽ ἐπ᾽ ἀκτάων ἐριδούπων μακρὸν ἀΰτει.	i 20.50
ἤτοι ὁ κὰπ πεδίον τὸ ἀλήιον οἶος ἀλᾶτο,	i 6.201
ὃν θυμὸν κατέδων, πάτον ἀνθρώπων ἀλεείνων,	i 6.202
δηρὸν τηκόμενος, στυγερὸς δέ οἱ ἔχραε δαίμων.	o 5.396
ἀφλοισμὸς δὲ περὶ στόμα γίγνετο, τὼ δέ οἱ ὄσσε	i 15.607
δεινὸν ὑπὸ βλεφάρων ὡς εἰ σέλας ἐξεφάανθεν.	i 19.17
χαῖται δ᾽ ἐρρώοντο μετὰ πνοίης ἀνέμοιο.	i 23.367
αἰεὶ δ᾽ ἀργαλέῳ ἔχετ᾽ ἄσθματι, κὰδ δέ οἱ ἱδρὼς	i 16.109
πάντοθεν ἐκ μελέων πολὺς ἔρρεεν, οὐδέ πη εἶχεν	i 16.110
ἀμπνεῦσαι· πάντῃ δὲ κακὸν κακῷ ἐστήρικτο.	i 16.111

And he came on with huge strides; his voice reached to the sky.
Taking his stand near the pomerium, outside the wall,
He shouts now and again a long distance along the roaring shore.
He wanders alone over the wandering plain
eating his heart out, avoiding the beaten path of men,
and has been wasting away for a long time. The heinous demon attacked
    him,

---

2. On Mary's lament over Jesus in late antique and early Byzantine literature, see Alexiou 1974:62-78.

and started to foam at the mouth. His eyes blazed
wickedly under his brow, like lightning.
And his hair tossed about with a gust of wind.
He kept panting terribly, and sweated profusely
all over all of his body: he couldn't catch
his breath. Evil through and through.

Christ meets this opponent, cast as a raging Homeric warrior, with vaunts typical of the Homeric hero (948-56). He boasts like Achilles over the doomed Asteropaeus (948-9), provokes his enemy as Ajax does Hector (950), and threatens him as Menelaus does Euphorbus (954-6):

"τίς πόθεν εἰς ἀνδρῶν, ὅ μευ ἔτλης ἀντίον ἐλθεῖν;	i 21.150 ✻
δυστήνων δέ τε παῖδες ἐμῷ μένει ἀντιόωσι	i 21.151
δαιμόνιε, σχεδὸν ἐλθέ· τίη δειδίσσεαι 'οὕτως';	i 13.810 @
δαιμόνιε, φθίσει σε τὸ σὸν μένος, οὐδ᾽ ἐλεαίρεις	i 6.407
ἄνδρα γέροντα, δύῃ ἀρήμενον, ἥ μιν ἱκάνει,	o 18.81
καὶ μάλα τειρόμενον καὶ ἐνὶ φρεσὶ πένθος ἔχοντα.	o 7.218
ὡς θην καὶ σὸν ἐγὼ λύσω μένος, εἰ κέ μευ ἄντα	i 17.29
στήῃς· ἀλλά σ᾽ ἔγωγ᾽ ἀναχωρήσαντα κελεύω	i 17.30
ἐς πληθὺν ἰέναι, μηδ᾽ ἀντίος ἵστασ᾽ ἐμεῖο."	i 17.31

"Where are you from, you who dare to engage me?
I assure you, only the children of unfortunate men encounter my strength.
Demon, come close; what are you afraid of?
Your own strength, demon, will destroy you; have you no pity
for an old man worn out with the misery that came his way,
completely tired, with grief in his heart?
Yes indeed, I will undo your strength, if you would stand
before me; but I command you to return to the crowd. Do not stand in my
   presence."

Appropriate to their context in Homer, the appropriated lines are linked together by the keyword μένος ("strength"). The word δαιμόνιε at 950-1, a characteristic Homeric form of familiar or coarse address, is used catachrestically here, as elsewhere in the Centos, for "demon"; this verbal icon is the basis for the generation of two successive lines, and is reinforced symbolically in that the identi-fication of the Homeric gods and heroes with biblical δαίμονες (based on the lexical match) was a topos in Christian apologetic.[3]

These are only a few of many *Iliad* appropriations. What is clear from these examples, however, is that Eudocia's assimilations are not based on a simple evaluative formula "X is good, Y is bad." As we see from Christ's response to the demoniac, the referents in Cento appropriations are not stable, nor the grounds for comparison consistent: Judas, the demoniac, and Jesus are all compared to Ajax; both Christ and the demoniac are compared to Achilles; in the earlier examples both Christ and Judas were compared to Hector. The referent alone is no reliable guide to interpretation, because in Cento intertextuality there is no one-to-one correspondence between Homeric and biblical characters. The grounds for comparison are variously tied to attribute and function. Sometimes the context suggests or reinforces one or more grounds; other times the ground itself overrides context, leading to *Verfremdung*.

Eudocia's activation of Homeric themes throws the intertextual and semiotic aspects of Cento composition into high relief, and calls attention to itself as a powerfully comparative reading of Homer and the Bible. Eudocia's assimilations are not allegories, not even her realizations based on symbolic grounds. They do not, in Northrop Frye's definition of allegory, "smooth out the discrepancies in a metaphorical structure by making it conform to a conceptual standard" (Frye 1982:10). It is not the case in the Centos, as it was for most pagan and Christian allegorical readers of Homer, that "the 'secondary' level of meaning is obtrusive and takes on a greater importance than the action itself, which has lost all claim even to a coherent 'surface' meaning" (Lamberton 1986:146). In the Centos, the surface meaning is not obliterated. Discrepancies are allowed to stand; indeed, they are fostered by the very act of appropriation, sometimes multiplied, as we have seen, by accommodation.

Eudocia is essentially a comparatist—a careful reader with an excellent memory who delights in the workings of plot and character.

---

3. E.g. Clement of Alexandria *Protrep.* 4.55.4-5 (citing *Il.* 1.22); Justin *Apol. 1* 5, 9; *Apol. 2* 5; Athenagoras *Leg.* 23-7 as cited in MacDonald 1994:20, 29.

Her Centos are an act of Homeric and biblical interpretation in which surface and symbol possess equal validity. Her art "is at once Surface and Symbol," the product, we might say, of an "anagogical" reading of Homer, in the sense defined by Dante (*Convivio* 2.1), whose validation of both surface and symbolic meanings stands in a tradition of poetic theory stretching back at least as far as the philosopher Proclus, Eudocia's younger contemporary (Liebescheutz 1995:196-7; Sheppard 1980:162-202).

Like the *Cantos*, Eudocia's Centos are at times "mannered, allusive, enigmatic, esoteric"; yet like Dante, Eudocia "clearly invites the reader to come at their ultimate meaning through a surface that is, within the limits of a very conventionalized mode of representing reality, real" (Damon 1961:334). As Dante himself declares of his own work, the sense of poetry, though "real," "is not simple, but may rather be called polysemous, that is, of many senses. For the sense that is gathered by the letter is one, and the sense that is gathered by the things signified by the letter another" (Dante in Wicksteed 1903:66). Roman Jakobson once explained that this is so because "The poetic function projects the principle of equivalence from the axis of selection into the axis of combination." "Similarity superimposed on contiguity imparts to poetry its thoroughgoing symbolic, multiplex, polysemantic essence." In the generation of poetry, to quote Jakobson's well-known slogan, "everything sequent is a simile" (Jakobson 1958:358, 370).

That, I suggest, is the poetry of the Homeric Centos, a rhapsodic, *parole* re-generation of Homer within the larger context of late antique aesthetics, where, in the words of one of its finest exponents, "Fragments of earlier poets, invested with brilliance and color by their original context, are manipulated and juxtaposed in striking new combinations, often exploiting the contrast with the previous text in sense, situation, or setting" (Roberts 1989:56).

The *Iliad* and *Odyssey* are a Bible of human experience. Somehow they contained all Eudocia needed to tell the Gospel story. Whenever and wherever Eudocia needed to express greatness, pain, truthfulness, deceit, beauty, suffering, mourning, recognition, understanding, fear, or astonishment, there was an apt Homeric line or passage ready in her memory to be recalled. As Robert Wood concluded in his great *Essay on the Original Genius and Writing of Homer*,

The more we consider the Poet's age, country, and travels, the more we discover that he took his scenery and landscape from nature, his manners and characters from life, his persons and facts (whether fabulous or historical) from tradition, and his passions and sentiments from experience of the operations of the human mind in others, compared with, and corrected by his own feelings. (Wood 1775:294)

That poet was also Eudocia.

References

Ahrens 1937   E. Ahrens. *Gnomen in griechischer Dichtung.* Halle: Triltsch.

Alexiou 1974   M. Alexiou. *The Ritual Lament in Greek Tradition.* Cambridge: Cambridge University Press.

Alfieri 1989   A. M. Alfieri. "Note testuali al Eudocia, Homerocentones." *Sileno*, 15:137-9.

Alfieri 1988   ————. "La tecnica compositiva nel centone di Eudocia Augusta." *Sileno*, 14:137-56.

Alfieri 1987   ————. "Eudocia e il testo Omerico." *Sileno*, 13:197-218.

Allen 1987   W. S. Allen. *Vox Graeca: A Guide to the Pronunciation of Classical Greek.* 3rd ed. Cambridge: Cambridge University Press.

Apthorp 1980   M. J. Apthorp. *The Manuscript Evidence for Interpolation in Homer.* Heidelberg: Winter.

Arend 1933   W. Arend. *Die typische Szenen bei Homer.* Berlin: Weidmann.

Baddeley 1990   A. Baddeley. *Human Memory: Theory and Practice.* Boston: Allyn and Bacon.

Bakhtin 1981   M. M. Bakhtin. *The Dialogic Imagination: Four Essays*. Trans. by C. Emerson and M. Holquist. Austin: University of Texas Press.

Bakker 1993   E. J. Bakker. "Activation and Preservation: The Interdependence of Text and Performance in an Oral Tradition." *Oral Tradition*, 8:5-20.

Bakker 1990   ———. "Homeric Discourse and Enjambement: A Cognitive Approach." *Transactions of the American Philological Associa-tion*, 120:1-21.

Bannert 1987   H. Bannert. "Versammlungsszenen bei Homer." In *Homer: Beyond Oral Poetry*. Ed. by J. M. Bremer, I. J. F. de Jong, and J. Kalff. Amsterdam: Grüner. pp. 15-30.

Barwick 1957   K. Barwick. *Probleme der stoischen Sprachlehre und Rhetorik*. Berlin: Akademie-Verlag.

Beazley 1963   J. D. Beazley. *Attic Red-figure Vase-painters*. 2nd ed. Oxford: Clarendon.

Bernand 1960   A. and E. Bernand. *Les inscriptions grecques et latines du Colosse de Memnon*. Cairo: Institut français d'archéologie orientale.

Bird 1994   G. D. Bird. "The Textual Criticism of an Oral Homer." In *Nile, Ilissos and Tiber: Essays in Honor of Walter Kirkpatrick Lacey*. Ed. by V. J. Gray. *Prudentia* 26.1:35-52.

Birnbaum 1985   H. Birnbaum. "Familiarization and its Semiotic Matrix." In *Russian Formalism: A*

Retrospective Glance. Ed. by R. L. Jackson and S. Rudy. New Haven: Yale Center for International and Area Studies. pp. 148-56.

Bloom 1994   H. Bloom. *The Western Canon: The Books and School of the Ages*. New York: Harcourt Brace.

Bloom and
Rosenberg 1990   ———, and D. Rosenberg. *The Book of J.* New York: Grove Weidenfeld.

Borges 1972   J. L. Borges. "The Gospel According to Mark." In *Doctor Brodie's Report*. Trans. by N. T. Giovanni and J. L. Borges. New York: E. P. Dutton & Co., Inc.

Bowie 1990   E. L. Bowie. "Greek Poetry in the Antonine Age." In *Antonine Literature*. Ed. by D. A. Russell. Oxford: Clarendon. pp. 53-90.

Brecht 1935-41   B. Brecht. "Neue Technik der Schauspielkunst." In *Bertolt Brecht Gesammelte Werke*. Vol. 15. Ed. by W. Hecht. Frankfort am Main: Suhrkamp (1967).

Brecht 1933-41   ———. "Über eine nichtaristotelische Dramatik." In *Bertolt Brecht Gesammelte Werke*. Vol. 15. Ed. by W. Hecht. Frankfort am Main: Suhrkamp (1967).

Bremond 1993   C. Bremond. "Concept and Theme." Trans. by A. D. Pratt. In Sollers 1993:46-59.

Brooker 1994   P. Brooker. "Key Words in Brecht's Theory and Practice." In *The Cambridge Companion to Brecht*. Ed. by P. Thompson and G. Sacks. Cambridge: Cambridge University Press. pp. 185-200.

Brown 1966   R. E. Brown. *The Gospel According to John (i-xii): Introduction, Translation, and Notes.* Vol 1. New York: Doubleday.

Browning 1983   R. Browning. *Medieval and Modern Greek.* 2nd ed. Cambridge: Cambridge University Press.

Burnyeat 1997   M. F. Burnyeat. "Postscript on Silent Reading." *Classical Quarterly,* 47.1:74-6.

Butler 1897   S. Butler. *The Authoress of the* Odyssey. Chicago: University of Chicago Press (1967).

Alan Cameron 1982   Alan Cameron. "The Empress and the Poet." *Yale Classical Studies,* 27:217-89.

Averil Cameron 1991 Averil Cameron. *Christianity and the Rhetoric of Empire: The Development of Christian Discourse.* Berkeley: University of California Press.

Cardinal 1994   R. Cardinal. "Toward an Outsider Aesthetic." In *The Artist Outsider: Creativity and the Boundaries of Culture.* Ed. by M. D. Hall and E. W. Metcalf. Washington, D. C.: Smithsonian Press. pp. 20-43.

Carruthers 1990   M. Carruthers. *The Book of Memory: A Study of Memory in Medieval Culture.* Cambridge: Cambridge University Press.

Cassidy and
Ringler 1971   F. G. Cassidy and R. N. Ringler, eds. *Bright's Old English Grammar and Reader.* 3rd ed. New York: Holt, Rinehart and Winston.

Chomsky 1985   N. Chomsky. *The Logical Structure of Lin-*

guistic Theory. Chicago: University of Chicago Press.

Clark 1997   M. Clark. *Out of Line: Techniques of Homeric Composition*. Lanham, Md.: Rowman and Littlefield.

Clark 1994   ———. "Enjambment and Binding in Homeric Hexameter." *Phoenix*, 48:95-114.

Crusius 1899   O. Crusius. "Cento." In *Paulys Real-encyclopädie der Classischen Alterumswissenschaft*. Ed. by G. Wissowa. Stuttgart: J. B. Metzler.

Culler 1975   J. Culler. *Structuralist Poetics*. Ithaca: Cornell University Press.

Damon 1961   P. Damon. "Modes of Analogy in Ancient and Medieval Verse." *University of California Publications in Classical Philology*, 15.6:261-334.

D'Assigny 1697   M. D'Assigny. *The Art of Memory: A Treatise Useful for Such as Are to Speak in Publick*. New York: AMS Press (1985).

Deledalle 1995   G. Deledalle. "Introduction to Peirce's Semiotic." *Semiosis: Internationale Zeitschrift für Semiotik und Äesthetik*, 79/80:5-31.

Delepierre 1875   O. Delepierre. *Tableau de la Littérature du Centon chez les Anciens et chez les Moderns*. 2 vols. London: Trübner.

DePorte 1985   M. V. DePorte. "Introduction to the AMS Edition." In D'Assigny 1697. pp. iii-xiv.

Dindorf 1855   G. Dindorf, ed. *Scholia graeca in Homeri*

References

Odysseam. 2 Vols. Oxford.

Doane and
Pasternack 1991   A. N. Doane and C. B. Pasternack. *Vox Intexta: Orality and Textuality in the Middle Ages.* Madison: University of Wisconsin Press.

Dresselhaus 1979   G. Dresselhaus. *Langue/Parole und Kompetenz /Performanz: zur Klärung der Begriffspaare bei Saussure und Chomsky.* Frankfort: Peter Lang.

Eco 1976   U. Eco. "Peirce's Notion of Interpretant." *Modern Language Notes*, 91:1457-72.

Edwards 1992   M. Edwards. "Homer and Oral Tradition: The Type Scene." *Oral Tradition*, 7:284-330.

Edwards 1991   ―――. *The Iliad: A Commentary. Volume V: Books 17-20.* Cambridge: Cambridge University Press.

Edwards 1987   ―――. *Homer: Poet of the Iliad.* Baltimore: Johns Hopkins University Press.

Edwards 1986   ―――. "The Conventions of an Homeric Funeral." In *Studies in Honor of T.B.L. Webster.* Ed. by J. H. Betts, J. T. Hooker, and J. R. Green. Bristol: Bristol Classical Press. pp. 84-92.

Empson 1966   W. Empson. *Seven Types of Ambiguity.* New York: New Directions.

Erlich 1965   V. Erlich. *Russian Formalism: History-Doctrine.* The Hague: Mouton.

Fabricius 1790   J. A. Fabricius. *Bibliotheca Graeca.* Vol 1. Hamburg: K. Bohn.

Fàj 1968

A. Fàj. "Probable Byzantine and Hungarian Models of *Ulysses* and *Finnegan's Wake.*" *Arcadia: Zeitschrift für vergleichende Literaturwissenschaft*, 3.1:48-72.

Faraone 1996

C. A. Faraone. "Taking the 'Nestor's Cup Inscription' Seriously: Erotic Magic and Conditional Curses in the Earliest Inscribed Hexameters." *Classical Antiquity*, 15.1:77-112.

Fehling 1969

D. Fehling. *Die Wiederholungsfiguren und ihr Gebrauch bei den Griechen vor Gorgias.* Berlin: de Gruyter.

Fenik 1968

B. C. Fenik. *Typical Battle Scenes in the* Iliad*: Studies in the Narrative Technique of Homeric Battle Descriptions.* Hermes Einzelschriften 21. Wiesbaden: Steiner.

Ferguson 1990

E. Ferguson, ed. *Encyclopedia of Early Christianity.* New York: Garland.

Foley 1991

J. M. Foley. "Orality, Textuality, and Interpretation." In Doane and Pasternack 1991:34-45.

Foley 1988

————. *The Theory of Oral Composition: History and Methodology.* Bloomington and Indianapolis: Indiana University Press.

Ford 1988

A. Ford. "The Classical Definition of PAΨΩIΔIA." *Classical Philology*, 83:300-7.

Fowler 1987

R. Fowler. *A Dictionary of Modern Critical Terms.* London: Routledge.

Fränkel 1921

H. Fränkel. *Die homerischen Gleichnisse.*

Göttingen: Vanderhoeck & Ruprecht.

Frazer 1906   J. G. Frazer. *The Golden Bough*. Ed. by R.
                   Fraser. Oxford: Oxford University Press
                   (1994).

Frye 1982   N. Frye. *The Great Code: The Bible and
                   Literature*. New York: Harcourt, Brace,
                   Jovanovich.

Gamble 1995   H. Y. Gamble. *Books and Readers in the Early
                   Church*. New Haven: Yale University Press.

Gavrilov 1997   A. K. Gavrilov. "Techniques of Reading in
                   Classical Antiquity." *Classical Quarterly*,
                   47.1:56-73.

Golega 1960   J. Golega. *Der Homerische Psalter: Studien
                   über die dem Apollinarios von Laokikeia
                   zugeschriebene Psalmenparaphrase*. [Ettal]:
                   Buch-Kunst-Verlag Ettal.

Graef 1963   H. Graef. *Mary: A History of Doctrine and
                   Devotion*. Vol. 1. New York: Sheed and Ward.

Green 1995   R. P. H. Green. "Proba's Cento: Its Date,
                   Purpose, and Reception." *Classical Quarterly*,
                   45:551-63.

Green 1991   ————. *Ausonius: Opera Omnia*, Oxford:
                   Oxford University Press.

Greimas 1966   A. J. Greimas. *Structural Semantics: An
                   Attempt at a Method*. Trans. by D. McDowell,
                   R. Schleifer, and A. Velie. Lincoln, Neb.:
                   University of Nebraska Press (1983).

Griffin 1980   J. Griffin. *Homer on Life and Death*. Oxford:
                   Clarendon.

Haffner 1996	M. Haffner. "Die Kaiserin Eudokia als Repräsentantin des Kulturchristentums." *Gymnasium*, 103:216-28.
Hainsworth 1993	J. B. Hainsworth. *The Iliad: A Commentary. Volume III: Books 9-12.* Cambridge: Cambridge University Press.
Hainsworth 1968	———. *The Flexibility of the Homeric Formula.* Oxford: Clarendon.
Harris 1898	J. R. Harris. *The Homeric Centos and the Acts of Pilate.* London: J. S. Clay & Sons.
Hawkes 1977	T. Hawkes. *Structuralism and Semiotics.* Berkeley: University of California Press.
Heath 1995	M. Heath. *Hermogenes* On Issues: *Strategies of Argument in Later Greek Rhetoric.* Oxford: Clarendon.
Herington 1985	J. Herington. *Poetry into Drama: Early Tragedy and the Greek Poetic Tradition.* Berkeley: University of California Press.
Higbie 1995	C. Higbie. *Heroes' Names, Homeric Identities.* New York: Garland.
Higbie 1990	———. *Measure and Music: Enjambement and Sentence Sructure in the* Iliad. Oxford: Clarendon.
Hilgard 1901	A. Hilgard, ed. *Scholia in Dionysii Thracis artem grammaticam.* In *Grammatici Graeci.* Part I, Vol. II. Hildesheim: Georg Olms (1979).
Hofmeister 1995	T. P. Hofmeister. "'Rest in Violence':

Composition and Characterization in *Iliad* 16.155-277." *Classical Antiquity*, 14.2:289-316.

Holum 1982   K. G. Holum. *Theodosian Empresses: Women and Imperial Domination in Late Antiquity*. Berkeley: University of California Press.

Hunger 1978   H. Hunger. "Der Cento und verschiedene Versspielereien." In *Die Hochsprachliche Profane Literatur der Byzantiner*. Vol. 2. Munich: Beck. pp. 98-107.

Hurwit 1985   J. M. Hurwit. *The Art and Culture of Early Greece, 1100-480 B.C.* Ithaca: Cornell University Press.

Jakobson 1958   R. Jakobson. "Closing Statement." *In Style in Language*. Ed. by T. A. Seboeck. Cambridge, Mass.: M.I.T Press. pp. 350-77.

Jakobson and
Waugh 1979   ———, and L. Waugh. *The Sound Shape of Language*. Bloomington: Indiana University Press.

Janko 1992   R. Janko. *The Iliad: A Commentary. Volume IV: Books 13-16.* Cambridge: Cambridge University Press.

Jousse 1925   M. M. Jousse. *The Oral Style*. Trans. by E. Sienaert and R. Whitaker. New York: Garland (1990).

Kahane 1994   A. Kahane. *The Interpretation of Order: A Study in the Poetics of Homeric Repetition*. Oxford: Oxford University Press.

Keaney and

Lamberton 1996	J. J. Keaney and R. Lamberton, eds. *[Plutarch] On the Life and Writings of Homer*. American Philological Association American Classical Studies 40. Scholars Press: Atlanta.
Kelly 1977	J. N. D. Kelly. *Early Christian Doctrine*. 5th edition. London: A & C Black.
Kirk 1990	G. S. Kirk. *The Iliad: A Commentary. Volume II: Books 5-8*. Cambridge: Cambridge University Press.
Kirk 1985	———. *The Iliad: A Commentary. Volume I: Books 1-4*. Cambridge: Cambridge University Press.
Kirk 1966	———. "Studies in Some Technical Aspects of Homeric Style." *Yale Classical Studies*, 20:75-152.
Knopf 1986	J. Knopf. "Verfremdung." In *Brechts Theorie des Theaters*. Ed. by W. Hecht. Frankfort: Suhrkamp. pp. 93-141.
Knox 1968	B. M. W. Knox. "Silent Reading in Antiquity." *Greek Roman and Byzantine Studies*, 9:421-35.
Krischer 1979	T. Krischer. "Unhomeric Scene-Patterns in Vergil." *Papers of the Liverpool Latin Seminar*. Vol. 2. Liverpool: Francis Cairns. pp. 143-54.
Labarbe 1949	J. Labarbe. *L'Homère de Platon*. Paris: Société d'Edition Les Belles Lettres.
Labourt 1953	J. Labourt. *Saint Jérôme, Lettres*. Vol. 3. Paris: Société d'Edition Les Belles Lettres.

Lamberton 1986   R. Lamberton. *Homer the Theologian: Neoplatonist Allegorical Reading and the Growth of the Epic Tradition.* Berkeley: University of California Press.

Lambros 1900   S. P. Lambros. *Catalogue of the Greek Manuscripts on Mount Athos.* Vol. 2. Cambridge: Cambridge University Press.

Lampe 1961   G. W. H. Lampe. *A Patristic Greek Lexicon.* Oxford: Clarendon.

Lane Fox 1989   R. Lane Fox. *Pagans and Christians.* New York: Albert A. Knopf.

Lemon and
Reis 1965   L. T. Lemon and M. J. Reis. *Russian Formalist Criticism: Four Essays.* Lincoln: University of Nebraska Press.

Lévi-Strauss 1960   C. Lévi-Strauss. "Structure and Form: Reflections on a work by Vladimir Propp." In *Theory and History of Folklore.* Ed. by A. Lieberman. Trans. by M. Layton. Minneapolis: University of Minnesota Press (1984). pp. 167-88.

Liebescheutz 1995.   W. Liebescheutz. "Pagan Mythology in the Christian Empire." *International Journal of the Classical Tradition,* 2.2:193-208.

Lord 1991   A. B. Lord. *Epic Singers and Oral Tradition.* Ithaca: Cornell University Press.

Lord 1960   ———. *The Singer of Tales.* Cambridge, Mass.: Harvard University Press.

Lord 1951   ———. "Composition by Theme in Homer and Southslavic Epos." *Transactions of the*

American Philological Association, 82:71-80.

Lord 1967

M. L. Lord. "Withdrawal and Return: An Epic Story Pattern in the Homeric Hymn to Demeter and in the Homeric Poems." *Classical Journal*, 62:242-48.

Louden 1995

B. Louden. "Categories of Homeric Word-play." *Transactions of the American Philological Association*, 125:27-46.

Ludwich 1897

A. Ludwich. *Eudociae Augustae, Procli Lycii, Claudiani Carminum Graecorum Reliquae.* Leipzig: Teubner.

MacDonald 1994

D. R. MacDonald. *Christianizing Homer: The Odyssey, Plato and* The Acts of Andrew. Oxford: Oxford University Press.

Maguire 1995

H. Maguire. "Magic and the Christian Image." In *Byzantine Magic*. Ed. by H. Maguire. Washington, D.C.: Dumbarton Oaks. pp. 51-72.

Makris 1995

G. Makris. "Zur Epilepsie in Byzanz." *Byzantinische Zeitschrift*, 88.2:363-404.

Maltomini

F. Maltomini. "P.Lond. 121 (=PGM VII), 1-221: Homeromanteion." *Zeitschrift für Papyrologie und Epigraphik*, 106:107-22.

Mango 1972

C. Mango. *Art of the Byzantine Empire 312-1453*. Englewood Cliffs, N.J.: Prentice-Hall.

Marrou 1956

H. I. Marrou. *A History of Education in Antiquity*. Trans. by G. Lamb. Madison: University of Wisconsin Press.

Matthews 1993

T. F. Matthews. *The Clash of Gods: A*

References

Reinterpetation of Early Christian Art. Princeton: Princeton University Press.

Migne *PG*

J-P. Migne. *Patrologiae cursus completus. Series Graeca.* Paris: Migne.

Miller 1982

D. G. Miller. *Improvisation, Typology, Culture, and the 'The New Orthodoxy': How Oral Is Homer?* Washington D.C.: University Press of America.

Miner 1979

E. Minor. *Japanese Linked Poetry: An Account with Translations of Renga and Haikai Sequences.* Princeton: Princeton University Press.

Mitchell 1986

W. J. T. Mitchell. *Iconology: Image, Text, Ideology.* Chicago: University of Chicago Press.

Moulton 1977

C. Moulton. *Similes in the Homeric Poems.* Hypomnemata 49. Göttingen: Vandenhoeck and Ruprecht.

Muellner 1990

L. Muellner. "The Simile of the Cranes and Pygmies: A Study of Homeric Metaphor." *Harvard Studies in Classical Philology*, 93:59-101.

Mukarovsky 1936

J. Mukarovsky. "Art as a Semiotic Fact." In *Semiotics of Art.* Trans. by I. R. Titunik. Cambridge, Mass.: M. I. T. Press (1976). pp. 3-9.

J. Murray 1980

J. Murray. "Reverend Howard Finster: Man of Vision." *Arts Magazine*, 55.2:161-64.

P. Murray 1996

P. Murray. *Plato on Poetry.* Cambridge: Cambridge University Press.

Nagler 1967   M. Nagler. "Towards a Generative View of the Oral Formula." *Transactions of the American Philological Association*, 98:269-311.

Nagy 1996a   G. Nagy. *Poetry as Performance: Homer and Beyond*. Cambridge: Cambridge University Press.

Nagy 1996b   ———. *Homeric Questions*. Austin: University of Texas Press.

Nagy 1990   ———. "Formula and Meter." In *Greek Mythology and Poetics*. Ithaca: Cornell University Press. pp. 18-35.

Nathhorst 1970   B. Nathhorst. *Formal or Structural Studies of Traditional Tales: The Usefulness of Some Methodological Proposals Advanced by Vladimir Propp, Alan Dundes, Claude Lévi-Strauss and Edmond Leach*. 2nd ed. Stockholm: P. A. Norstedt & Soner.

Neitzel 1977   S. Neitzel. "Apions Γλῶσσαι Ὁμηρικαι." In *Sammlung griechischer und lateinischer Grammatiker*. Vol. 3. Ed. by K. Alpers, H. Erbse, and A. Kleinlogel. Berlin: de Gruyter. pp. 185-328.

Norbrook 1993   D. Norbrook. "Introduction." *Penguin Book of Renaissance Verse, 1509-1659*. Ed. by D. Norbrook and H. R. Woudhuysen. London and New York: Penguin.

Nöth 1990   W. Nöth. *Handbook of Semiotics*. Bloomington: Indiana University Press.

O'Neill 1942   E. G. O'Neill, Jr. "The Localization of Metrical Wordtypes in the Greek Hexameter."

162 *References*

Yale Classical Studies, 8:105-178.

Ong 1982

W. Ong. *Orality and Literacy: The Technologizing of the Word*. London and New York: Methuen.

Parry 1933

M. Parry. "The Traditional Metaphor in Homer." In *The Making of Homeric Verse: The Collected Papers of Milman Parry*. Ed. by A. Parry. Oxford: Clarendon (1987). pp. 365-75.

Parry 1929

————. "The Distinctive Character of Enjambement in Homeric Verse." In *The Making of Homeric Verse: The Collected Papers of Milman Parry*. Ed. by A. Parry. Oxford: Clarendon (1987). pp. 251-65

Pecorella

G. B. Pecorella, ed. *Dionisio Trace ΤΕΧΝΗ ΓΡΑΜΜΑΤΙΚΗ. Testo critico e commento*. Bologna: Cappelli.

Peirce 1955

C. S. Peirce. "Logic as Semiotic: The Theory of Signs." In *Philosophical Writings of Peirce*. Ed. by J. Buchler. New York: Dover (1955). pp. 98-119.

Peirce 1867

————. "On a New List of Categories." In *Peirce on Signs*. Ed. by J. Hoopes. Chapel Hill: University of North Carolina Press (1991). pp. 23-33.

Pépin 1982

J. Pépin. "The Platonic and Christian Ulysses." In *Neoplatonism and Christian Thought*. Ed. by D. J. O'Meara. Norfolk, Va.: International Society for Neoplatonic Studies. pp. 3-18.

Perin 1994

C. Perin. "The Reception of New, Unusual,

and Difficult Art." In *The Artist Outsider: Creativity and the Boundaries of Culture*. Ed. by M. D. Hall and E. W. Metcalf. Washington, D. C.: Smithsonian Press.

Plett 1991   H. Plett. *Intertextuality*. Berlin and New York: de Gruyter.

Preminger and Brogan 1993   A. Preminger and T. V. F. Brogan, eds. *The New Princeton Encyclopedia of Poetry and Poetics*. Princeton: Princeton University Press.

Propp 1966   V. Propp. "The Structural and Historical Study of the Wondertale." In *Theory and History of Folklore*. Ed. by A. Lieberman. Trans. by A. Y. and R. P. Martin. Minneapolis: University of Minnesota Press (1984). pp. 67-81.

Propp 1928   ———. *The Morphology of the Folktale*. Trans. by L. Scott and L. Wagner. Austin: University of Texas Press (1968).

Reece 1993   S. Reece. *The Stranger's Welcome: Oral Theory and the Aesthetics of the Homeric Hospitality Scene*. Ann Arbor: University of Michigan Press.

Richards 1928   I. A. Richards. *Principles of Literary Criticism*. 3rd ed. New York: Harcourt Brace Jovanovich.

Roberts 1989   M. Roberts. *The Jeweled Style: Poetry and Poetics in Late Antiquity*. Ithaca: Cornell University Press.

Roberts 1985   ———. *Biblical Epic and Rhetorical Paraphrase in Late Antiquity*. Liverpool: Francis Cairns.

Rubin 1995   D. C. Rubin. *Memory in Oral Traditions: The Cognitive Psychology of Epic, Ballads, and Counting-out Rhymes*. New York and Oxford: Oxford University Press.

Ruijgh 1971   C. J. Ruijgh. *Autour de 'τε épique': Etudes sur la syntaxe grecque*. Amsterdam: Hakkert.

Russell 1983   D. A. Russell. *Greek Declamation*. Cambridge: Cambridge University Press.

Russo 1976   J. Russo. "Is 'Oral' or 'Aural' Composition the Cause of Formulaic Style?" In *Oral Literature and the Formula*. Ed. by R. S. Shannon and B. A. Stolz. Ann Arbor: University of Michigan Press. pp. 31-71.

Rutherford 1905   W. G. Rutherford. *A Chapter in the History of Annotation*. Scholia Aristophanica Vol. 3. London: Macmillan & Co.

Salanitro 1997   G. Salanitro. "Osidio Geta e la poesia centonaria." *Aufstieg und Niedergang der Römishen Welt*. Part 3. Vol. 34.3. Berlin and New York: de Gruyter.

Salanitro 1987   ———. "Omero, Virgilio e i Centoni." *Sileno*, 13:231-40.

Sattler 1904   G. Sattler. *De Eudociae Augustae centonibus*. Bayreuth: L. Ellwanger.

Schaff 1919   P. Schaff. *The Creeds of Christendom*. Vol. 2. New York: Harper & Brothers.

Schembra 1995   R. Schembra. "Analisi Comparativa della redazioni lunghe degli *Homerocentones*." *Sileno*, 21:113-37.

Schembra 1994 ———. "Varianti di christianizaione e δοιάδες nella 'quarta' redazione degli *Homero-centones.*" *Sileno,* 20:317-32.

Schembra 1993 ———. "La 'Quarta' Redazione degli *Homerocentones.*" *Sileno,* 19:277-95.

Schneemelcher 1991 W. Schneemelcher. *New Testament Apocrypha.* Vol. 1. Ed. by R. McL. Wilson. Louisville, Ky: Westminster/John Knox Press.

Scott 1974 W. C. Scott. *The Oral Nature of the Homeric Simile.* Leiden: Brill.

Sealey 1957 R. Sealey. "From Phemios to Ion." *Revue des études grecques,* 70:312-55.

Shapiro 1993 H. A. Shapiro. "Hipparchos and the Rhapsodes." In *Cultural Poetics in Archaic Greece: Cult, Performance, Politics.* Ed. by C. Dougherty and L. Kurke. Cambridge: Cambridge University Press. pp. 92-107.

Sheppard 1980 A. D. R. Sheppard. *Studies on the 5th and 6th Essays of Proclus' Commentary on the Republic.* Hypomnemata 61. Gottingen: Vandenhoeck & Ruprecht.

Slatkin 1996 L. M. Slatkin. "Composition by Theme and the Mêtis of the *Odyssey.*" In *Reading the Odyssey: Selected Interpretive Essays.* Ed. by S. L. Schein. Princeton: Princeton University Press. pp. 223-37.

Smolak 1979 K. Smolak. "Beobachtungen zur Darstellungs-weise in den Homerzentonen." *Jahrbuch der Österreichischen Byzantistik,* 28:29-49.

Sodano 1970   A. R. Sodano, ed. *Porphyrii Quaestionum Homericarum Liber I*. Naples: Giannini.

Sollers 1993   W. Sollers, ed. *The Return of Thematic Criticism*. Cambridge, Mass.: Harvard University Press.

Stallbaum 1825   J. G. Stallbaum, ed. *Eustathii commentarii ad Homeri Odysseam*. Hildesheim: G. Olms (1970).

Stanford 1939   W. B. Stanford. *Ambiguity in Greek Literature*. Oxford: Oxford University Press.

Stanley 1992   K. Stanley. *The Shield of Homer*. Princeton: Princeton Universtiy Press.

Stehlíková 1987   E. Stehlíková. "Centones Christiani as a Means of Reception." *Listy Filologicke*, 110:11-15.

G. Steiner 1996   G. Steiner, ed. (with A. Dykman). *Homer in English*. London and New York: Penguin.

P. Steiner 1984   P. Steiner. *Russian Formalism: A Metapoetics*. Ithaca: Cornell University Press.

Sykes 1987   S. W. Sykes. "The Role of Story in the Christian Religion: An Hypothesis." *Journal of Literature and Theology*, 1:19-26.

Thomas 1992   R. Thomas. *Literacy and Orality in Ancient Greece*. Cambridge: Cambridge University Press.

Todorov 1973   Tz. Todorov. *Introduction to Poetics*. Trans. by Richard Howard. Minneapolis: University of Minnesota Press.

Uhlig 1883

G. Uhlig, ed. *Dionysii Thracis Ars Grammatica.* In *Grammatici Graeci.* Part 1, Vol. 2. Hildesheim: G. Olms (1979).

Usher 1998

M. D. Usher. *Homerocentones Eudociae.* Stuttgart and Leipzig: Teubner.

Usher 1997

————. "Prolegomenon to the Homeric Centos." *American Journal of Philology,* 118.2:305-21.

van der Valk 1971

M. van der Valk. *Eustathii archiepiscopi Thessalonicensis commentarii ad Homeri Iliadem pertinentes.* Leiden: Brill.

van Deun 1993

P. van Deun. "The Poetical Writings of the Empress Eudocia: An Evaluation." In *Early Christian Poetry: A Collection of Essays.* Ed. by J. den Boeft and A. Hilhorst. Leiden: Brill. pp. 273-82.

Verweyen and
Witting 1991

T. Verweyen and G. Witting. "The Cento: A Form of Intertextuality from Montage to Parody." In Plett 1991:165-78.

von Kamptz 1982

H. von Kamptz. *Homerische Personennamen: sprachwissenschaftliche und historische Klassification.* Göttingen: Vandenhoeck and Ruprecht.

Walz 1835

C. Walz, ed. *Rhetores Graeci.* Vol. 8. Stuttgart and Tübingen: J. G. Cottae.

West 1981

M. L. West. "The Singing of Homer and the Early Modes of Greek Music." *Journal of Hellenic Studies,* 101:113-29.

West 1978

————. "Die griechischen Dichterinnen der

Kaiserzeit." In *Kyklos: griechisches und byzantinisches* (Festschrift Rudolf Keydell). Ed. by H. G. Beck, A. Kambylis, and P. Moraux. Berlin and New York: de Gruyter. pp. 101-15.

Whitman 1958   C. H. Whitman. *Homer and the Heroic Tradition*. Cambridge, Mass: Harvard University Press.

Wicksteed 1903   P. H. Wicksteed. *The Convivio of Dante Alighieri*. London: Aldine House.

Wilde 1891   O. Wilde. "Preface to *The Picture of Dorian Gray*." In *The Artist as Critic: The Critical Writings of Oscar Wilde*. Ed. by R. Ellmann. Chicago: University of Chicago Press (1982).

Wilken 1967   R. L. Wilken. "The Homeric Cento in Irenaeus, Adversus Haereses I, 9, 4." *Vigiliae Christianae*, 21:25-33.

Wilson 1983   N. G. Wilson. *The Scholars of Byzantium*. Baltimore: Johns Hopkins University Press.

Wood 1775   R. Wood. *An Essay on the Original Genius and Writings of Homer*. New York: Garland (1971).

Zumthor 1987   P. Zumthor. *La lettre et la voix: De la 'littérature' médiévale*. Paris: Editions du Seuil.

Index

About the Author

M. D. Usher is assistant professor of classics at Willamette University in Salem, Oregon. His publications include a critical edition of the Homeric Centos, and articles on Propertius, Ezra Pound, and the Sibylline Oracles.

DATE DUE